DRAMA EDUCATION AND SPECIAL NEEDS

A HANDBOOK FOR TEACHERS IN MAINSTREAM AND SPECIAL SCHOOLS

Editor: Andy Kempe

Stanley Thornes (Publishers) Ltd

First published in 1996 by:
Stanley Thornes (Publishers) Ltd
Ellenborough House
Wellington Street
CHELTENHAM GL50 1YW
England

A catalogue record for this book is available from the British Library.

ISBN 0–7487–2273–4

Typeset by Tech-Set, Tyne and Wear
Printed and bound in Great Britain at The Bath Press

To Tiz and Sue

ACKNOWLEDGEMENTS

This book has grown and grown from my original idea of a short, informal little trot through some practical ideas for drama in the special classroom. A good deal of this expansion has been due to the tremendous enthusiasm for the project and careful critical support offered by friends and colleagues, many of whom, I have no shame in admitting, have far more experience of teaching young people with special needs than I. I would like to thank Marigold Ashwell, Margaret Burke, Sally Mackay, Helen Nicholson and my colleagues at Reading University, Rosemary Ayles, Paul Croll and Keith Postlethwaite, for their comments on the text. Special thanks are due to the staff and students of The Avenue School, Reading and to Barbara Jones who first encouraged me to apply my knowledge of drama to special education. Finally, I am very grateful to the contributors to this book who have given their time so generously and were always so gracious in addressing the reams of comments and questions I gave them.

Andy Kempe

The publishers would like to thank the following:

Steve Beaumont for taking the photographs in Chapter 4.
Gary Harman for taking the photographs in Chapters 7 and 8.
Mr I. MacLean of Reading University for taking the photographs in Chapter 9, and the pupils of Elmfield School for Deaf Children in Bristol, who appear in them.

The Bodley Head Children's Books for permission to reproduce the illustration from *Rosie's Walk* by Pat Hutchins on page 66.
Macmillan Children's Books for permission to reproduce the illustration from *Whatever Next!* by Jill Murphy (1983) on page 74.
Walker Books Ltd, London, for permission to reproduce the illustration from *PIGGYBOOK* by Anthony Browne © 1986

CONTENTS

ABOUT THIS BOOK

The purpose of this book is to offer an insight into how teachers can use drama in their work with young people who have special individual needs. Although this may seem a simple enough statement, there are some contentious elements to it. For example:

- The phase 'use drama' suggests that drama is a tool to be applied in order to achieve something else. Perhaps it is, but some people might argue that working in drama is an end in itself. To achieve its full potential, they might say, the work must help students see how they can manipulate the art form for themselves.

- The statement refers to people who have 'special individual needs' rather than 'special educational needs'. Is there a real difference or is this just a case of semantics?

- Finally, the statement promises 'an insight'. This suggests that having an insight would be useful for you, the reader, and that the different contributors are somehow worthy to provide it.

The easiest of these contentions to deal with is the last, though the other two will be fully dealt with in due course.

The contributors to this book are all teachers with considerable experience in teaching young people who have a wide variety of special educational needs. They have all come to believe that in essence there is no difference between the drama activities used in mainstream classrooms and those used in the special school or any class in which the participants have some kind of special educational need. What is often different, though, is the reason for using drama with different groups, the way in which the activities are introduced and developed, and the way in which the outcomes are most appropriately evaluated.

The second contention is thornier, for the very concept of what constitutes a special educational need is undergoing considerable review. For many, images of children so disabled that they are dependent on others will spring to mind, while others will think of those children with behavioural or learning difficulties. The fact is that all manner of physical, mental, social and emotional conditions may manifest themselves as special educational needs. It is a very broad term – so broad, in fact, that it makes more sense to talk about students as having special *individual* needs (as we shall discuss in more detail in Chapter One).

Many teachers new to special education sense that the active, physical aspects of drama may be an invaluable contribution to their classes. This book will provide them with an insight into a wide range of techniques and ideas upon which to draw for practical classroom work. Conversely, while this book does not purport to be an introduction to special education in general, it will give the drama specialist an insight into how the art can contribute to that field.

The chapters in Section One give an overview of the relationship between drama and special education. They set drama in the context of the National Curriculum and outline the role it may play across the curriculum. A range of drama techniques are discussed and illustrated with specific examples of classroom practice.

Section Two contains a number of chapters which outline in more detail drama activities and projects that have been used in a wide array of special education situations. These have been organised in a sequence according to the age-band that each writer has principally worked with.

Melanie Peter describes how she uses popular and familiar stories as the basis of her work with children with severe learning difficulties. She offers a range of practical ways into the stories which will help utilise and extend the imagination of young children.

Gill Brigg focuses on how to plan drama sessions for children with moderate learning difficulties in order to develop language skills. Her practical examples have a wide application across age ranges (one is picked up and developed in Jan Beats' and Penny Barratt's chapter).

Bernard Hodgkin discusses what he learned when he transferred from a comprehensive school to a centre for young people with physical disabilities and learning difficulties. His chapter focuses on how to approach GCSE and production work with young people aged 14 plus. He offers a fascinating insight into how a text as challenging as Lorca's 'Blood Wedding' can be adapted to offer students such as his the chance to perform.

Jan Beats and Penny Barrett work with young people in the 16–19 age group who have general learning difficulties. They describe the strategies they have evolved to work together as teacher and assistant in a special school in order to engage their groups with ongoing dramas.

Andy Kempe's chapter reviews the benefits and problems of making links between special and mainstream schools. This chapter provides an agenda for such projects and describes an example in which a group of sixth-formers worked with students who had a broad range of learning difficulties.

Finally in Section Two, Daphne Payne offers invaluable practical guidance on organising and presenting yourself in the drama classroom. Her particular focus is on working with deaf children but her advice has far wider application. She outlines how she prepares students, most of whom are deaf or hearing impaired, to enter the classroom as teachers and drama leaders. A number of games and exercises designed to enhance physical communication are described, and examples are given of how these can feed into a stylised piece of theatre or serve as the foundation for a structured classroom drama.

Although the chapters are organised in terms of the age-group discussed, this is not a coursebook. The capabilities of students you teach, who are described as having special educational needs, may not relate to their age and it would be inappropriate to follow through the ideas presented here without selecting and adapting them to your own particular situation. However, by describing their work, the teachers who wrote this book hope that you will come to understand why they have gone about things in the way they have. It is not their intention to promote their way of working as the best or only way, or give you answers to the individual problems you face in your teaching situation. Rather, by considering their failures as well as their successes, you may come to steer your own path with a clearer sense of direction and purpose – and if that's not useful, what is?

In Section Three you will find guidance on how to organise the drama experience so that it is a coherent one for the pupils, and understood by parents, governors and inspectors.

At the end of the book you will find details of resources which the contributors have found valuable in the development of their own work, and a number of useful addresses.

ABOUT THE AUTHORS

Penny Barrett worked in comprehensive and primary schools as a teacher's assistant and cook before moving to Addington Special School. She has an NVQ in Child Care with three endorsements – one in Special Education. She has lived in Berkshire all her life and is adamant that she learns more from children than she will ever be able to teach them.

Jan Beats worked as a playleader in an inner-city adventure playground in Liverpool before training to teach children with learning difficulties. She has taught 11 to 19-year-olds in Liverpool, Cornwall and Berkshire and obtained a Certificate of Further Professional Studies in Drama Education from the University of Reading. She is currently curriculum leader for the 14 to 19-year age group at Addington Special School in Reading.

Gill Brigg is a freelance drama teacher and consultant based in Suffolk. She was an advisory teacher for seven years with a particular interest in supporting drama work with children with special educational needs. In addition to delivering in-service work for teachers, she devises and directs theatre in education programmes with a specific emphasis on language development.

Bernard Hodgkin taught in comprehensive schools for sixteen years before moving to the National Star Centre College of Further Education where he is currently Co-ordinator for the Performing Arts. He has taken his students' innovative work to Poland and Italy and in 1994 opened the Cheltenham Festival of Literature with a multi-media production of Ralph Steadman's 'I Leonardo'.

Andy Kempe taught Drama in comprehensive schools in England for ten years and is now a lecturer in Drama Education at the University of Reading. Among his publications are:

Drama Sampler (1988) Basil Blackwell – a collection of play extracts and new approaches to the study of plays.
The GCSE Drama Course Book (1990) Simon & Schuster – a major coursebook for students aged 14–16 studying Drama to examination level.
Imaging (1994) Hodder & Stoughton – a series of three books designed for use in classrooms for 10 to 13-year-olds. Each book uses drama to explore a topic. A Teacher's Book explains the techniques used, and offers different approaches to the resource materials.
Dramascripts Extra (1993–95) Thomas Nelson & Sons – a series of fourteen professionally written playscripts suitable for use with children aged 10 to 16. Each book contains extensive notes on follow-up and research activities.

The Arts and Environmental Education (1995) Council for Environmental Education – a package of ideas designed to help teachers in the arts see how their work can develop knowledge and understanding of the environment in children of all ages.

Andy Kempe has worked in Germany, Norway, Poland and Australia, introducing teachers and teacher-trainers in those countries to different aspects of drama education.

Daphne Payne has been profoundly deaf since the age of 4 but attended a mainstream school where she struggled to lip-read the largely unsympathetic teachers. Rescued from the inevitable academic rubbish-dump by an English teacher who cast her in school plays, she went on to study at the Birmingham School of Speech and Drama and Leeds University. After obtaining a PGCE from Oxford she was forced to teach abroad for three years before being granted a DES number (being unable to pass the medical because of her deafness!) and taking up posts in London and the south-east of England. She moved to Bulmershe College (latterly the University of Reading) in 1985 in order to develop the now highly successful Theatre of the Deaf course. She has worked extensively with the National Deaf Children's Society and as far afield as Russia. She is currently researching physical theatre as a teaching method for students with linguistic disadvantages.

Melanie Peter graduated from Cambridge in 1980 and worked in long-stay hospitals in the creative therapies. After training to teach, she worked in a variety of educational fields concentrating on developing practice in the arts and special education. She is currently an advisory teacher in Norfolk and delivers in-service training in Britain and abroad. She has written three books:

Drama For All (1994) David Fulton
Making Drama Special (1995) David Fulton
Art For All (1995) David Fulton

SECTION ONE

CHAPTER ONE

SPECIAL EDUCATION – NEEDS AND APPROACHES IN DRAMA

INDIVIDUAL NEEDS

In his book simply called *Special Education,* Jonathan Solity discusses the report of the Committee of Inquiry into Special Education which led to the 1981 Education Act on Special Needs. The report, chaired by Baroness Warnock, claimed that about one in six children at any one time and perhaps one in five at some point in their school career, may be in need of special educational provision. The figures were based on a number of large-scale studies but, more recently, Lady Warnock has stated that the figure may just as well have been 'plucked out of the air'.

Solity's point is that the actual figure is irrelevant. What is important is the attitude towards the children to which it refers. 'Seeing that a child in a wheelchair requires a special school rather than a mainstream placement', he says, 'is as much a reflection of our beliefs as an indication of the child's needs'. There are very different implications, he goes on to say, to believing that one in five children are going to experience some kind of difficulty, to thinking that in any one class approximately 20 per cent of the children may not be receiving adequate support. The former perspective makes us regard the problem as being centred in the children themselves; the latter position helps us to see that it is the learning environment that needs changing.

To gather people together under the heading 'special needs' is intrinsically problematical. It suggests that there is a similarity in their needs, whereas in truth the specific special needs of individuals might be wildly disparate. The severity and persistence of different special needs are of course independent of one another. For example, a child who, for some reason, is under great stress at home, may exhibit quite severe learning difficulties but these may, with adequate attention, be overcome. Accident victims similarly might need special attention while they overcome both the physical and mental trauma. On the other hand, a number of medical or social conditions may restrict a person's learning during their whole life though not necessarily in a severe way.

In their helpful book entitled *Classroom Responses to Learning Difficulties,* Bridie Raban and Keith Postlethwaite suggest that:

> "in categorising pupils we are in danger of implying that special educational needs arise because of some deficit on the part of the pupil. A more realistic way of thinking about special needs is to see them arising out of

the interaction between the characteristics of the pupil on the one hand and those of the education system on the other."

It is for this reason that it might be more helpful to think of children as having individual needs. Clearly, there is a correlation between how easy it is to recognise the specific needs of an individual, and how easy it is to deal with them: making sure that a child with poor eyesight sits close enough to the board to see what's written on it, and dealing with a child who is completely blind, are fundamentally different problems. Similarly, dealing with a child who becomes frustrated in the classroom as a result of not understanding a piece of work is a very different problem from dealing with a child who is consistently emotionally disturbed.

In order to come to an understanding of how best to accommodate individual needs, let us look at three contrasting approaches to teaching in general.

THE CHILD-CENTRED APPROACH

The child-centred approach to education may be characterised by the notion of 'starting from where they are'. The teacher pays close regard to how the individual child expresses his or her particular needs through the work and play they engage in. In essence, the child is allowed to set the agenda for that child's own learning.

There is much about this philosophy that is appealing and educationally sound, but it also produces some conundrums which teachers should consider. A negative stereotype of this approach in terms of drama would be that the teacher simply tells the children to make up a play about whatever they like and then watches what they come up with. In 1969, *The Black Papers*, edited by Cox and Dyson, made a sharp criticism of the very notion of child-centred education:

"child-centred education, free activity, no rules, no streaming, no examinations, no teaching and therefore no learning."

Cox and Dyson's position may be seen as extreme but in retrospect their statement can be seen as signalling a move away from the notion that, left to their own devices, children can and will teach themselves: a notion of which many teachers of children with special educational needs have always had good reason to be sceptical.

On the face of it, the idea that young people with special educational needs actually have highly individual needs rather than being part of a cohesive group, may suggest that the most appropriate way of teaching them would be to adopt a child-centred approach. In one sense, this could involve recognising in what ways they are personally challenged and offering them opportunities to work within the parameters dictated by that challenge. Such a philosophy, however, might reinforce the idea that the educational difficulty lies within the child as opposed to within the system or, as Raban and Postlethwaite would have it, in the interface between the two.

For drama teachers, the philosophy of 'child-centred education' throws up an apparent contradiction. Many aspects of 'child-centredness' have been a dearly held factor of much drama teaching in the last forty years. However, its attendant aims of self-expression and creativity have had to be set against the fact that drama, as an art form, is essentially a social activity and demands a negotiation of meaning and method which may negate the very possibility of complete individualism.

David Hargreaves has referred to 'the fallacy of individualism' which has 'led teachers to deny and fear the social functions of education'. This is nowhere more apparent than in the social art form of drama where teachers have become aware that it may not be justifiable or 'good' simply because that expression has come from the child. If an expression is totally incomprehensible and seems unrelated to anything else the child has done, how can anyone judge it to have actually expressed anything?

A key facet of drama as an art form is communication. This assumes that somehow the bridge between what a child wants to express and what an audience (I use the term in the widest possible sense) perceives is crossed in some way. This may involve use of spoken language or, in drama, the use of facial expression, gesture, sound and movement. Whatever the form of expression, it must be comprehensible – that is, convey some meaning to another party – for it to be deemed drama. Seen this way, drama would seem to demand some element of tuition and critical response in order to help the child appreciate which elements of the work are communicating meaning and which are not.

The other aspect of the social function of the drama teacher's work concerns the group as a whole. If the expression chosen by one individual is in some way offensive in form or content to the rest of the group, then the teacher surely has a responsibility to address that. Here again we see that to argue for the absolute right of the individual to express him or herself may not be automatically assumed to be educationally acceptable because the resultant behaviour may not be socially acceptable.

Some specialist therapists have, of course, made notable use of drama when working with individual clients in order to deliberately release responses which would be unacceptable in the social situation of most classrooms. The difference between such 'drama therapy' and drama as either a method used across the curriculum or as an art form in its own right is discussed below. Suffice it to say here that social dynamics are a fundamental part of most educational drama work just as they are an essential factor of any experience grounded in dramatic art.

THE TEACHER-CENTRED APPROACH

Apparently contrary to a purely child-centred approach would be a purely teacher-centred one. This can be characterised by the teacher (who may simply be acting on behalf of the institution) dictating the classroom activity. In its most recognisable form, all the children engage in the same activity at the same time, following the teacher's instructions. Again, many teachers of children with special educational needs saw the folly of this approach long ago. Given the different individual difficulties their pupils experienced, expecting them all to be able to tackle a task at the same rate was always unlikely to bring anything but frustration. In drama, grouping the children prudently can sometimes enable them to help each other and so even the pace at which different groups work, but grouping children can also sometimes exacerbate their differences.

The teacher-centred approach is often seen as being essentially traditionalist and holding to the paradigm that children are either empty vessels needing to be filled up with facts, machines that need to be programmed to perform new tasks, or naive innocents who needs their attitudes and ideas changing to fit the more acceptable views of the teacher. Curiously, a good deal of drama teaching which has purported to be child-centred may fit into this category by merit of the fact that whole classes are often required to engage in the same activity in order to pursue a theme selected as being worthwhile by the teacher. To genuinely empower children to develop the skills they regard as worthwhile and provide classes with equal opportunities surely suggests differentiation of activity rather than working towards an end determined largely, if not solely, by the teacher.

It may be that a more realistic look at the part teachers play in learning is needed if both they and the children they work with are to reach their full potential.

THE INTERVENTIONIST APPROACH

Many commentators on teaching young people with learning difficulties would agree that the principles of good teaching are the same no matter what the make-up of the class. No special or mysterious methods which aren't already in the employ of any sound teacher need be utilised. The underlying question is always the same: 'What is it that teachers do which leads to successful learning?' The simple answer is that they teach. That is, they take account of the individuality of the members of the group but design a programme of learning around a number of objectives that they, as teachers, deem desirable, and steer the group towards them. Centring the teaching approach on the needs of each child in the group is not the same as promoting individuality above all factors.

This view is consistent with that of Russian psychologist Vygotsky. In his work he describes how children have a 'zone of proximal development' or ZPD.

That is, because of children's individual circumstances they are always limited in just how far they can progress from any given starting point. By actively stimulating the children, the teacher in effect puts them onto a new starting point and consequently provides a new ZPD. Left to their own devices, the child may stand still or, worse, regress to the original point of departure. Through careful observation, the teacher recognises the direction in which the child appears to be progressing, and through intervention ensures that another forward step is taken.

At the risk of being simplistic and flippant, I liken the process to that of a frog sitting on a lily-pad. Should someone touch it, the frog can jump up to one metre. What we don't initially know is in which direction the frog will jump. So we touch the frog and find out. He jumps and lands on a second lily-pad. His ability range is still one metre, but from his new pad the frog has new horizons; neither he nor we, his 'stimulators', should see any purpose to his returning to the first lily-pad. So it is with teaching. The model is child-centred in that we want children to develop as individuals, but we do this by stimulating and intervening in a way that recognises the nature of the wider environment: the size, shape, dangers and opportunities of the pond, if you like. Successful teaching takes account of the social functions of education. To stretch the analogy even further, it is clearly important not to tickle the frog all over; if you over-stimulate it, it may not know in which direction to jump at all!

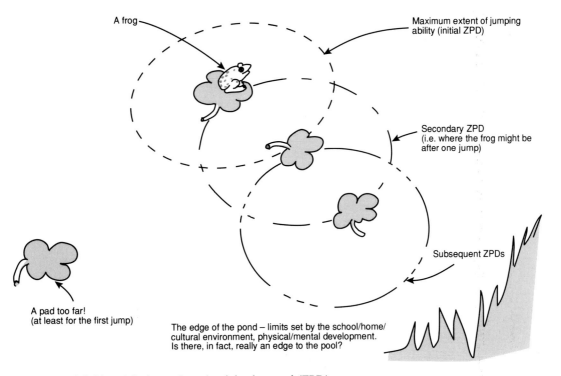

Figure 1 Vygotsky's idea of the 'zone of proximal development' (ZPD)

A seminal work in the field of special educational needs published in 1965 was Tansley and Gulliford's *The Education of Slow Learning Children* – not, perhaps, a title that would find much support today, but nevertheless a book which addressed a broad spectrum of individual needs and was one of the first in this field to draw from the child-centred philosophy favoured at the time by many educationalists. In the book the authors state that:

> *"The benefits derived from creative and expressive activities such as art and craft, drama, music, movement and dance are not so obvious and there is a tendency to think of these rather as relaxation after the more serious work of school is done. Our view is that they provide experiences which are essential for the full development of pupils."*

I suspect that while some schools may still think of the arts only in terms of 'relaxation', a greater number do accept that they have an essential part to play in 'the full development of pupils'. However, what may have been thought about less is 'Why?'

To create something that successfully expresses a feeling or belief, is to engage with those cultural aspects of human life which join people together regardless of any individual physical or mental differences. Using the arts as a vehicle by which people can acquire new social, physical, communicative or mental skills will of course help them to understand and survive in the world outside the drama session. To promote self-advocacy is to acknowledge and respect the dignity and integrity of the individual. Tansley and Gulliford, in their promotion of the arts as an essential part of children's education, adopted the stance that the arts stimulated intelligence. There is another view, but to understand that it is necessary to go further back to the fundamental ways in which we come to know the world.

It can be argued that all children, whatever their individual needs, should be entitled to an arts education not because of how the arts might serve other elements of the curriculum or stimulate intelligence, but because they are a manifestation of intelligence in themselves. The relationship between the cognitive and the aesthetic is discussed in greater detail in David Best's book *The Rationality of Feeling*.

Psychologist Jerome Bruner and educational philosopher Louis Arnaud Reid have variously proposed that there is a kind of knowledge other than that which concerns itself with objective facts which exists only in the cognitive domain. Rather, it is based in sensate experience and as such is of a fluid and personal nature yet still offers insights and structures for understanding and assessing one's place in the world. This type of knowledge has been termed 'aesthetic knowing'. On the basis of this thinking, David Ward has explained why a recognition of the existence of aesthetic knowing is crucial in the education of children with special educational needs by considering the five following constituent factors.

Sensation

In the first instance, we come to know the world through our senses. In the case of most people, there are five senses that can give information about the world but some people have fewer, which inevitably results in their coming to know the world in a different way.

Perception

When we perceive, we register what we have sensually experienced. This involves fitting the sensation into a scheme. This is essentially a cognitive process. For example, if I stuck my finger in someone's back, their skin would give under the pressure. Assuming they have the sense of touch they will feel this pressure. Whether or not they register this, though, is dependent on a cognitive ability which, in the case of some people, is not fully functional.

Representation

This is a particularly strong feature of aesthetic knowing as it involves a person using their own body to represent a sensate experience. For example, if I asked someone to show me what happened when I stuck my finger in their back they might physically replay their reaction or, interestingly for the drama specialist to witness, they might adopt the role of me and actually replay the action using a classmate to represent themselves. The degree to which any of us is able to do this depends upon our ability to utilise a potentially artistic medium. Some children are extraordinarily gifted in some modes of representation; for example, take the child who may be able to reproduce in phenomenal detail something she has heard, yet may not be exercising any 'artistic' choices in the way she does it; she is simply 'playing back' the experience.

Sometimes people represent things in surprising ways. For example, asked to represent the experience of the finger in the back they may show what they think the person was doing by jabbing their finger into thin air, or perhaps even their other hand. It is surely a fundamental point for arts education that teachers realise people simply don't always represent experiences in the same way.

Synthesis

Human beings with unimpaired senses relate to things through multi-sensory activity. For example, on feeling a sharp pressure in the back most people would turn around to use their eyes to see what was going on. However, should they be standing at a cash point with a wad of twenty-pound notes in their hands, they may prefer to prick up their ears in order to try to pick out other clues as to what is going on. The point is that many people have the ability to support one sense with another. By the same token, if a person is without one of the senses, the others may be employed to compensate the deficiency in order that they come to know the world; many of us can cite examples of people who, though sensorily disabled in one way, can demonstrate exceptional ability in the use of other senses.

Structuring

Humans seem to have a desire to 'close' an experience and pigeonhole it for future reference. On checking exactly what it is that is sticking into one's back, the experience can be closed by treating it as a joke, an accident or perhaps a deliberate assault. We cannot assume though that people structure things in the same way. There are other factors concerning context and previous experience which will inevitably affect the way in which any given experience is construed. A person who has actually been held up at gunpoint might react in a very alarming way to having a finger stuck in her back because of her previous experience. It might be that a person is deemed to have a special individual need because of the way they appear to interpret and structure situations.

The arts educator working in the field of special needs must be able to pinpoint which area or areas seem to be impeding aesthetic developing, and try to emphasise other areas in order to support it. In essence, the work emphasises what the children can do rather than confronting them with what they can't do. In the case of severely mentally disabled people it may be that any reaction to a visual, aural or physical stimulus represents the beginnings of aesthetic knowing.

K. J. Weber's book *Yes, they can!* outlines a number of practical ways in which teachers can help young people with learning difficulties to achieve more. I believe that Weber's suggestions support Ward's proposal that teaching should be a more sensate experience. For example, Weber suggests that problems are presented in a variety of ways in the classroom. Perhaps most important is the teacher's personal communication with the children when there is the possibility of supporting the instruction with facial expression, gesture, tone and modulation of voice. Pupils were found to solve problems better when they were given relevant materials and allowed to physically move things around. Similarly, when problems were presented in concrete rather than abstract terms, so that the children could visualise a 'real' situation, their performance improved.

All of these things might seem obvious and the everyday 'meat' of drama teaching but we should not underestimate the importance of paying special attention to the part they play in the drama session. A central problem in some children's ability to learn is a lack of spatial awareness. For example, the symbol on a map may be the same as that shown in the key but because they might be oriented differently the child does not recognise them as being the same. Children beginning to read often get the letters b and d and sometimes p mixed up. The problem may rest in their inexperience of dealing with space and what happens to objects when they are revolved or reflected.

In a similar vein an understanding of time often creates problems for young children and those with learning difficulties. Time is relative. 1956 is a date in their past but it was in the future to people living 100 years ago!

Both space and time are essential elements of drama. By making special use of them drama teachers may be helping their pupils overcome their learning difficulties at a fundamental level; that is, by addressing the way they come to know the world aesthetically rather than through abstract cognition alone.

SOCIOLOGICAL FACTORS IN SPECIAL EDUCATION

It would be naive, and certainly misleading, to suggest that most children with special educational needs had learning difficulties arising out of some physical or mental disability. Sadly, in many schools, the very terms 'learning difficulties' and 'special needs' are all too often loosely (and sometimes pejoratively) applied to children whose behavioural response to education makes them difficult to accommodate in the mainstream classroom.

The fact that certain social and racial groups seem over-represented in samples of children receiving special education, begs the question of whose interests are being served by identifying these children as having special needs. Any system that seeks to segregate children according to ability works through the establishment of a norm. If learning difficulties were wholly a matter of medically definable conditions there might be less contention surrounding the identification of and provision for those in need of special education. As it is, a great many children are categorised, either through formal statements or in the popular conceptions of teachers, as having special needs on the grounds of rather more subjective views as to what the norm is. Segregating children who do not tend to fit into the norm of the mainstream classroom may be seen as a way of controlling them and offering them something more suitable to their individual needs. More cynically, it may also be seen as a means of getting them out of the way of those who can learn without too much difficulty providing there isn't too much distraction.

Many drama teachers in mainstream schools find themselves teaching classes in which pupils who are segregated in other lessons are re-integrated with their peers for the drama lesson. Sometimes this causes no problem. A child who has difficulty reading or working with numbers may have no reason to experience difficulty in drama. On the other hand, a pupil who is segregated from lessons because of anti-social behaviour may be as much a nuisance for the drama teacher as for anyone else. The problem lies not so much in any easily definable need of the child, as in the policy of the school or the personal ability of the teachers to cope with the situation. To re-state Raban and Postlethwaite, 'special needs' may be seen as 'arising out of the interaction between the characteristics of the pupil on the one hand and those of the education system on the other'. Much as it sounds like a disclaimer, it is regrettably true that neither this book nor any one teacher can produce a solution to all of the problems that arise from the tensions created by different interests of social groups.

THERAPY OR THERAPEUTIC?

Teachers who use drama in their work with children with special educational needs are sometimes wrongly assumed to be involved in 'dramatherapy'. The assumption is that because the child has some kind of learning disability, the only type of drama they might usefully engage with is designed to help them with their particular individual need.

The practice of dramatherapy is built on the belief that there are elements of drama which can actually help with and heal specific problems. Dramatherapy is the intentional use of these elements with individuals or groups of people who broadly share the same kind of difficulty or problem. Sometimes this involves helping people to be creative or to express themselves in order to give form to the problem. Sometimes the work is task-centred and designed to furnish the participants with physical or social skills.

Some forms of dramatherapy have been quite highly publicised. One-to-one work with abused children and group work with violent prisoners have, for example, been the subject of numerous documentaries. The purpose of using drama with these clients is to help both the therapist and therefore the clients to understand and deal with the psychological background and implications of events in the individual client's life.

Dramatherapy is a developing approach to the treatment and education of specific groups. While some children with special educational needs might benefit from the approach, it should not be assumed that any child needs dramatherapy any more than they need physio- or electro-convulsion therapy. *Dramatherapy with Families, Groups and Individuals* (1990) and *Dramatherapy, Theory and Practice* (Vol. 1 1987, Vol. 2 1992), by Sue Jennings give a fuller account of current thinking in this field.

Any reservation about the applicability of dramatherapy for children with special educational needs should not be confused with the belief that any well structured and carefully monitored work in the arts can be therapeutic by merit of the fact that it can give the individual a greater sense of competence and self-worth. The act of externalising and making concrete some inner impulse so that it can be reflected upon, proves to us that we have an independent existence which draws from and feeds back into the world around us. Aesthetic activity proves we are alive (just as an anaesthetic will send us to sleep); it doesn't have to be a treatment, but it is a manifestation of our humanity.

REFERENCES

Best, D. (1991) *The Rationality of Feeling*, The Falmer Press

Bruner, J. (1962) *On Knowing – Essays for the Left Hand*, Harvard University Press
(1986) *Actual Minds, Possible Worlds*, Harvard University Press

Cox, C.B. and Dyson, A.E. (1969) *Fight for Education: A Black Paper*, Critical Quarterly Society

Hargreaves, D. (1982) *The Challenge for the Comprehensive School*, Routledge & Kegan Paul. See also pp. 30–31, 51, 82, 174, 226–27

Jennings, S. (1987) *Dramatherapy, Theory and Practice 1*, Routledge
(1990) *Dramatherapy with Families, Groups and Individuals*, Jessica Kingsley
(1992) *Dramatherapy, Theory and Practice 2*, Routledge

Raban, B. and Postlethwaite, K. (1988) *Classroom Responses to Learning Difficulties*, Macmillan

Reid, L.A. (1986) *Ways of Understanding and Education*, Heinemann

Solity, J. (1992) *Special Education*, Cassell Education

Tansley, A.E. and Gulliford, R. (1960) *The Education of Slow Learning Children*, Routledge & Kegan Paul

Vygotsky, L. (1978) *Interaction Between Learning and Development in Mind and Society*, Harvard University Press

Ward, D. (1989) 'The arts and special needs' in Ross, M. *The Claims of Feeling*, The Falmer Press

Weber, K.J. (1978) *Yes, they can!* Oxford University Press

CHAPTER TWO

DRAMA IN THE SPECIAL CURRICULUM

A MULTITUDE OF SINS

Since Drama first started to become an accepted subject in schools some forty years ago it has accrued something of a mystique. Grand claims have been made about its potency as an educative and liberating force. It has been said that the subject:

- promotes self-expression
- aids self-confidence
- enhances creativity
- encourages co-operation

These are laudable aims and it may well be true that Drama meets them, but many teachers other than those using Drama might claim that their work was serving similar purposes.

In practice, activities labelled as 'drama' have covered a vast spectrum. They have included:

- physical and mental games
- role plays
- discussions
- simulation exercises
- physical, mental and vocal warm-up activities
- trust exercises
- movement and dance work
- working with masks and puppets.

For many parents, school governors, and indeed anyone else who might have had occasion to look in on some of these sessions, calling the activities 'drama' must have been rather confusing. The relationship between these active, and usually fun-filled, sessions and what people have seen on the professional or school stage or television under the heading 'drama' has frequently been far from clear.

This isn't to say that many of the practical, physical and usually group-based activities done under the banner of 'drama' aren't useful. Far from it. What this book is interested in is looking at work which does bear a clear relationship to the most widely accepted meaning of the term 'drama'.

DRAMA AND THE DRAMATIC

We often talk about 'real-life dramas' or describe something as being 'dramatic' yet accept that there is a difference between these events and what we recognise as 'drama' when we see it on television or the stage. The simple difference is that the dramatic events of our real lives tend to happen in spite of us; they are the result of various circumstances conspiring together in a way that we personally can't always control. When we watch a play or film, however, we know that the events depicted have been selected and carefully crafted in order to achieve particular effects. It is the difference between standing in a bank queue and suddenly finding yourself involved in a hold-up, and watching a bank raid in a TV cop show.

Perhaps this suggests that the drama work described in this book is all about making up and performing plays. In a way, that's right, though the projects described in this book illustrate ways of making that process an appropriate educational experience for the children, rather than a vicarious one or one geared solely towards the entertainment of onlookers. The final product may not be packaged in the same way as a professionally written and produced play, but it will have many, if not all, of the same essential ingredients.

What is at the heart of the thing we call 'drama in education'? Look at these definitions:

> *"Drama in schools is a practical artistic subject ... It relies on the human ability to pretend to be someone or something else."*
>
> HMI, *Drama from 5 to 16*

> *"It involves the creation of imagined characters and situations which are enacted within a designated space."*
>
> Arts Council of Great Britain, *Drama in Schools*

> *"Drama occurs when one or more human beings isolated in time and space present themselves in imagined acts to another or others."*
>
> Bernard Beckerman, *The Dynamics of Drama*

> *"Any activity which involves human beings in projecting themselves into an imaginary situation and using their voices and bodies to act out the characters and events they have imagined, may be described as drama."*
>
> Ann McClintock, *Drama for Mentally Handicapped Children*

Such attempts to economically define drama are of course many and various but from these alone one may see that drama involves the following.

Characters

Someone must be in the drama. It may be that the people are playing themselves or someone (perhaps something!) else. Either way, drama involves asking the question *Who are we?*

Place

Drama takes place somewhere. At one level we could say that it takes place in the school hall or classroom. But just as we can imagine being someone else, it often suits our purpose to imagine that we are somewhere else. So the question is *Where are we?*

Time

Drama is a temporal art; that is, unlike the visual or literary arts, time itself is an element. When the event has passed, it has passed for ever. The drama session may take place every Tuesday morning or whenever it suits the teacher to dip back into it. But whenever they dip back in, the group need to know *When is this taking place?*

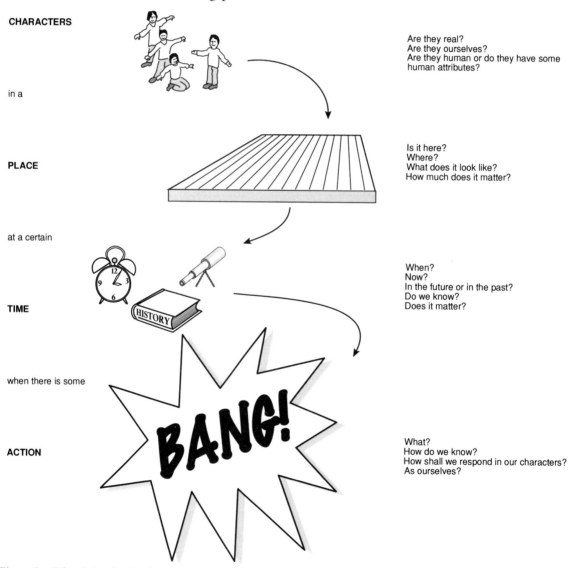

CHARACTERS

in a

PLACE

at a certain

TIME

when there is some

ACTION

Are they real?
Are they ourselves?
Are they human or do they have some human attributes?

Is it here?
Where?
What does it look like?
How much does it matter?

When?
Now?
In the future or in the past?
Do we know?
Does it matter?

What?
How do we know?
How shall we respond in our characters?
As ourselves?

Figure 2   What is involved in drama

Event

The question here is '*Why* are we who we say we are, when and where we say we are?' In other words, what is there about the situation that is going to make the whole enterprise engaging for those involved? What's 'dramatic' about it?

Somewhere or other, fiction is a central element. In drama, a story is told in an enactive way. It may be that the children, playing themselves, are magically transported to a different time or place. The insights they gain there might help them to see themselves in a new light. Or perhaps they play other people, who find themselves in our here and now. What insights about their world might children gain by trying to see it through the eyes of someone else?

It may well be that teachers build, develop and begin to explore the fictional world of drama through careful use of games, exercises, movement, written plays or improvisation. Notwithstanding the constraints of the National Curriculum, there is no need to be precious about where one subject ends and another begins in classroom practice. The most important factor is whether the teacher considers the activity, whatever its nature, to be of benefit to the pupils. If working through the fiction of drama can do the job, teachers should use it.

DRAMA IN SCHOOLS

Schools have tended to make use of drama in the following four ways.

PRESENTING PLAYS

Most schools annually present a play to parents and visitors. It's a whole school event and one that usually generates tremendous excitement and satisfaction. Sometimes the children work from a script, sometimes from their own ideas. In many schools, members of staff take on a part themselves and this can add to the excitement and fun of the occasion. Such plays are a means by which schools can celebrate themselves and demonstrate the culture that exists in their micro-society. David Hargreaves has called the school play 'an exemplar of differentiated team work' and in that description he clearly signals that no matter what the ability of the individual, everyone can play some part in the making and presenting of the venture.

In many schools, children regularly perform short plays in assemblies or by way of sharing with others the work they have been doing in their class. Sometimes, the time put aside for drama consists almost entirely of small groups of children preparing short plays which they then show to their classmates.

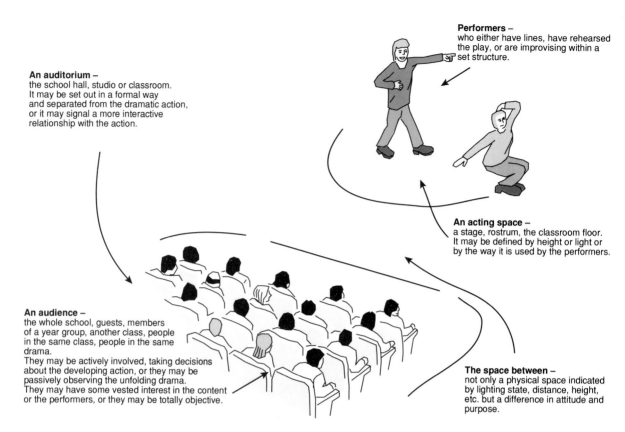

Performers –
who either have lines, have rehearsed the play, or are improvising within a set structure.

An auditorium –
the school hall, studio or classroom. It may be set out in a formal way and separated from the dramatic action, or it may signal a more interactive relationship with the action.

An acting space –
a stage, rostrum, the classroom floor. It may be defined by height or light or by the way it is used by the performers.

An audience –
the whole school, guests, members of a year group, another class, people in the same class, people in the same drama.
They may be actively involved, taking decisions about the developing action, or they may be passively observing the unfolding drama.
They may have some vested interest in the content or the performers, or they may be totally objective.

The space between –
not only a physical space indicated by lighting state, distance, height, etc. but a difference in attitude and purpose.

Figure 3   Presenting plays

COMPLEMENTING WORK ACROSS THE CURRICULUM

Elements of drama are often used in other curriculum areas. For example, in some schools personal and social education has a separate time on the timetable and the teacher will use drama to explore issues as part of the programme. Role play is sometimes used to prepare young people for specific situations such as interviews, or to review incidents that seem important to the group. Role play is often used to help foster skills in both the mother tongue and foreign languages. Melanie Peter, in her book *Drama for All,* spells out the contribution that drama may make to the development of language. She discusses how symbolic understanding, vocabulary, articulation, accuracy, conversational competence, oracy and literacy are all key features of drama work, giving the subject particular relevance to pupils with special educational needs.

The National Curriculum Council produced a poster which illustrated how drama could be used to fulfil some of the requirements of other subjects. Though this poster is largely out of date now, Figure 4 illustrates how drama can 'service' other areas of the whole curriculum.

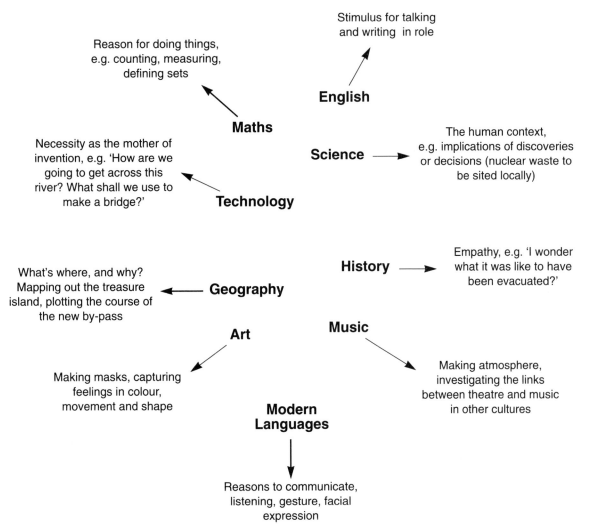

Figure 4   Drama as a way of complementing work across the curriculum

AS A FRAMEWORK FOR THE CURRICULUM

In some schools, drama is placed at the very centre of the curriculum. The tension of the unfolding fiction is used to motivate the pupils in a broad range of tasks.

EXAMPLE

In a drama about Columbus, the children are not simply recruited as sailors, but are employed to measure the hold of the ship, work out exactly what provisions can be stowed there, and how long they will last. Maps are studied, times and speeds calculated, log entries are made, and so on.

Such a project can quickly grow tentacles which touch every part of the National Curriculum; drama becomes the device the teacher uses to give relevance and import to the work. You will find some excellent examples of this kind of approach in the Department for Education's *The Teaching and Learning of Drama*.

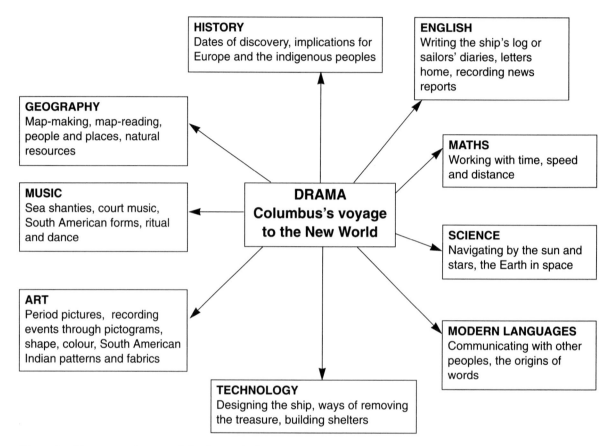

HISTORY
Dates of discovery, implications for Europe and the indigenous peoples

ENGLISH
Writing the ship's log or sailors' diaries, letters home, recording news reports

GEOGRAPHY
Map-making, map-reading, people and places, natural resources

MATHS
Working with time, speed and distance

MUSIC
Sea shanties, court music, South American forms, ritual and dance

DRAMA
Columbus's voyage to the New World

SCIENCE
Navigating by the sun and stars, the Earth in space

ART
Period pictures, recording events through pictograms, shape, colour, South American Indian patterns and fabrics

MODERN LANGUAGES
Communicating with other peoples, the origins of words

TECHNOLOGY
Designing the ship, ways of removing the treasure, building shelters

Figure 5   Drama as a framework for the curriculum

AS A SUBJECT IN ITS OWN RIGHT

In the mainstream secondary school, Drama and Theatre Studies continue to attract a large number of candidates at both GCSE and A Level. Drama has its own history and traditions which can be taught. Like all the other arts, it also involves practical skills related to the form itself which children can be introduced to and tutored in.

In music, children learn the properties of rhythm, tone, pitch, melody, pace, and so on. In art, line, colour, texture, pattern and scale are seen as key elements of the work.

In the above discussion on drama and the dramatic, we stated that drama involves an enacted pretence. It tells a story about some characters. The content of the story and the nature of the characters obviously changes from drama to drama, but at heart the work makes use of certain key elements which might be listed as:

- use of space
- gesture and facial expression
- use of sound and voice
- costume, make-up and other design elements
- use of light and colour.

If we accept that teaching art or music or history or geography can be useful and interesting for children with special educational needs, there can be no logic in suggesting that drama, as a subject in its own right, is somehow different. What may be particularly appropriate is to dig a little below the surface and recognise not just what knowledge exists in the subject, but how it came to be there, and what its use is. In history, for example, teachers may see more purpose in giving their pupils the skills to ask questions about how and why things happened rather than just teaching them that they did happen. So it is in drama. It may be far more fruitful to explore how things acquire meaning and how that meaning is effectively communicated than simply to re-enact a story. If this sounds complicated and beyond the abilities of your pupils, consider the powerful effect that might be achieved by re-telling a story from a different point of view or in a different way.

EXAMPLES

The children in a drama about Columbus's voyage, having cheered at the sight of land, are then asked to imagine themselves as people on the shoreline watching and commenting on the strange boats full of shouting, wild men which appear to be coming closer and closer. Having discussed both perspectives, the teacher invites them to re-enact the jubilation of the men on the boat and then slowly move across the room changing their expression as they do so until they are representing the scene on the beach.

Another example: After the teacher has read out an extract from the daily log of one of the officers, the class are asked to mime what they think the daily life was like for the ordinary seamen. As they laboriously go about the gruelling work, the teacher sits at a desk and again reads the officer's log.

In both cases, the stark contrasts are captured for the children.

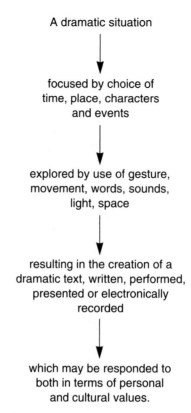

A dramatic situation

↓

focused by choice of
time, place, characters
and events

↓

explored by use of gesture,
movement, words, sounds,
light, space

↓

resulting in the creation of a
dramatic text, written, performed,
presented or electronically
recorded

↓

which may be responded to
both in terms of personal
and cultural values.

Figure 6   Drama as a subject

There is a place for all of these approaches in schools, just as there is a place for any activity that can challenge children and help them develop new skills and knowledge about themselves and the world in which they live. The projects described in Section Two of this book encompass all four of these manifestations.

DRAMA, SPECIAL EDUCATION AND THE NATIONAL CURRICULUM

A criticism of the National Curriculum, when it was first imposed, was that it largely ignored the possibilities offered by a view of learning based in sensate rather than cognitive experience (though Bruner would certainly argue that 'aesthetic knowing' was cognitive in its own way – see Chapter One). It is a curious thing, though, that in the National Curriculum Council's booklet *Curriculum Guidance 9: The National Curriculum and Pupils with Severe Learning Difficulties,* it is stated that:

> *"access to National Curriculum subjects alone cannot meet all the needs of pupils. The whole of the curriculum should seek to do this. For all pupils with SEN the content of the whole curriculum will be particularly important."*

In one sense, this seems to offer encouragement for those teachers who wish to use drama in their work with pupils with special individual needs. Drama is not a foundation subject and so could be completely ignored in schools (though it is, to some degree, accommodated within the English Orders). But here, teachers are being told to recognise the value of things other than the foundation subjects.

Many teachers welcomed Drama's exclusion from the list of National Curriculum subjects because it meant they were released from what they saw as reductive and restrictive practices of assessment which dictated how the time was to be spent in sessions. On the other hand, the absence of Programmes of Study for Drama threw teachers back on their own resources and, for many, generated a feeling of not knowing what to do for the best. This is a situation which hasn't been resolved by Sir Ron Dearing's report, and suggests that both drama specialists in mainstream schools, and teachers simply wishing to use drama with pupils with learning difficulties, need other forums in which to share and develop examples of actual classroom practice.

My own curiosity about the NCC statement above is that it suggests that 'the whole curriculum' is more important to pupils with special educational needs than to others. Why? Perhaps the statement is suggesting that there are things outside the National Curriculum that are more potent educative tools than the foundation subjects. What a shame it is, therefore, that many children – that is, those in mainstream education – are being denied the same degree of access to these as children deemed to have special educational needs! The point is that the *Guidance* may be fallaciously grouping children with individual needs into a cohesive body, a trap that I have already discussed above, not so much to their detriment in this case, but to the detriment of children in the mainstream.

Teachers of drama in the mainstream have, however, found powerful arguments to defend their practice despite its exclusion from the foundation subjects. These range from promoting the efficacy of drama as a method of delivering other subject areas and the required cross-curricular themes, to pointing out the continued growth of drama as an examination subject at GCSE and A Level. It is not appropriate to rehearse or represent those arguments here but it may be sufficient to point out two things. Firstly, if arguments can be found for using drama in mainstream education, they must surely be applicable to children with special individual needs on the grounds that children in mainstream education are individuals also. Secondly, if there is the perception that work outside the foundation subjects is somehow 'particularly important' to children with special individual needs, then teachers who want to use drama and can match their work to the needs of their pupils should take this as a licence to do so. The practical ideas and advice contained in Section Two of this book will help them do so, as will the explanation of drama methods discussed overleaf.

Ann Cattanach, drawing on earlier work by Sue Jennings, offers three models of learning in drama. I believe that it is best to resist seeing these models as being mutually exclusive. Any drama-based project may be seen to have elements of all three, though the balance and emphasis can be seen to change depending on how the teacher perceived the needs of the group (or, indeed, how the group perceive their own needs and recognise the opportunities that drama offers them).

CREATIVE AND EXPRESSIVE

In the 'creative–expressive' model, the work is designed to cater for what is deemed to be the natural, healthy desire of the group to explore both their own environment and ideas, and the world beyond their personal experience, through whatever physical or linguistic means seem appropriate. Part and parcel of this exploration is the communication of the responses to it. Sometimes this may be to some kind of passive audience, as in the presentation of a piece of work to parents or another class. More often the communication is an integral part of the process of self- or group expression.

EXAMPLE

A group of secondary-age children with a wide array of learning difficulties met weekly to take part in a drama set on a spaceship. Posed with the problem of whether or not to rescue a group of aliens who were pleading for help, the participants had to communicate with each other in order for the drama to move on. What was communicated was, of course, personal expressions of fear, hope and moral uncertainty.

Sometimes the work is more abstract; the expression takes the form of movement or use of sounds other than words. In this model, the teacher may intervene not only to stimulate the creativity of the participants, but to offer other ways of expressing the feelings and ideas generated. Positive intervention does not dictate what the participants express or how they do it, but it does offer them new choices. One might say that the focus of this model is on the thing made.

TASKS AND SKILLS

In the 'tasks–skills' model, the work focuses on clearly recognisable deficits in the participants' experience and ability. The intervention of the teacher here is designed to offer highly focused activities which confront the participants with their weakness and aim to help them overcome it. While this sounds rather drastic, the educational practice being espoused is no different to the teacher of reading who spends a little extra time listening to slower readers read, or the tutor who encourages a child to talk about what is upsetting him. Within this model would fall many of those highly specialised activities such as 'dramatherapy' or 'playtherapy'. Here, the focus is on the participants' engagement with 'making' rather than on the thing made.

EXAMPLE

In one special school class of 11-year-olds, there were three pupils who were quite good readers, and the other children tended to rely on their skill to avoid having to read for themselves. A half-day workshop was devised in which the three readers worked with an assistant on designing and building a dummy time-bomb. Their classmates, meanwhile, worked as detectives with their teacher who presented them with a series of cryptic clues as to the bomb's whereabouts. The first letter of each clue formed an acrostic. To solve each clue, the children had to interview a number of different characters (played by the teacher in role), look up words in dictionaries and spend some time re-arranging words into sentences then letters into words. They eventually set off around the school to find the bomb. The fiction of the drama had motivated these children to handle words with more confidence and purpose.

The main skills promoted in this example were to do with reading; drama was used to complement another area of the curriculum. As has already been discussed, though, drama demands the use of certain skills integral to its own form. In this example, the moments when the children had to interview the teacher in role as another character, gave them the opportunity to use language appropriate to their role as detectives. The teacher also cleverly used her own language to give the pupils the chance to use movement and gesture appropriate to the situation:

> *"You want to talk to me about that stranger that was round 'ere do you? Well, you'd best come in then but mind you wipe those muddy feet and watch your 'ead as you come through this doorway – it's a bit low even for you!"*

SELF-ADVOCACY

In this mode, the group set out to identify themselves as a group and register what they see as their own abilities and weaknesses. Drama is used to explore their personal situation and maybe even change it. Clearly, just coming to recognise one's own strengths and weaknesses might represent a positive change for some young people.

One way of achieving 'self-advocacy' is to employ role play. Simple everyday situations might be re-enacted in the classroom in order to give the young people the chance to explore the dynamic of the situation and practice in dealing with it. In this sense it could be seen as an extension of the 'tasks–skills' model. However, there may not be much room for creative expression in this type of work.

In his book *Disability, Theatre and Education*, Richard Tomlinson, a founder-member of the Graeae Theatre Company, describes why and how disabled people might make theatre. The main quest, in his view, is to theatricalise real events and thereby take power over them. There is a strong social function in the work both for the participants and the audience: 'The aim would be to present a play so that the physically handicapped factor is seen as a common denominator to be ignored rather than patronised.' Interestingly, Tomlinson argues that while it is imperative to recognise the individual differences between people, there is sometimes a positive purpose in promoting commonalities:

> *"To fight for his individual rights, a disabled person has to relinquish his more cherished desire – that is, to be seen as just another member of society. It is conventional to condemn the labelling or lumping together of disabled people. And yet the only way to fight for rights and against discrimination is to accept this label and try to organise an effective political lobby."*

Tomlinson's work throws out many important challenges for both disabled students wanting to use drama and those who work with them. The philosophy has helped Graeae to become a well-respected and internationally recognised theatre company. However, it may be that teachers have good reasons for not wanting to present the work of their students publicly yet are interested in the notion of using drama to promote self-advocacy. In this they may find considerable support in the work of Augusto Boal. Some of his techniques such as 'forum theatre' and 'image theatre' were originally designed to help oppressed people in South America to take a critical look at their own situation and explore ways of changing it. These techniques have now been used around the world with many different types of group. The techniques involve elements of performance but the performance isn't so much for show as a way of demonstrating a problem and speculating on the effectiveness of various solutions. Those watching the performance are engaged because they also have the right to suggest new ways of playing the scene or changing the image. The techniques, which are described more fully in Boal's book *Games for Actors and Non-Actors,* are very flexible and adopted in many of the projects described in this book.

A group of physically disabled young people had been offended by a report in a local newspaper which described them as being 'victims' of certain medical conditions (spina bifida, cerebral palsy, etc.). They set out to create a number of scenes which demonstrated, through a variety of dramatic forms, some everyday situations in which they were hampered not by their medical conditions, but by other people's attitudes towards those conditions. The finished piece of theatre was then shown to a number of other local schools and used as the stimulus of a debate regarding the facilities for disabled people in the town.

THE PROCESS OF DRAMA

In 1992, The Arts Council's *Drama in Schools* booklet was sent to all schools in an attempt to help fill the gap left by the absence of any official programmes of study in drama. The booklet suggests that when people are involved in dramatic activity they are involved in one of three activities: *making, performing* and *responding*. Sometimes, as we shall see, these modes of activity run concurrently in a drama activity. However, recognising the features of these activities can help a teacher plan a balanced programme in drama and lead to recognising where individual pupils have particular strengths.

MAKING DRAMA

The activity of 'making drama' may be seen as stretching along a scale which goes from having an idea, to writing or directing a play. Sometimes we have ideas as a result of mystical, blinding inspiration. More often we have them in response to something we have seen or heard. This implies that making drama involves:

Researching

Discussing

Questioning

Thinking

Sharing and shaping ideas

Experimenting

The scale between having an idea and knowing how to put it into practice isn't linear. Age and academic ability may have little to do with coming up with good ideas. What is needed is an environment that stimulates thought and which encourages people to voice their ideas without fear of being told they are wrong.

In addition to the purely creative side of making, there is a technical side. For ideas to be valuable, they have to be realised. Some young people have tremendous tenacity and practical skills which can be employed to make ideas work. In this sense, 'technical' doesn't only relate to building sets or handling lights, but to finding the words a character might say in a given situation or capturing a feeling in a movement. It is here that making drama becomes blurred with the second type of activity, 'performing drama'.

> *'Making drama' encompasses those activities which involve generating and shaping ideas in order to capture and express meanings in an enactive way.*

PERFORMING DRAMA

One of the elements of drama that distinguishes it from other art forms is the way in which it uses – and indeed exists – in time. It is a 'temporal art form'.

If drama is about capturing and expressing meanings, the notion of 'text' becomes important. Understandably, you may think of 'text' as the words that characters actually say in a play. Certainly, a playscript is a kind of text, and one that most people are quite familiar with in terms of what it looks like and how it can be read. But 'text' can mean many other things; anything, in fact, that holds a meaning which becomes apparent when considered by someone looking at it. Given this wider view of 'text', one can see that storyboards, pictograms and even sequences of shapes and colours might be used as texts for drama.

In music, teachers talk of 'notation' to cover the variety of ways in which the actual sounds made in music can be recorded on paper. Similarly, in drama, there are many ways of recording or notating the action of a play. Certainly, one way is to write down what is said, but pictograms might show better what is done, and sequences of shapes and colours might be well used to show what feelings are running through the play. David Hornbrook has referred to the 'written text' of drama, but it may serve our purpose better to think of this as covering all the ways in which we get children to record what they want to do or have done in their drama.

David Hornbrook goes on to describe what he calls the 'electronic text'; by this he simply means what is recorded by sound or video equipment. The point of recognising this type of text is that while it clearly records a performance in one way, it doesn't actually capture the same elements that an audience perceived in a live performance. Anyone who has seen the same play in the theatre and then on television will be aware that the camera behaves in a more selective way than the human eye and that the dynamic between an audience and the actors on a stage is very different from that which exists between a person and a television screen.

The third category of dramatic text is the 'performance text' itself.

The word 'performance', like the word 'text', is rather unfortunately imbued with connotations, many of which are very unhelpful. When we initially think of 'a performance' we are likely to think of actors and actresses presenting something on a stage to an audience sitting expectantly in the dark of the auditorium. The thought of a performance in a school might, in its most negatively stereotyped form, conjure up images of children stumbling through lines and dropping the baby Jesus in front of parents, teachers and friends who are at once delighted with the effort but sceptical of the artistic quality.

But these are narrow views of a word which simply means 'to carry into effect' – that is, to give form to an idea. (In its very broadest sense of the word, the act of notating a play takes on an element of performance as does the rehearsal.) Neither does this broader sense of the word indicate the need for any audience other than the people who are actually involved in the enterprise. Most of us have a strong sense of what we look like and sound like to others; we are an audience to our own performance in any social setting. In drama, this facility for an internal audience is made use of not only to change and make our performance clearer, but to objectively judge the meaning of what we are doing. For example, in an improvisation I might play a boy who is lost in a busy marketplace. By listening to myself and being aware of how others in the drama are reacting to me, I can change my performance to become sadder, more desperate, more frightened. But I also become aware of my own feelings associated with being lost. By stepping into someone else's shoes in the fictitious situation offered by the drama, I gain an insight into a potentially real situation.

Performance then can be seen to encompass the work of a group who have been given time to prepare and then share their ideas through some kind of enactment. It would include the activity that happens after a teacher says to some pupils, 'Stop! Show us that bit again.' It includes the spontaneous role play that would occur when a teacher enters in role (a practical idea which is explained later) as a different character and the children react to the teacher accordingly. In fact, it includes any activity that involves people presenting dramatic ideas to an audience (which might be themselves) for whatever purpose (which might simply be to entertain invited guests, or to explore more deeply a fictitious situation).

Performance can be notated or electronically recorded. But when it is, its meaning inevitably changes because one of the key elements of drama, time, is being used in a different way.

In performance the notion of audience is crucial, even if that audience is oneself. The presence of an audience raises the question: 'In whose interest and for what purpose are we performing?' Such a question must be fundamental if drama is to have an educational purpose. As discussed in Chapter One, an avoidance of addressing such a question may result in children being described as having special needs because their interests do not cohere with those of the educational establishment.

> *'Performing drama' involves communicating with an audience through the dramatic form. It is the physical process of imparting meaning.*

RESPONDING TO DRAMA

Responding to drama might simply be what is happening when we say 'I liked that'.

Of course, we could be responding to a number of things about the drama when we say this. We could be responding to the *content* of the drama; perhaps we liked the story or the characters or the theme. Or we could be responding to the *form*, the way it was done. Our responses could be at a purely felt level:

> *"It moved me/It didn't move me."*
> *"It was good to watch."*

Or they could be intellectual:

> *"I thought it made a good point about ..."*
> *"It was interesting the way you did that ..."*

Responses to drama do not always have to be verbal. Asking children to draw a picture that represents the scene they liked or remembered best could be as valid a way of assessing their perception as discussing or writing a review. Other ways of responding might include drawing a kind of graph to show how they perceived the way the play built up excitement, or ascribing colours or patterns to the different characters: 'If this person was a colour, what colour would they be? If they were a line, would they be a squiggly line, or a jagged line or a curvy line?'

Sometimes our response has more to do with the people playing in the drama than either its form or content, and perhaps you feel that in the teacher's case this should always be so. For when we, as teachers, respond to a piece of drama we want to assess what development the children have made both in the ideas they have come up with and the way they have used them. Just as this evaluation of personal performance is important for us, we should consider how important it is for children also to be able to evaluate fairly their own and each other's work. This implies that they need to see their own work in a context and have something to compare it with. It clearly isn't always appropriate to compare children's work against that of professional actors, but it is fair to consider what they did this term against what they did last term. To do this for themselves, children not only need to be asked about their work, but also to learn how to ask questions of themselves, of each other and of the dramas they experience through television, film and theatre.

'Responding to drama' involves expressing an understanding of what the drama is saying and how it is saying it.

The way in which children engage with this matrix of *making, performing* and *responding* is informed by other factors. Their own feelings and their actual ability or desire to express those feelings are factors. Their existing knowledge and experience becomes part of the equation along with the cultural context in which they are working (this includes both the wider culture outside the school and the social dynamics of the class itself). Figure 7 attempts to show the ingredients of the drama process.

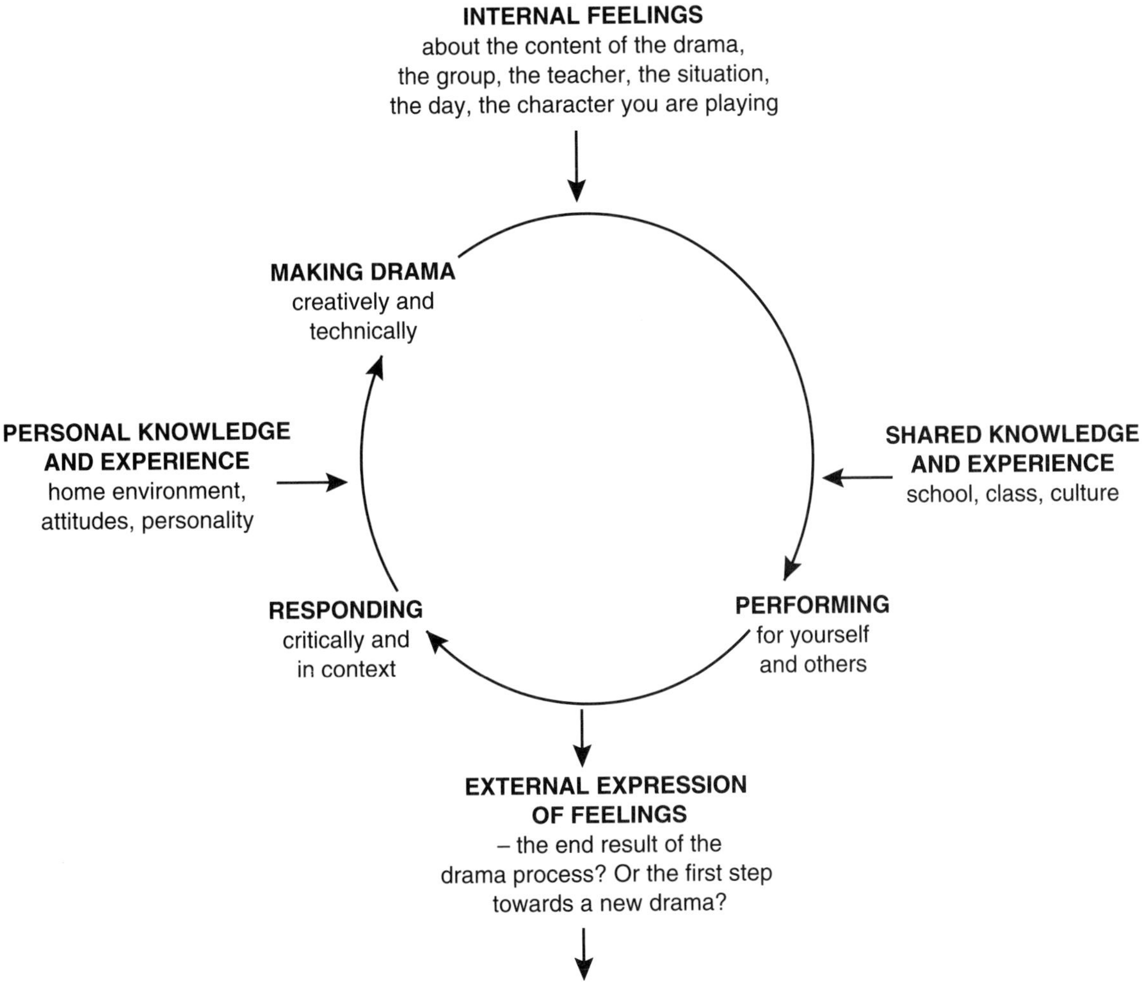

INTERNAL FEELINGS
about the content of the drama,
the group, the teacher, the situation,
the day, the character you are playing

MAKING DRAMA
creatively and
technically

**PERSONAL KNOWLEDGE
AND EXPERIENCE**
home environment,
attitudes, personality

**SHARED KNOWLEDGE
AND EXPERIENCE**
school, class, culture

RESPONDING
critically and
in context

PERFORMING
for yourself
and others

**EXTERNAL EXPRESSION
OF FEELINGS**
– the end result of the
drama process? Or the first step
towards a new drama?

Figure 7   The influences at work in a drama

SUMMARY

So far I have outlined different ways of thinking about drama and noted that activities which could be called drama manifest themselves in four ways:

- the presentation of plays
- complementing other subject-based work
- as a framework for the whole curriculum
- as a subject in its own right.

A consideration of what educational purpose these activities actually affords has produced three 'models' for educational drama:

1 Creative and expressive
2 Tasks and skills
3 Self-advocacy.

We can perceive three types of dramatic activity:

- Making
- Performing
- Responding.

While teachers may favour some types of activities over others or see one model as being more pertinent to their pupils than others, I believe it is best not to see these categorisations as mutually exclusive, but to constantly address the question of what individual needs the children appear to have and how their interests may best be served by any given activity. Chapter Three outlines more specifically what those activities might look like in practice.

REFERENCES

Arts Council of Great Britain (1992) *Drama in Schools*, ACGB

Beckerman, B. (1970) *The Dynamics of Drama*, Drama Book Specialists, New York

Boal, A. (1992) *Games for Actors and Non-Actors*, Routledge

Cattanach, A. (1992) *Drama for People with Special Needs*, A & C Black

Dawson, S.W. (1970) *Drama and the Dramatic*, Methuen

Department for Education (1990) *The Teaching and Learning of Drama*, HMSO

HMI (1989) *Drama from 5 to 16*, HMSO

Hornbrook, D. (1991) *Education in Drama*, The Falmer Press

McClintock, A. (1984) *Drama for Mentally Handicapped Children*, Souvenir Press

National Curriculum Council (1991) *Drama in the National Curriculum* (poster), NCC
(1992) *Curriculum Guidance 9: The National Curriculum and Pupils with Severe Learning Difficulties*, NCC

Peter, M. (1994) *Drama for All*, David Fulton Publishers

Tomlinson, R. (1982) *Disability, Theatre and Education*, Souvenir Press

CHAPTER THREE

DRAMA IN PRACTICE

TOOLS FOR THE TEACHER

Just as children give special names to the games they play, so drama teachers have tended to name the different devices they use to make planning and discussing sessions easier. The problem is that just as 'Cat and Mouse' might signify a particular set of rules in one part of the country, it may be the title of a very different game in another region. We can't be certain therefore that there is necessarily any agreement regarding the exact nature of terms given to drama strategies. Indeed, the fact that there are so many variations is encouraging in that it indicates that the strategies are flexible enough to suit many situations and purposes.

The discussion of terms and strategies that follows represents an honest attempt simply to provide examples of some of the ways in which children can engage with drama. They should certainly not be seen as prescriptive or exclusive. Where appropriate, references have been given to other books which contain more detailed discussions of the strategies.

SOME GENERAL TERMS

IMPROVISATION

This is a very general term which may be seen as covering most of the work done in drama. The word itself implies something newly made from whatever resources are available. Children moving spontaneously to capture the atmosphere of a piece of music are improvising, as are children who have adopted a fictitious role and are answering questions posed by the teacher: 'We've been on this island for a week now. You've all had a good look around. What have you seen?'

Improvisation covers the work that occurs when small groups of children re-enact a story through drama, or the activity resulting from the teacher saying: 'Show me some different ways in which aliens might explore this space.'

Children need some freedom in the way they use a stimulus as the basis for an improvisation if their creativity and technical skill are to develop. An important resource which is always at their disposal is, of course, their own imagination and their own body. Teachers will recognise that it is through their improvisation that children reveal what they already know and can do. In the interventionist model, the teacher's job is to then guide the participants into new areas of experience which will stretch the way they use their own resources.

Useful books on improvisation include:
Impro by Keith Johnstone
Improvisation for the Theatre by Viola Spolin

ACTING

It is not the intention of educational drama to produce young actors and actresses for the entertainment industry (though if children discover they enjoy being involved in the theatre as a result of participating at school that is surely a bonus for them). The notion that drama in schools is somehow explicitly vocational doesn't fit in with most teachers' aspirations and expectations of it and so the term 'acting' has sometimes attracted some negative connotations.

In essence, though, 'acting' can be seen simply as the activity in which a person pretends to be someone or something else. It is quite useful to distinguish here between *characterisation* and *role play*.

Creating a character who has his or her own background story and personality traits can provide tremendous insights for the actor and for anybody who is watching or directly responding to that character.

EXAMPLE

One Year 9 girl in a withdrawal class in a comprehensive school developed the character of a mother whose son had died in a household accident. The rest of the class asked her questions about the incident and soon began to take on the characters of other people she mentioned in her story. The girl was frequently bullied in the class but played the part with such conviction, using a quiet voice, a sad expression and slow, heavy movement, that at no time in the hour-long lesson did any of her classmates do anything that undermined the story she unravelled.

At other times, playing a role is what is necessary to make the drama move along. In this case, it is not the personal traits of the character that matters as much as their function within a given situation.

TEACHER IN ROLE

This is an extremely effective technique to use in the drama situation but the comments above on the difference between characterisation and role play should be borne in mind. The purpose of this strategy is not to demonstrate to the class what a brilliant actor the teacher is and therefore set some kind of example for them to try and follow. Rather, the role should have a very clear function which will get the children responding within the drama.

The most useful type of role for the teacher to adopt is the one that presents the children with some kind of problem. Sometimes this takes the form of an obstacle:

"I'm sorry, you can't come in here without a very good reason indeed."

Sometimes a challenge:

"I'd like to help you but you'll need to show me exactly what you want."

Sometimes a role is used to give the class control of the situation:

"Can you help me, please? I'm completely lost and must find a shelter for my children before nightfall."

Or sometimes to give the class a new piece of information that will move the drama along:

"I've been sent by the king to tell you that he expects you to perform a dance at his daughter's wedding tomorrow, or else!"

There is an excellent short chapter on the teacher in role in Brian Woolland's book *The Teaching of Drama in the Primary School,* and a longer discussion in *Teaching Drama* by Norah Morgan and Juliana Saxton.

These examples are all verbal but a teacher can work in role in a very physical way, particularly if there is another teacher or assistant to help with the session. Costume and make-up can be very stimulating as they signify a role without having to use language.

After finding a tattered treasure map, the class teacher has accompanied his class of Year 7 children in a special school to a desert island (the hall). On arriving, they discover a person (the assistant) dressed like a pirate. Without resorting to speech, the pirate shows that he is astonished at the way these visitors are dressed. He also shows that he is very concerned to keep them away from one particular corner of the hall ...

Children can extract huge enjoyment out of creating a character for the teacher to play and then acting opposite them.

The teacher tips a pile of colourful and bizarre clothes onto the floor and tells the children that they belong to a certain Mrs Bippo. Today is a very special day for her (the children decide why) and she has asked them to help her choose the right clothes for the occasion. As they choose the clothes, the teacher dons them until the group agree she is ready. The teacher then asks the class to advise her on how to play Mrs Bippo: how does she sit, walk, eat, etc? Finally, the teacher explains that on her journey to wherever it is she is going, Mrs Bippo meets a number of other people. The teacher sets off on her journey, giving the class a cue to help them see how they can join in the drama:

"Ah! Here is the flower shop. I think I should wear a flower today. Excuse me, is there anyone serving in this shop?"

WHOLE GROUP DRAMA

In some ways, working as a whole group seems to be a self-evident aim for drama which is, after all, a social art form. However, one danger with the notion is that it might suggest that the teacher adopts a wholly teacher-centred approach and simply sets a series of tasks which every member of the group must undertake. This would clearly be to stifle the creativity of the participants and leave them bereft of the feeling that the drama is theirs.

The most useful way of seeing the term 'whole group drama' is as an organisational device which gives the work a clear context and purpose. Sometimes the whole group might well be involved together. At other times they may be working in smaller groupings or even on their own but the central storyline of the drama will stay the same.

On meeting the pirate on the desert island, the whole class try to communicate with him but he is scared and obviously worried by their presence. The teacher suggests they work in pairs to try and find a way of enticing him out from behind his rock. The children discuss and practise this on their own for a few minutes, then take it in turns to see if their strategy is effective.

Just as the groupings may change from step to step of a whole group drama, so the teacher may suggest new roles for the children and adopt new roles himself if this will give new opportunities to make the story exciting. Sometimes it may be necessary to drop the fictional roles altogether and reflect on what has happened from a personal viewpoint.

There are a number of drama handbooks which explain and offer good examples of whole group work. Teachers new to the idea may find *Drama Structures* by Cecily O'Neill and Alan Lambert particularly helpful.

DRAMA GAMES

A great many sessions purporting to be drama lessons consist almost entirely of games. This is curious and rather depressing because games are not, in themselves, drama and may not even be dramatic. One can see why some confusion arises when the similarity between drama and games is considered:

- both contain elements of play
- both contain elements of tension
- both involve an active engagement
- both frequently require more than one person.

Some of the overall aims of drama in education pertain to many games also:

- they can develop a sense of trust by being non-threatening
- they can promote group co-operation
- they help children understand the need for rules and codes of behaviour
- they can help develop physical and mental dexterity
- they can promote intellectual and emotional flexibility
- they can be used to inject energy into a lethargic group or calm down an over-excited one
- they can help children manipulate space and time.

None of these aims relates specifically to drama, though they can serve as useful physical, mental and social warm-ups across a wide range of abilities. Teachers need to be able to adapt games to suit their own classes, as the following examples show.

Fruitbowl

The class sit in a circle and are labelled, in turn, Orange, Apple, Banana. One member of the group stands in the middle of the circle and calls the name of one of the fruits. Everyone in that set must move from their place and find another place. The person in the middle also tries to grab a vacant place, so someone else is now left in the middle. An alternative to calling the name of one fruit is to call 'Fruitbowl' which makes everybody move.

In the drama context, the players might be responding to some code, for example animals in a zoo who must come out of their cages when they are called for dinner.

An adaptation of this would be to use a semi-circle and play the game using British Sign Language or Makaton.

Crisps and crackers

Two teams face each other in straight lines. When the session leader calls 'Crisps', team A must retreat over a line behind them before their opposites from team B can touch them. When 'Crackers' is called, it is team B's turn to move to cover.

A drama context might be that the players are on an adventure with Indiana Jones. When they hear a certain sound they know that a deadly booby trap will spring, so they must jump back to avoid capture. Children in wheelchairs can have a terrifyingly good time by wheeling backwards over a tape on the floor to safety.

Hot cakes

The teacher repeatedly asks the class to get into smaller groups of a given number. The emphasis is on watching and moving quickly. The game is made more challenging by asking the groups to construct a particular shape or object.

In a drama in which the children are exploring the house of a giant, they have decided to freeze whenever they hear the giant coming. The giant has very good hearing so they must communicate in silence, but he is very short-sighted; if they are clever he will easily mistake them for household objects! Words for numbers may be replaced by simply holding up fingers or cards with shapes or simple drawings of objects.

I'm going on holiday

This is a well-known memory game that can be very helpful for some children with learning difficulties because of the need for repetition. The teacher starts with the line, 'I'm going on holiday and I'm going to take a toothbrush'. The child sitting on the teacher's left repeats the line and adds something of their own:

'I'm going on holiday and I'm going to take a toothbrush and my bag", and so on around the group. The game can easily be adapted to fit the drama context. For example, Columbus's sailors run through their list of provisions before setting off for the New World, or the group make up their shopping list in preparation for some celebration.

No mobility is required for this game which can be good for groups that include non-ambulant children. Objects can of course be mimed and a combination of word and action can help reinforce the memory of the growing list.

Good source books for games are *The Gamesters' Handbook 1 and 2* by Donna Brandes. Brian Woolland gives a detailed example of how a game can be used as the starting point for a whole group drama in *The Teaching of Drama in the Primary School.*

SOME SPECIFIC STRATEGIES

DESIGN

Sketching costumes for characters or drawing places can help build belief in the drama and helps to introduce the way meaning is contained in the way things look. A simple and fun way of actually making costumes is to use a large sheet of card and to draw a life-sized costume onto it. This can be cut out and worn like an apron. See Figure 8.

HOT-SEATING

A character from the drama sits on the hot-seat and answers questions about herself and her situation. Children love to talk to an adult in the hot-seat, but teachers may also think that individual pupils could handle the situation very well. The types of questions asked can vary according to the situation.

EXAMPLE

The teacher pretends to be a lost child. The class ask questions in order to help him find his way home.

The teacher pretends to be a teenager who has run away. The class take on the roles of people who know him (friends, family, teachers, etc.). Before asking their question, the children say who they are. The teacher, in role as the runaway, can then respond in different ways (perhaps *sulkily* to parents, *brazenly* to friends, *resentfully* to the teacher, etc.) in order to demonstrate how different relationships affect behaviour.

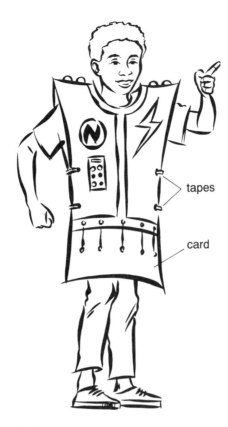

Figure 8   A costume for drama

IMAGING

Participants in a drama are asked to try and capture their own thoughts and feelings by making an image of them. This may involve sound and movement. They may work on their own or in pairs or groups. The purpose is to abstract the feeling. Children who communicate principally through words can find this difficult because they just want to give a name to their feelings, but verbally challenged children can use their physicality extraordinarily well once they are unshackled from the expectation that they must use words.

SUGGESTION

Ask the children to *show* what something is rather than describing it. For example, how can you show 'winter' without showing what people do in winter?

Help the whole class to make an environment by joining together in the space and using movement and sound to capture the atmosphere of, for example, an undersea world or a dark jungle (Figure 9).

Figure 9   Making an environment

MEETINGS

What happens in meetings is that people have discussions. The only productive meetings are those that have a clear purpose and are well managed; so it is in drama! Drawing together the characters or participants in a drama can serve as a useful brake on the action, giving the teacher the chance to take stock of what is going on and to re-focus the work. This is best done by stating clearly at the start what the problem in the drama seems to be. The characters or participants then discuss it from their perspective. The teacher's job is always to try and help the group find some way forward and to make the next step plain at the end of the meeting.

A special school class have discovered that a girl who has been visiting their class has stolen some money they were collecting for the Christmas party (the situation is fictitious). With their class teacher they discuss what the implications would be if a) they just pretended it had never happened or b) they reported the girl to her headteacher. They decide to confront her themselves and plan what they are going to say.

MIME, MUSIC AND MOVEMENT

Mime is a highly specialised form of acting, and it may not be very relevant or useful for many children. However, as an alternative to words, gesturing and signing can be very useful options for some children.

Try to give the work a very clear purpose. For example, a group of children in role as visitors to another planet must show the uncomprehending inhabitants three things about their life on Earth, or demonstrate that they come in peace.

Children can benefit enormously from movement and dance work, and activities such as stretching, curling, jumping and rolling can be woven into a drama context. Veronica Sherborne's book *Developmental Movement for Children* is a particularly useful source book.

Music is obviously an excellent stimulus for movement work and can be extended into drama in a variety of ways.

A lilting piece of music was played to a group of adolescents in a special school. They were initially asked just to use their index finger to write their name in the air in front of them while the music played. The action was repeated again and again, each time using a larger movement; first writing from the wrist, and so on, all the while trying to let the music guide the speed and style of the movement. Keeping the idea of their name firmly in mind helped the students develop a fascinating and beautiful piece of movement without any conscious intention of 'dancing'.

The group were then asked to think what sort of physical jobs would fit the music they had heard. It was played again and in small groups the students mimed the work using its rhythm.

The teacher explained that he was going to enter the space as someone keen to learn how to do their job. Again the music was played and each of the small groups helped the 'new recruit'. This situation was then explored in other ways. Why, the new recruit wanted to know, did the workers seem so slow and sorrowful in their work? Perhaps he could repay them for sharing their skills with him by giving them new pieces of music to work to? This led to a number of situations being acted out to different styles of music.

NARRATION

Young children often narrate their individual play quite naturally whereas some older ones tend to use it as a clumsy alternative to showing action. Narration is a good way of linking things which can't be shown for some reason, and pupils in the drama lesson need to be helped to understand this. One way of doing this is for the teacher actively to use narration as a means by which the class are moved from one part of the drama structure to the next.

EXAMPLE

The class have been preparing to go on an expedition into the jungle and now the teacher wants to move them on to a situation in which their preparations are put to the test. The class sit and listen while she narrates their story:

"The journey into the jungle took seven days. They paddled upstream in their canoes. It was the hardest week of the explorers' lives. They managed to escape from an attack by crocodiles and only narrowly survived when they had to paddle through some terrifying rapids. All of them were bitten by mosquitoes. By the time they reached their destination they were all tired and hungry but knew that they must set up camp before night came."

The teacher now adopts the role of an explorer:

"So, here we are. I guess we'd better get set up before nightfall. Come on ..."

SOUNDSCAPING

This activity involves the participants creating a scene by sound alone. Real and invented sounds can be used and it can be great fun to actually tape-record the work and play it back to the group. Very brave teachers might choose to give the children instruments to work with rather than relying solely on voices and hands to make noise.

EXAMPLE

The children talk about what noises the sailors might have heard on board Columbus's ship. The teacher 'conducts' the class by bringing in one child at a time so that everyone can hear their contribution. They begin to creak and groan and make the noises of the waves splashing against the side of the ship. The teacher can suggest a change in the situation; at first the boat is gently sailing through a calm sea but then the wind picks up, the sails begin to flap, a storm draws closer …

SPEECH BALLOONS AND THINKS BUBBLES

Large cartoon-type balloons and bubbles can be cut out of card and laminated. This allows the teacher to use a chinagraph on them and makes them re-usable. Children are generally familiar with these devices from comics and cartoons. Their main purpose in a drama session is to demonstrate that what someone is saying may not be what they are thinking. To demonstrate this it is necessary to freeze the action; by physically placing the balloon or bubble by a character's mouth or head, the class can consider what is really going on.

EXAMPLE

A class are exploring a giant's castle. One of the children has suggested stealing his money. Just as they are about to drag the bag out of the door the teacher asks them to freeze and suggests they they can hear the giant coming. She brings out the 'speech balloon' and asks the characters what they would say at that moment. Next she brings out the 'thinks bubble' and, after reminding everyone of what one or two of the characters have actually said, she asks other members of the group what they might really be thinking.

TABLEAU

This is sometimes called 'freeze-frame' or 'still image'. It involves the children capturing a specific moment of tension or interest as if they are caught in a photograph. The exercise has many uses including the one described in the example above. Sometimes, if the tableau involves just a small group, the rest of the class can be invited to ask questions of the characters in the tableau or discuss the kind of atmosphere and feeling it seems to show. Tableau is a good introduction for children into the way that visual images communicate meaning. Tableau work requires good concentration and the ability to stand still – not something all children can do, though some teachers might feel that, in the context of a drama, this would be a good exercise for their pupils.

SUGGESTION

Work on tableau and speech balloons/thinks bubbles can be combined to make photo-stories. Like comics, these are popular and familiar forms of story telling. The process of selecting images before actually going out to photograph them involves careful planning. Balloons and bubbles can be stuck onto the developed photographs but because they are inevitably limited in size, children have to think carefully about what to actually write in them.

WORKING OUTSIDE

A great deal of use can be made of the school's local environment. Many schools have playground apparatus which lends itself to drama. The same range of drama strategies can be employed out of doors but here the exciting thing is that it is the setting itself which is being used to inspire the story and, consequently, there is sometimes less of a need to imagine a situation.

Using the natural environment gives an opportunity to bring drama together with visual art.

EXAMPLE

A class of comprehensive school Year 7 children considered as having special needs were working with sixth-formers. They were told the story of a millionaire who set off around the world through sheer boredom. On his return he set about making a series of remarkable sculptures in the grounds of his house. Each sculpture reflected a place he had been to or something that had happened to him on his journey.

Working in small groups, the children made sculptures in the school grounds out of bits of wood, leaves, stones, etc. Some non-natural materials such as string proved helpful. As they worked, the story to which the sculpture related grew and, on completing their structures, each group shared its story by acting it out.

OTHER CLASSROOM STRATEGIES USEFUL FOR DRAMA

Some of the strategies described above may seem to require the use of space and perhaps a special allocation of time. Although the availability of a good space and a special time is desirable for drama, these are by no means essential. Drama can take place in short bursts and may be the better for being integrated with other types of work.

The activities noted here are common practice in many classrooms and can provide both a complement to and a reason for the drama activities.

AUDIO/VISUAL RECORDING

Using tape and video recorders isn't just good fun, it can give the child a sense of responsibility and importance. Some teachers are frightened that pupils will damage the equipment through misuse. In many cases though, children know how to handle the machines better than the teachers, and often have sophisticated equipment at home. Recording can give the work itself more focus and serve as a way of getting the children to respond to what they've done. Moreover, the recording can usefully play a part in the ongoing drama rather than simply being a way of recording a finished product.

EXAMPLE

The teacher has introduced the idea that a class in a different country have written asking for details about what the life of children in Britain is like. The class gather ideas about how they spend their time at home, at play, at school, etc. and use the video to record scenes that will show something of their lives. When the video is complete, the teacher asks the children to imagine that they live in a very different place, perhaps a very icy place, a desert or a very poor country. After watching the video, the class discuss what these children might have made of it all.

CREATIVE WRITING

This is something of a catch-all phrase used to describe many different types of writing. The purpose and value of getting children to write is self-evident but what is often lacking is the motivation. Drama isn't a panacea to all the problems teachers and children have, but it can provide a strong stimulus, a reason to write. Letters and diaries can be written by the characters in a drama, while newspaper reports or headlines can capture the events of the drama. As with audio/visual recording, the writing done in one lesson can provide an exciting start to the next one.

Having explored the desert island, the class are told that they have discovered an old chest full of maps and documents. The children spend a lesson creating these. For the start of the next lesson, the teacher has placed the work in a box. The class re-enact the moment when it is opened and they look at each other's work. The teacher asks them what they think should be done next ...

DISPLAY

Using children's own work to enrich the classroom environment promotes a sense of achievement and acts as a stimulus. Most usually, it is creative writing or art work that is displayed and often this is presented in a two-dimensional way on the classroom walls. Some of the ideas discussed above may present alternatives, though. Certainly, photo-stories, maps or letters or documents written in role can cover the walls. Journals and diaries might actually be made up into books.

Some children might best respond to work in drama by making shapes and using colours to capture their feelings. These might not look much against a flat wall, but could make great mobiles! Similarly, to complement acting out a drama in a particularly stimulating environment, the class might use a part of the room to make that environment. (One classroom I visited recently was resplendent with huge jungle leaves and hanging creepers. The exciting look and feel of the room was comment enough on how engaged the children were with the ongoing drama).

ASSESSING WORK IN DRAMA

For many years the prevailing view was that work in drama could not be assessed. The work of the Arts in Schools project (which is reported in a very accessible way in the National Curriculum Council's *The Arts 5–16: A Curriculum Framework*) has strongly suggested otherwise.

The key to any assessment is the criteria that are being used. If a teacher knows what he is trying to do with a class, he will surely be able to assess the extent to which he has managed it. Clearly, other learning and development may be recognised alongside the teacher's main purpose.

Vygotsky's model of how children develop (see page 5) is helpful in assessing drama work as it suggests that the development of knowledge and skills is not always linear and certainly not common across cultures. This argues strongly for criterion-referenced assessment rather than norm-referenced assessment. In other words, the teacher sets targets pertinent to individual pupils depending on the work in hand, rather than comparing pupils' progress against each other and against a perceived 'norm'.

If a teacher is using drama to complement work in other subject areas of the curriculum, then what should be assessed is the children's progress in that subject area. Similarly, if the teacher wishes to use drama to assist in the development of specific physical, mental or social skills, then progress should be measured accordingly.

One group of teachers and advisers in Wigan who considered the problem of what to assess in drama devised a model which consisted of four elements. These were identified as:

- content
- 'the real'
- form and language
- the aesthetic.

In the light of what we have said so far about drama and special education needs, these elements can be explained as follows.

CONTENT

The content of a drama session might be drawn from many areas. It might, for example, be primarily concerned with telling a story from history, a local event, a news item. The story might be entirely fictitious or grounded in the lives and experiences of the pupils themselves. In any event, *drama is about something*.

It might be the teacher's aim to help children acquire an explicit knowledge of facts and attitudes through the drama.

EXAMPLE

In the Columbus drama, the learning area is principally about his voyage and its implications.

In the drama about a theft in the school, the learning area had a strong moral dimension. The participants were engaged in isolating and testing their own judgements.

Drama is a physical art form which is most effective as a learning medium when personal feelings are engaged. It involves the whole person in the learning process. Cognitive development occurs as a result of emotional and physical as well as intellectual involvement in the content. This suggests that if it is the teacher's aim to assess the pupils' developing understanding and knowledge of a given content, then the content must be able to engage the children in all of these ways.

'THE REAL'

When children start a drama session they bring with them a mix of personal experiences, feelings and attitudes. Drama is a social art form. It involves people working together and it might be the teacher's aim to use the session to help pupils develop their social skills.

EXAMPLE

In a drama about a group of explorers lost in space, the children are required to rely on each other in order to survive. The teacher devises a number of situations in which the participants have to physically help each other and talk to members of the group whom they would not normally mix with.

Drama also involves, as we have seen, exploring a given content, and this too may have direct relevance to the child's 'real' life in or outside the classroom.

EXAMPLE

In a drama about some teenagers who have been involved in an accident after joy-riding, some of the participants seemed to be using personal knowledge to feed the fiction. Within the safe confines of the drama session, they could personally reflect on that knowledge and those experiences and see them in a more circumspect way.

Drama tends not to work well when it preaches to the participants or confronts their existing attitudes and experiences head-on. Children need to feel safe from personal exposure. Like any other art form, drama works through its use of symbols. This implies that teachers who want to tackle aspects of the child's 'real' life experience need to consider how to do this from inside the fiction of the drama.

FORM AND LANGUAGE

Drama has its own set of conventions which make it recognisable as drama rather than anything else. This is not to say that it cannot or should not be linked closely with other forms such as dance, visual art or literature. It may be that the teacher's aim is to extend the pupils' practical ability to use the art form to express their own ideas and will therefore need to recognise that the language of drama consists of more than spoken or written language; it also, as outlined earlier, implies the language of space, movement, visual impact and gesture.

The Arts Council's *Drama in Schools* booklet offers a model of how teachers might assess children's progress in terms of their ability to *make, perform* and *respond in drama*. The model is matched to the National Curriculum Key Stages and the examples are not applicable to some children with special educational needs. Nevertheless, teachers may find it useful to comment under these headings when reporting on the contribution, activity and understanding of their pupils in drama sessions.

THE AESTHETIC

In Chapter One I discussed how aesthetic awareness may be seen as underpinning all learning. Children may already have the ability to use their senses, perceive, represent, synthesise and structure their experiences but the teacher's principal aim may be to enhance these abilities in order to help the pupils make and articulate responses to the aesthetic qualities of their own or other people's work in drama. A developing understanding of the form and language of drama is necessary to make such responses.

EXAMPLE

In the space exploration drama, pupils in role as the crew of a starship devised some ways to show the inhabitants of a planet that they came in peace. They shared the scenes and talked about whether or not they were likely to have the required affect. The children were having to judge the appropriate use of the different elements of the form for the targeted audience.

It may be that a group of children do not have all of the abilities to engage aesthetically with the environment that other children have. In this case, the teacher might use drama-related work to focus on either developing an underdeveloped ability or helping the child use other facets of aesthetic knowing to compensate for a specific disability.

One teacher used the story of *The Iron Man* by Ted Hughes as the basis for a drama session with a group of severely disabled children. The children became the different parts of the Iron Man's body which lay scattered around the hall. Helpers joined in with the drama and helped the children roll, crawl and slither to the middle of the hall where they made the shape of the Iron Man's body. The work involved close contact with other people and lots of physicality to represent the Iron Man.

THE MODEL

The four strands of this model are interrelated. In any drama session all four will be present but what may change is the teacher's focus – that is, what she has decided it is most valuable to accentuate and assess. The more clearly a teacher is regarding why she is actually doing a drama session, the easier she will find it to comment on the development each child is making in the selected learning area.

Diagrammatically, the Wigan team suggest the model looks like Figure 10.

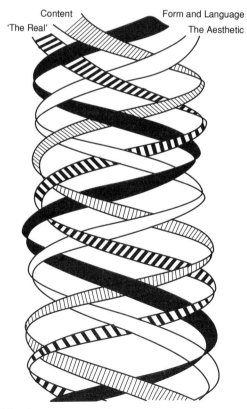

Content   Form and Language
'The Real'   The Aesthetic

Figure 10   A model for the assessment of drama

For further discussion on assessing the different elements of drama, see *Teaching Drama* by N. Morgan and J. Saxton, and *Imaging: A Teacher's Guide* by A. Kempe and R. Holroyd.

REFERENCES

Arts Council of Great Britain (1992) *Drama in Schools*, ACGB

Brandes, D. (1977 and 1982) *The Gamesters' Handbook (1 and 2)*, Stanley Thornes

Johnstone, K. (1981) *Impro*, Methuen

Kempe, A. and Holroyd, R. (1994) *Imaging: A Teacher's Guide*, Hodder & Stoughton

Morgan, N. and Saxton, J. (1987) *Teaching Drama*, Stanley Thornes

National Curriculum Council (1990) *The Arts 5–16: A Curriculum Framework*, Oliver & Boyd

O'Neill, C. and Lambert, A. (1982) *Drama Structures*, Stanley Thornes

Sherborne, V. (1990) *Developmental Movement for Children*, Cambridge University Press

Spolin, V. (1963) *Improvisation for the Theatre*, Northwestern University Press

Wigan Education Authority (1987) *'Evaluation and assessment in drama'*, *2D Magazine*, Vol. 7 No. 1

Woolland, B. (1993) *The Teaching of Drama in the Primary School*, Longman

SECTION TWO

CHAPTER FOUR

DEVELOPING DRAMA FROM STORY

Melanie Peter

INTRODUCTION

The idea of developing drama from story is not a new one. By this, I mean a 'story' as found in children's literature, as opposed to the kind of narrative that necessarily evolves through developing an 'idea' in drama. Certainly many established practitioners in textbooks on drama in education recognise the value of using story as a starting point for drama work. Many teachers venturing into drama for the first time look to a story for a ready-made framework.

The National Curriculum Council, in *English: Non-Statutory Guidance,* has lent official endorsement to children exploring and responding to stories through the use of drama, particularly for developing speaking and listening skills. Dorothy Heathcote, one of drama in education's pioneering figures in recent years, has noted, however, that opportunities are often missed in drama work with 'slow learners', through material being dealt with at a relatively superficial level (see *Dorothy Heathcote, Collected Writings*). In particular, she referred to the way events are often simulated but not explored, and also how stories tend to be hurried through (in straightforward re-enactments) but not *experienced*. She was drawing attention here not only to the missed potential of developing drama from story, but also implying that pupils with learning difficulties might be capable of more in-depth experience in drama.

In this chapter, I intend to bring these two issues together in an exploration of possibilities for using story-based drama as an educational learning medium with pupils with severe learning difficulties (SLD). Some commonly held approaches to drama with pupils with SLD purport to be story-based. However, it is possible to achieve more in-depth understanding by approaching story more obliquely and flexibly using methods established in mainstream drama in education. Certain adaptations, modifications and considerations need to be made, to take account of the particular challenges that pupils with SLD present for working in drama. The second half of this chapter describes examples of lessons carried out with pupils with SLD based on a mainstream model for developing drama from story.

SOME MISCONCEPTIONS

For many teachers unfamiliar with educational drama, it can appear a potentially threatening and exposing way of working, particularly with unpredictable and highly idiosyncratic pupils. Unsurprisingly, when using drama with pupils with SLD, many teachers commonly opt for controlled, structured drama games, in order to develop the 'social health' or cohesion of their group, or predictable role plays for social skills work (e.g. making a telephone call). Acting out stories can seem to offer a comfortable, 'safe' alternative, but with a more spontaneous open-ended 'feel'. Certainly acting out familiar stories offers a clear structure and the chance for the children to take on a role and to use language and initiative to bring the story to life: 'OK, what happened next? … Right! Let's do that bit shall we? …' It is always difficult, however, to have to deal sensitively with a pupil who contributes a 'wrong idea' that isn't faithful to the storyline. There can actually be considerable mileage in veering away from the familiar rendition – but more of this later.

It can be problematic too if older pupils with SLD 'act out' stories that are not age-appropriate through a mismatch of material by the teacher, even if developmentally the content is at a level they can cope with. This can become exacerbated if they end up being walked or wheeled through their paces, supposedly 'acting out' a story to an invited audience (e.g. an assembly or end-of-term show), when maybe they have little or no understanding or engagement with what they are doing. I'm not one to deny all pupils the chance to perform: it can be a real confidence-boost as well as a fine celebration of the whole school community. The experience can be made much more meaningful, however, if the pupils have had the chance to explore the story in depth first in class-based drama, and have been enabled to engage with the issues and themes embedded in the story. It may be then that significant moments can be selected and given shape, which will enable the pupils to communicate material more meaningfully to their audience. By contrast, a straightforward 'acting out' of the story (without previous in-depth exploration through the teacher's intervention) would merely swing along, conveying the narrative with more attention to acting skills, rather than reflecting the pupils' actual *understanding*.

Similarly, developing an emerging storyline in an elaborate spontaneous improvised narrative risks never exploring the potential of using drama as a medium for learning. An example is the all-too-familiar bus ride, where the bus breaks down, out they get and change the wheel, on we go … and on and on and on! Letting the ideas flow in this way, and going along with easy solutions to situations, really amounts to the teacher giving shape and clarity to the same kind of make-believe play that happens in the home-corner or playground. It fails, however, to heighten the pupils' understanding of the *significance* and *implications* of their suggestions and events. It can certainly provide a motivating context for language work, and be empowering for the pupils to see their ideas acted upon. The point is that make-believe play will become drama when the teacher *challenges* it, and slows the drama down: 'Hang on a minute – have you seen the size of that wheel? You won't catch me changing a wheel like that, not in these clothes …'. In this way pupils with SLD, as with their mainstream counterparts, may be brought to some development of insight, and put on their mettle to resolve a situation.

STORY INTO DRAMA

Many traditional stories and folk tales contain adult themes, which may provide quite sophisticated drama and areas of learning with older pupils too: for example, the implications of disregarding parents ('The Gingerbread Man'); the dangers of wandering off alone and into other people's houses ('Goldilocks'); the danger of divulging personal information to complete strangers ('Red Riding Hood'). Similarly, many stories aimed at younger children contain themes that may offer potential areas of learning to be explored in drama at all ages and ability levels. Take Quentin Blake's 'Mr Magnolia', for example (behaviour towards an eccentric?); or 'Humpty Dumpty' (did he jump or was he pushed … and why?). I've witnessed secondary mainstream pupils engaged in role as social workers at the case review of a young girl going by the name of Cinderella! Simply acting out the storyline would be unlikely to engage the participants sufficiently in depth for the underlying issues to affect them on a feeling level. This is particularly the case with a story that is already familiar to the participants, as this tends to create its own tension and momentum through awareness and preoccupation with the superficial storyline, at the expense of more in-depth understanding of the significance of events. So what can you do?

The story as known (even unknown to the pupils at this stage) should be considered as a *starting point* and *framework*, a ready-made context in which to explore issues and themes relating to human behaviour. David Sheppard, in his paper 'Developing drama and art in primary schools', has developed a useful model for considering teacher intervention to develop drama from story (Figure 11). How does it work?

STAGE ONE

First of all, the storyline itself, the narrative, may be considered as a series of incidents or events linked sequentially.

- That sequence can be recounted by working *forwards* in time: 'Once upon a time there was a young girl called Cinderella, who lived with her two sisters …'.

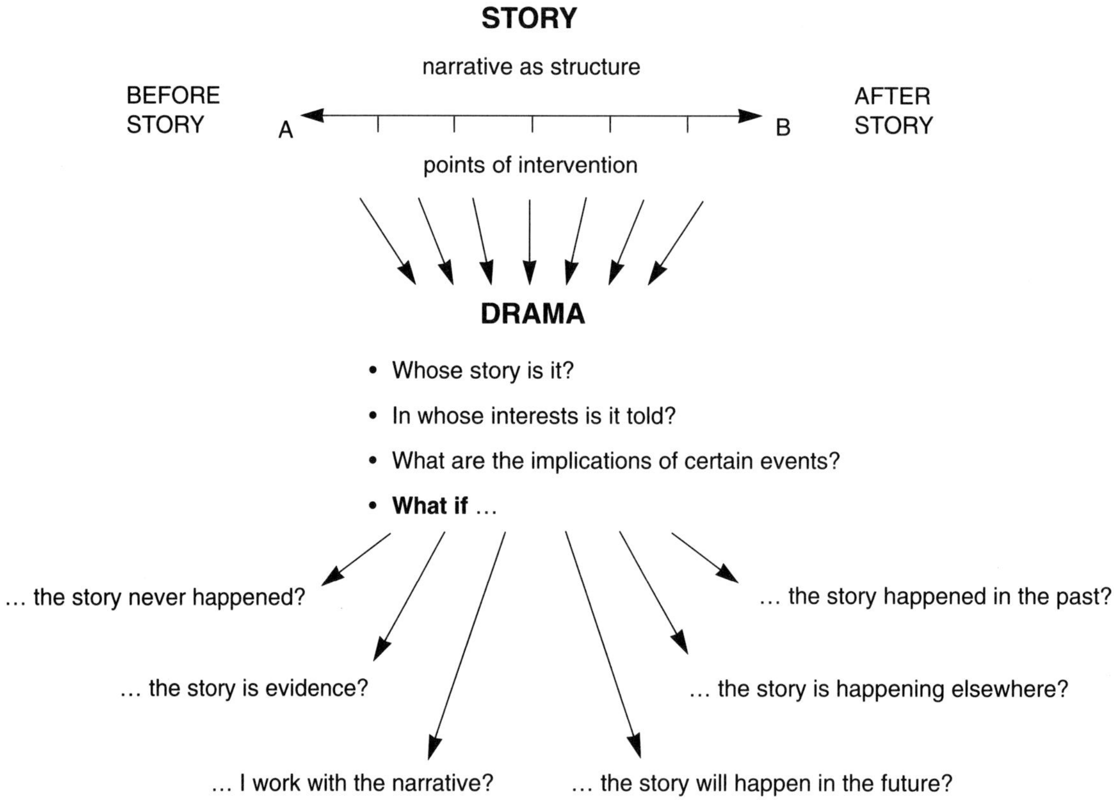

STORY

narrative as structure

BEFORE
STORY

A

B

AFTER
STORY

points of intervention

DRAMA

- Whose story is it?
- In whose interests is it told?
- What are the implications of certain events?
- **What if** …

… the story never happened?

… the story happened in the past?

… the story is evidence?

… the story is happening elsewhere?

… I work with the narrative?

… the story will happen in the future?

Figure 11   Developing drama from story

- The story could begin by telling the *ending* first, and working backwards: 'There was once a beautiful queen called Cinderella; it is said she married the Prince as he was in those days, because her foot fitted a glass slipper. You see, that slipper was left behind by … and so on.
- A rendition of the story could begin somewhere in the middle: 'There was once a magnificent ball held at the king's palace; all the people in the kingdom were invited, but one person almost missed her chance … etc.

I'm not suggesting that you begin a story-telling session using those exact words with pupils with severe learning difficulties. Rather, the point I wish to make is that any story may be explored by moving forwards and/or backwards in time. Any incident or event occurring in a narrative may provide a starting point for developing drama work – for accessing more in-depth understanding of moments in a story. These can be 'dipped in' to, before continuing forwards or backwards in time to consider a related incident. The narrative therefore can be considered as a series of related events – possible hooks – any one of which may provide a potential point of intervention for developing drama work.

STAGE TWO

This all still begs the question, however, at which point does *our* story (the drama) start? Which moment of the story offers a way in? The answer is that there can be umpteen points of entry, depending on what your agenda as teacher is and how you wish to explore the content, themes and significant moments of the narrative.

Ask yourself key questions:

- *Whose story is it?* Would Cinderella's version be the same as that of one of her sisters – or is Disney's the same as Grimms', come to that? The point is that there can be many different angles on the same narrative, and a sense in which nobody 'owns' a story.
- *In whose interest is this story being told?* There may be a moral message or learning point embedded in the narrative.
- *What are the implications of certain events in the story?* Exploring key moments of tension may offer fertile ground for learning.

What is required is a flexibility in approach and attitude to a story . It is possible to consider the narrative in a more elastic kind of way: our 'story' (the drama) doesn't have to unfold at life pace sequentially in time – there may be much to be gained from moving forwards and backwards in time. The analogy of drama being like 'making a video story' is useful, and I often describe drama to pupils, including those with severe learning difficulties, in the following way.

- *It can be rewound a little* – a chance to repeat a scene, very useful for consolidating a learning point, to remind participants what happened: 'Let's see that bit again … did you notice his face?'
- *It can be rewound a long way,* even back to the beginning – a chance to recall an incident or earlier scene, to go back in time – or to *before* the beginning.
- *It can be paused* – the freeze-frame can capture a moment at a high point of tension, maybe to question participants about what is happening and how they are feeling, etc.
- *It can be stopped* – to discuss the drama out of role, perhaps to deal with a management problem, to clarify a point, or to carry over the drama to a future session: a cliff-hanger!
- *It can be played* – the drama being lived through, and a moment in time explored.
- *It can be fast-forwarded* – to speed up the drama and find out what happened, which is useful when time is pressing, or when it seems the drama is getting bogged down: 'Let's fast-forward our drama to one day, when …'.
- *It can become a sequel,* like *Superman 2,* e.g. 'Goldilocks 2'.

The unfolding drama may be developed by moving forwards, backwards or taking a sideways step in time in the narrative (storyline), and actually departing from the known 'plot'. Consideration has to be given to some pupils with severe learning difficulties, however, who may end up very confused by jumping about in 'time' and who have difficulties generally with concepts of time. Nevertheless, it is still possible, in this video age, to access this elastic view of time to very many pupils by using the terminology of 'fast-forwarding' and 'rewinding'. Scenes may need to be very clearly demarcated, however – for example a change of space or lighting to indicate a flashback.

STAGE THREE

The next key question to ask yourself concerns the 'what if …?' factor! At this point, the teacher begins to consider ways to offer insight into the inherent themes and issues, by brainstorming how to offer an alternative angle on the course of events. This may entail consciously manipulating people and events in the story as known, and going off at a tangent. This is not to be clever for the sake of it; rather, to teach children that things can be different, and that *they* can be proactive in bringing about change and living through the consequences. Using story as a starting point offers immediate contexts for challenging the pupils in this way. This insight may come with more revelatory impact to the participants through diverting from a familiar narrative, the inherent tension of knowing what is coming next, and by knowing that it has 'gone wrong' and wondering how to get back to the story. All of the following examples were carried out with pupils with severe learning difficulties, who were already familiar with the story in question, in order to challenge their expectations and put them on their mettle.

What if …

- *… the story never happened?*

Here, the pupils are in role as certain characters, who, if they had been around at the time of a particular moment in the story, could have significantly influenced the course of events.

EXAMPLE

'The Three Little Pigs'
Invite the pupils to adapt space and furniture to make the house of one of the pigs. Explain to the class that they will be a family of pigs – agree which room they could all happen to be in, and install them in the 'house'. Explain that you (teacher) will pretend to be their friend –

---

remove yourself at a slight distance from the pigs' house. When they are ready (pregnant pause!), enter in role and knock on their door. You have called to warn them to watch out because there are some people coming round trying to sell shoddy roofing materials. Discuss in role what are good/bad materials and why, before making an excuse to leave. Assistant in role then enters in first guise (distinguished hat) as travelling salesperson, selling straw: what do the pigs do? You can return just in the nick of time (in role still as their 'friend'), to send the assistant in role packing, if the pupils' initiative is unforthcoming. Repeat for a second guise (different hat), this time selling sticks … and then for a third time (bricks). Stop the drama, take off hats and return the room to its original state. Out of role, discuss what happened, to consolidate learning – can you always trust callers at the door? What should you do if someone you don't know calls at your house?

- *… the story is evidence?*

The idea is to refer to the story as it is known, in order to add significance to the opening frame of a new story (drama) involving a central character.

EXAMPLE

'Goldilocks'

Place an empty chair strategically in full view of the group. Tell the pupils that in a moment the drama will begin, and you will be pretending to be somebody else. Put on a simple prop or item of clothing in their view, to indicate the change (hat or scarf). Talk in role (implicitly as Goldilocks' parent) to the empty chair. If this is confusing, use an assistant in role as Goldilocks, indicated by a headscarf or bold ribbon, who looks sheepish but does not speak. This moment of 'theatre' should be watched by the pupils:

> *"I remember what happened the last time you wandered off – it got you into terrible trouble, you remember with those bears. Look at the state of your clothes …"*

> *"Where have you been? Whatever have you been doing?"*

Stop this piece of theatre after a short while, and discuss out of role: What was going on? Who were the characters? What do they think Goldilocks has done this time? Depending on the ability of the pupils, the scene could be illustrated through an improvisation. On a call of 'freeze', the action could be suspended momentarily, and individual pupils questioned about their thoughts. Resume role as Goldilocks' parent, and call the group together to ask for their help:

> *"Perhaps Goldilocks will listen to them? Could they please talk to her and tell her what they think of what she has done?"*

The group (in role as villagers) could then consider how Goldilocks should be dealt with, *before* telling Goldilocks (teacher or assistant in role, wearing the headscarf or ribbon as before) and offering her advice. Having had a chance to think through their ideas (a practice – drama within the drama), the group should be better placed to help Goldilocks successfully repair the situation.

- *... the story is happening elsewhere?*

This is the soap-opera genre: exploring a scene which by implication could have taken place in parallel to the main course of events. The notion of 'forgotten characters' can be a useful one, entailing taking a sideways step from the narrative to develop a scene not in the usual rendering of the story.

EXAMPLE

'Patrick' by Quentin Blake
Patrick is a mystical charmed figure, who wanders about the countryside: every time he plays his violin, previously drab things become transformed into a world of colour. He meets up with two small children (Kath and Mick), who follow him in his travels.

Immediately after a telling of the story, sit the group comfortably together, and brief them that in a moment, when you next speak to them, you will be pretending to be somebody else. Enter in role as a parent, a 'forgotten character' who doesn't appear in the actual story: 'Have you seen my little boy, Mick and my little girl Kath? Someone told me he saw them following a man playing a violin – is this true?' Enlist the children's help as villagers to organise a search party – incorporate movement (walking on tiptoe) and follow-my-leader exercises (e.g. wading through mud, climbing over stiles, etc.) to deepen their belief and commitment and to add tension. Use a narrative link to move the drama on to the moment when Kath and Mick are found (e.g. 'After many hours of looking, at last Kath and Mick were found safe'). Discuss what they should say to the children, especially on how to stay safe in the future. To reinforce the learning point, switch roles to become one of the children (Kath or Mick – wear an obvious prop). What do they say? Can they teach the pupils about 'stranger danger'?

Drama based on 'Patrick' by Quentin Blake.

(a) *Teacher in role, as Patrick, greets senior pupils with severe learning difficulties, in role*
    as villagers about their daily tasks. These pupils are able to co-operate in improvisation
    without the use of props, but with the teacher keeping them 'on task' by questioning in
    role.

(b) Teacher in role, as a young girl, is instructed by senior pupils, in role as villagers, not to go off with Patrick. The teacher's original role as Patrick (see photograph (a)) has been transferred to the supporting member of staff, to enable the teacher to elicit 'stranger danger' strategies from the pupils, through a role-reversal situation.

- *... the story happened in the past?*

  Here, a thread from the main story can be picked up, to explore the implications of the original story's outcome.

EXAMPLE

'Cinderella'

Establish pupils in role as servants at a palace about their duties. Let them suggest appropriate jobs as far as possible, and indicate whereabouts in the drama space ('the palace') they are carried out, by positioning themselves accordingly. For those pupils who 'blank', offer them a choice: 'Are you the person who does the washing-up? Or is it your job to scrub the floors?' Once everyone has been allotted tasks, let the improvisation run for a short time. Use an assistant in role as 'housekeeper' to go round questioning everyone about their work to keep them on task. Then draw everyone together to explain that it is now that time of day when Queen Cinderella speaks to her staff. Do they remember how to behave towards a

---

dignitary? Practise bowing and curtseying, and saying 'Your Majesty'. Implicitly in role as the head servant, instruct them to form a line, ready for Queen Cinderella's arrival. Pause the drama momentarily if necessary, to explain that you will now pretend to be Queen Cinderella (put on a crown in view of the group). Enter in role as Queen Cinderella: greet your staff, thanking them for their hard work, and comment what a change it is now that other people do all the cleaning and housework! There was a time when things were very different … Stop the drama, and invite the pupils to develop a short improvisation to show Cinderella's previous lifestyle. Depending on the ability and social maturity of the group, this could become a series of small group scenes to show different tasks Cinderella had to do. Discuss whether the things Cinderella *said* to other characters in the story were the same as what she actually *thought*.

The drama could also be 'fast-forwarded' in time. Ask the pupils to consider what kind of Queen they thought Cinderella turned into. Did she change at all, now that she was rich with loads of money? Was there anything she missed? How did other people think of her, such as her old friends, or her sisters? Depending on the ability and social maturity of the group, short scenes could be devised to illustrate what Cinderella was like once she became Queen. As an alternative to improvisations, scenes could be depicted statically as 'frozen moments' – still tableaux or pictures. Participants could be questioned directly to explain their contributions. Whilst these drama conventions may be challenging conceptually and in terms of physical control and mental concentration, they can help circumvent difficulties with sustaining dialogue in improvised conversation, and give legitimacy to those with limited physical expressive ability.

- *… the story will happen in the future?*

The implication here is to question a central point of tension in the story: in other words, if a particular situation had never arisen, then the 'story' as such would not have happened. (See also the 'Old Bear' example later in this chapter.)

EXAMPLE

'Rosie's Walk' by Pat Hutchins
This very simple picture book portrays Rosie the hen going for a walk round the farmyard, unaware that she is being pursued by a fox, whose attempts to catch her are thwarted by various obstacles. She finishes up back at her coop in time for dinner, whilst the fox has been chased off by a swarm of angry bees.

Immediately following a telling of the story, alert the group that in a moment, when you next speak to them, you will be pretending to be somebody else (put on farmer's hat in view of the group). Greet the pupils in role as farmworkers: 'Good morning. Thank you for coming to work at my farm. Now is everybody here? Who looks after the horses? Ah yes! Who feeds the chickens? Thank you. What work do you do? ...' Introduce a new farmworker (assistant in role) to them: they will have to train the new worker to do the farm jobs. Remind everyone of the importance of shutting in the animals safely at the moment, as there is a dreadful fox about. Still in role, tell them that it is now time for them to do their jobs. Allocate them to different parts of the 'farm' (the drama space), using their ideas as much as possible, e.g. where the cowshed is, etc. When everyone is ready, on a signal (e.g. call of 'Action', or drumbeat), the farmworkers resume their duties. The assistant in role as the new farmworker can question them about their work (keeping them on task). Before long, the assistant in role goes round trying to convince the other farmworkers that the farmer is wrong, and that the animals should be allowed to run about. (Reactions?) 'Fast-forward' to 'dinner time', later that day. In role as the farmer (clearly still wearing the hat), you are angry because the farmyard is a tip: sacks of flour upset, beehives all damaged, the haycocks all destroyed ... and Rosie the hen in her coop with the door open – a lucky escape. Reactions? Do they blame anyone? Whose fault is it? Theirs? The fox's? The new farmworker's? Does the farmer believe them? The farmer is impatient ... How can the situation be resolved? ... Do they need to speak to the trainee farmworker again (assistant in role)? What do they say to him? Discuss out of role what they can do in real life if they are wrongly accused of something, e.g. in the workplace.

'Rosie's Walk'

It may be that with certain groups of pupils with severe learning difficulties, it is more viable for them to 'live through' events in chronological sequence, rather than moving forwards and backwards in time. Following the familiar narrative is embraced within David Sheppard's model outlined in the previous section, but for the sake of clarity, it is worth explaining here how to harness the ongoing inherent tension contained within the narrative, to avoid it running superficially onwards. Whilst this approach may entail sticking rather more closely to the known narrative, the intention for the drama remains the same: to offer an insight into the inherent content and tensions of the story. Digressing from a familiar narrative to slow things down, and to explore in detail what is going on at some critical moment in the 'story', may create its own tension. As Brian Woolland points out:

> *... the importance of a strong narrative in drama cannot be underestimated – you have to 'hook' the children into the work – but the really valuable learning takes place when you intervene in the action to slow it down, to examine what's going on between people at the moment of high tension, not when the narrative is flowing quickly.*

B. Woolland, *The Teaching of Drama in the Primary School, pp. 20–21*

The following examples were all carried out with pupils with severe learning difficulties across the age and ability range.

- *Meeting a character afterwards*

  The point of this exercise is to gain insight into a particular character's perspective on events. It can also be a useful way for the teacher to overcome the psychological hurdle of going into role: talking to the pupils as a character from the story! This in itself may comprise a short ten-minute drama, perhaps at the end of 'story time' – the pupils will need to have the story fresh in their minds. Ask the children who they would most like to meet. Beware of going into role as a 'wicked person': remind them that it's you really, but be prepared for ambivalent reactions and to soak up the responses. However, Geoff Davies, in *Practical Primary Drama*, points out the potential of *challenging* stereotypes through the apparently incongruous or paradoxical. He lists several possibilities, including the friendly ghost, the gentle giant, the unhappy princess.

Wicked fairy Carabosse ('The Sleeping Beauty')

> "It's not fair. Everybody else got an invitation to the special party for the baby princess. Well I was fed up. I felt like I wanted to get my own back. Do you *like it*, if other people go to a party and you don't go? ... All right, so perhaps I overdid it a bit ... OK, a lot ... I suppose it was *bad of me to put the spell on the baby to make her go to sleep* ... (pretending to sob) ... *I'm so lonely. I haven't got any friends* ... (reactions?) ... Do you *go round doing bad things if* you *feel fed up with other people*? ... *You don't*? ... Oh ... so how do you show people you still want to be friends with them, then? ... Oh, I see, so if I did the same as you – show me again ... then maybe people would be my friend ... What else could I do? ..."

and so on.

The idea is to engage the pupils in discussion about feelings and how to cope with them, with consideration for another person's view, and leading to a point in this example, where they reflect on whether Carabosse was right to take revenge in this way, and advise on what would be appropriate behaviour. If this starts getting complicated in role, stop the drama to explain and discuss out of role: 'What do you do in real life if someone forgets to invite you to their party?'... 'Is it good to go round being wicked like Carabosse?'... 'What's a nice way to show that you still want to be friends with someone?'... 'Can you each think of something nice to do for, or to, another person?' The point here is to help them make connections between the fiction and real life, to consider how things could be different, and how *they* can be instrumental in this.

- *Meeting a character at a point during the story*

  This is a similar approach to the one above, but the difference is that the pupils are invited into the context of the story – wherever that character happens to be at the time. The 'space' or 'set', therefore, will need to be established before they meet the character. The pupils will most likely have a collective kind of role (e.g. villagers or friends of the character) – fairly indeterminate roles that really enable them to be caught up in the fiction. It may not always be necessary for the pupils to know the story beforehand: it may be that during a reading of the story the teacher stops and invites the pupils into the 'story' at a significant moment, to meet one of the characters; the story-reading can be resumed after this brief digression. The point is to make the pupils more aware of the significance of an event or of a situation to a particular character.

Angelina in 'Angelo' by Quentin Blake
Angelina is incarcerated by her wicked uncle, who makes her work all the
time. She has no opportunity to go out into the world outside, until one day
when Angelo and his family (a band of roving performers in Italy) engineer
her escape.

Read the story up to the point where it is revealed that Angelina is sad
because she has to do chores endlessly and look after her mean and
gloomy uncle. Then tell the pupils that in a moment they are going to
meet Angelina (you, in role) – they will know, because you will be wearing
Angelina's apron. Which room in her uncle's house will they be in? Adapt
furniture and space according to their ideas, and install them in the
'room'. Enter in role as Angelina (use an apron as a prop), looking around
furtively, and emphasising secrecy: thank them for coming to see you, it's
lucky uncle has gone out shopping. Explain how lonely you are, and how
much work you have to do. Could they help? Use a feltboard with picture
prompts of various chores, to enable each pupil to choose a task. This can
be ritualised with a song or chant, e.g.

Scrubbing floors for Angelina, Angelina, Angelina,
Scrubbing floors for Angelina, Susan gets it done.

The drama can be extended: Angelina can hear footsteps – it's uncle back
home early. Will they promise not to tell that they have spoken to you or
helped you? Angelina hides, assistant in role enters as grumpy uncle, who
greets them grudgingly: have they seen Angelina? She must be here, the
place looks so clean. How come she's managed to get all this work done
already? Do they keep the secret? Do they challenge the uncle about being
unreasonable? Uncle then makes an excuse to leave. Re-enter in role as
Angelina, and tell the group that you're that fed up you feel like running
away ... (Reactions?) Do they think that's a good idea? Why not? What
would make it possible to stay? Can they make any suggestions to the
uncle? ... Can a reconciliation be made possible? Stop the drama and
discuss it briefly out of role, particularly the advisability of running away
from home, before resuming the story. Return to the notion of running
away afterwards – were the two versions the same? Did they think that
Angelina in the story was wise to do what she did? Why not? What can they
do in real life if they feel fed up?

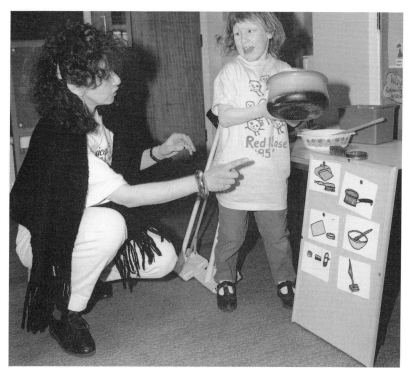

Drama based on 'Angelo' by Quentin Blake.

(a) Infant pupil with severe learning difficulties selects a required item to help Angelina (teacher in role) with her daily chores. Visual prompts enable the pupil to make a creative choice: the teacher is wearing a simple item of costume to indicate her role, and to set the make-believe context.

(b) Infant pupils with severe learning difficulties, in role as friends of Angelina (teacher in role), help her with her daily chores. They are enabled to work together in a group improvisation, through the use of props, which give a clear focus for their chosen tasks.

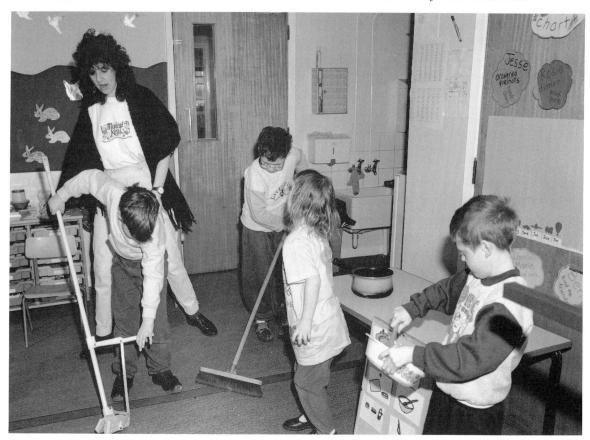

- *Turning tables unexpectedly*

  There may be much to be gained from leading the children through a much closer 'dramatisation' of a story (the very thing I've been advocating *not* to do!), *but* with the important proviso that this is in order to bring the pupils to a dramatic point where suddenly the lid is taken off the whole thing, to blow holes in their expectations. In this way, the brakes are very sharply applied on the 'story', and the participants are immediately confronted with the implications of an alternative outcome. It is not crucial that the participants are thoroughly familiar with the story beforehand, although if they are, insights may be sharpened.

EXAMPLE

'The Snowman' by Raymond Briggs
A picture story (now a renowned animation) of a young boy who creates a snowman that comes to life and befriends him, and leads him on an adventure during the night.

Cultivate a serene, enchanted atmosphere to contrast with the turn of events planned towards the very end of the story. Mark out the boy's house and garden using masking tape on the floor and moving furniture, according to suggestions from the pupils. Establish the group sitting in a huddle in one part of the house, and explain that they will pretend to be friends of the boy in the story, and that you (teacher) will pretend to be the boy (using a dressing-gown as a prop). Enter in role, thanking the group for coming round in the middle of the night to help build a snowman (assistant in role). Emphasise tension and secrecy, looking round furtively, and checking nobody else is listening. Build the snowman out in the garden (assistant in role wearing sheet, hat and scarf) – pupils mime shovelling on snow, and the snowman 'grows' taller and taller. As in the familiar story, bring the snowman to life (using a tambourine shake and clang on the cymbal). The pupils can teach him how to use certain objects correctly (e.g. a tin-opener), and practise how to land and roll over safely (contextualised movement). The snowman takes them 'flying', and 'dancing' at the North Pole, to the taped accompaniment of the Howard Blake music score. Transfer role (dressing-gown) to one of the pupils, to enable you to slip away and assume a different guise (e.g. headscarf or shawl) to play a new role. After they have landed safely, greet them in role as a fraught and angry parent: 'There you are! I've been worried sick. I looked in your room and your bed was empty. Where have you been? … You mean you've gone off with someone? … A nice snowman? But you mustn't go off with anyone, even if they do look nice … Why didn't you tell me where you were going?' This should not be aimed at any one individual – by implication, they can all have become 'the boy' or indeterminately 'friends of the boy'. Do not prolong: they may well be stunned and bemused by the turn of events, and be unable to take in too much verbal flow. It is probably more viable to discuss the implications of this 'stranger danger' out of role.

- *Living through the story in parallel to the central character*

  This entails the pupils going through the same experiences or course of events as the main protagonist, but one step removed – with a particular angle or objective. This way, they may gain some insight into the motivation of the main characters, but have an additional perspective cast upon the sequence of events.

EXAMPLE

Jack and the Beanstalk

Prepare the group (sitting on chairs or on the floor) by telling them that in a moment you will be pretending to talk to them as somebody else. Enter in role as Jack's mother: 'Can you help me? Have any of you seen my boy? He set off to market this morning to buy a cow … he's been gone ages, have you seen him? … You know, my boy Jack … I'm very worried about him, he's always climbing things and getting into mischief … And what's that great big plant growing over the way in my garden … Do you know anything about it?' Gradually bring in snippets of information connected with the story until they grasp that it is Jack and the Beanstalk. Alternatively, if you tell them beforehand that the drama will be about Jack and the Beanstalk, this will not actually detract from the momentum of the ensuing drama. React shocked and horrified, and pretend to burst into tears at their explanation. Will they help get Jack back? Stop the drama momentarily to create the beanstalk (rolls of green paper, snipped down and pulled up from the centre), and mark out the giant's castle using masking tape and re-arranging furniture according to the pupils' ideas. Practise wading through giant grass, tiptoeing quietly so that they won't be heard, and also practise appropriate ways to make requests – an opportunity to practise skills they will need later on, as well as generating tension and deepening their belief and commitment. To get round any logistical difficulty here, you could 'fast-forward' to the giant's castle, where they now have to wade through long grass, tiptoe past a sleeping guard (assistant in role). Make an excuse to slip away (e.g. tell them that you will just check there's nobody coming and will catch them up). Quickly switch props (change of headscarf), and install yourself in the giant's castle. Can they negotiate effectively to get Jack back?

An additional dynamic may be to turn the tables (see above): an idea of Cecily O'Neill's was that instead of the giant confronting them, they meet the giant's mother (assistant in role): 'What do you mean, you want to kill my boy? … Oh dear, I just don't know what to do with him, I've tried everything … How can I teach him to go round being nice to people? … What are kind things to do to people?' Out of role, discuss behaviour towards parents and others, to help the pupils to make the connections between the make-believe and the real world.

- *Continuing the story*

This can follow a straightforward telling of the story, where the familiar narrative is open-ended, maybe ending in a question. For example, Quentin Blake's 'Mrs Armitage' customises a bicycle, only for it to crash and be rendered useless; the story ends with her contemplating a pair of roller skates! The idea would be to engage the pupils in story-making, drawing on characters from the original story and adding new ones of their own. The teacher has to consolidate the emerging storyline, and as with the known story, look to find a way in that will allow the teacher to slow the drama down and make the participants consider the implications of choices, decisions, suggestions and events.

EXAMPLE

'Whatever Next!' by Jill Murphy
In this picture story book for young children, a young bear goes to the moon in a cardboard box via the chimney. He finds it all much less interesting there than he supposed. On arriving back home, his mother is waiting to give him a bath and is shocked at his state, and unimpressed at his tale: 'You and your stories,' she says, 'whatever next!'

Develop what *does* happen next! Invite the pupils to come to the moon with teddy (a real ted, for which you supply a 'voice'). Gather round an empty cardboard box and make plans and preparations. Can they each think of one item of food for the picnic? Ritualise this by singing or chanting about each person's contribution: e.g. 'Susan wants a banana, and in the box it goes'. Use pictures of items on a feltboard as prompts for those that 'blank', to enable everyone to suggest something to bring. In addition, they could each think of a treasured possession they want to bring, *or* that they will miss. To deepen their commitment and belief further, pull on pretend boots and practise moon-walking. Everyone then gathers around the cardboard box, and holds on to it with one hand. Simulate take-off and flight (with a countdown, and a whirly-tube to make sound of the engines, followed by a bumpy landing). Go for a moon-walk (feed in through role how dull it is: no trees, etc.). Draw everyone together again to have a picnic – make an excuse to leave. Pause the drama momentarily to explain that in a moment you will pretend to be an alien (with bullet-proof vest if necessary!). Re-enter in role as a terrified alien (challenging the stereotype): 'Agh! Aliens! What are you doing here? This is *my* moon …' etc. Reactions? Lead the group to consider why it's so boring: 'It used to be lovely here, now it's just dust.' How did this happen? … Can they do anything to help improve things (e.g. plant seeds,

---

dig a river, etc.)? The alien can be very grateful. The group then return to Earth (everyone holding on to the picnic box, with countdown and whirly-tube as before). Switch roles quickly (put on apron) ready to greet the group as 'mother': 'Where have you been? ... Whatever next!' Stop the drama and discuss out of role what things spoil our planet Earth, and how we can keep it a beautiful place.

'Whatever Next!'

- *Edging along, one step ahead of the 'story'*

  This can be more effective if the pupils *don't* know the story beforehand. The teacher identifies and selects certain strategic moments to be 'lived through' by the pupils, taking on roles that could legitimately enable them to be on the scene at the time. There can be a choice over the direction of the drama once a scene has been explored, if it differs significantly in outcome from that in the original 'story': either follow through the pupils' emerging story, or alternatively pick up and revert back to the original one. There can be insight to be gained from the latter, in that the pupils are brought to consider and compare two courses of action, with the notion that they can be instrumental in affecting the course of events. It may be that the outcome of *their* scene is the *same* as that in the original story, in which case, again, some understanding has been offered as to why this should be so. This approach can be very useful for tackling stories that have grizzly endings: rather than 'live through' blood and gore, the teacher can intervene *ahead* of the pupils knowing the actual 'ending', to challenge them to find a way to make this a happy ending. Alternatively, an unhappy ending can be told as in the original story, and the pupils subsequently invited to reflect on it with the benefit of hindsight. They could then suggest how this could have been avoided: what would have been a happy ending?

EXAMPLE

'The Willow Pattern Story' by Allan Drummond
An old Chinese mandarin has arranged a marriage for his daughter, Koong Shee, to a wealthy ageing merchant, Ta Jin, and keeps her incarcerated in his pagoda and grounds. Koong Shee, however, has fallen in love with her father's clerk, Chang. They elope, but are eventually hunted down and killed, to be forever immortalised as two doves.

Possible points at which to pause:

- Mandarin (teacher in role) has a disobedient daughter who will degrade herself by wanting to marry below her class (hot-seating – pupils question the mandarin and discuss issues with teacher in role).
- Scene between father and daughter when he forbids her to see her lover (pairs improvisation or theatre – two staff in role, followed by discussion).
- Scene between father and clerk (pairs improvisation or piece of theatre between two members of staff) when he forbids him to see his daughter (speech bubbles and thinks bubbles made out of paper – are they the same?).
- Thoughts of the lovers banned from seeing each other (pairs – pupils or staff in role in different parts of the room: thought-tracking, thinks bubbles).
- Daughter and clerk elope and go into hiding (pupils in role as members of a household, teacher and pupil in role as the lovers, begging for asylum – soldier (assistant in role) turns up looking for them – will they be betrayed?).

'The Willow Pattern Story'

- *Exploring significant scenes in depth*

  In some ways, this approach is similar to the one outlined above. The difference is that key moments have already been highlighted by the author. For example, 'Window' by Jeannie Baker captures, through a series of pictures, the gradual despoilation of a landscape over time, as viewed through a window. The teacher's job is to bring this purposefully to life, where the pupils are enabled to grasp the significance on a feeling level. It tends not to matter whether or not the pupils know the story beforehand in terms of the quality of understanding that may be achieved; however, it may make a difference to the kind of insight and awareness they may bring to a particular scene.

EXAMPLE

'Piggybook' by Anthony Browne
A surreal children's picture story book about a nuclear family, where the father and two sons are totally idle and take the mother for granted. One day she leaves; the males degenerate into utter slobs and turn into pigs. Gradually they begin to fend for themselves. She returns, ends up staying, and they all live happily ever after, having redefined their roles.

Possible points at which to pause:

- Tableaux (frozen pictures) of the scenes before and after the mother left (questioning, thinks bubbles, improvised conversations between members of the family).
- Where did the mother go? (short improvisations to show what she did).
- Questioning mother about her thoughts and feelings ('hot-seating' mother – teacher or pupils in role).

- What do the neighbours think? (teacher-led improvisation: teacher and pupils, in role, discuss the 'problem family' – gossip, issues).
- Tableau (frozen picture) of the moment mother returned (questioning characters, thinks bubbles).
- How she came to stay for good (teacher in role as mother, with pupils in collective roles as other members of the family, negotiate new living arrangements).

'Piggybook'

STORY-BASED DRAMA IN ACTION: AN EXAMPLE

'OLD BEAR' BY JANE HISSEY

This children's picture book is about an old forgotten teddy bear who had been put up in the attic because the children were treating him too roughly. The actual storyline (narrative) is about how his soft toy friends rescue him. It occurred to me that a significant scene must have occurred *before the story*, whereby the teddy had been packed away. This could provide a valuable learning area ('treatment of toys') for a particularly boisterous group of 8 to

10-year-old pupils with severe learning difficulties. This would need to be presented directly rather than trusting to them to make connections by implication. I opted therefore for exposing them to the scene that must have occurred *before the story* of 'Old Bear' began, but safely distanced. Putting them in role as the 'naughty children' could potentially become a licence for reinforcing the very behaviour I was wanting them to reconsider. The situation might also potentially get out of hand, with risk literally to the toys used as props, not to mention to other people. Notionally it is *possible* to do this, provided the make-believe context is made very clear and that the pupils are in role: possibly miming damaging toys (pupils with severe learning difficulties may find working in the abstract like this very difficult, however), with the teacher in role as the angry parent who banishes the toys as a result – how do they feel about that? etc. Much more viable, however, was to adopt a more positive and constructive approach: much better to lead the pupils to a point in the drama where they are put in a position of demonstrating what is appropriate. There were three adults on this occasion, who all took roles: myself (advisory teacher), the class teacher and teaching assistant. This was fortunate, though two adults (or even one) would have sufficed by taking on more than one role, clearly indicated by change of props. The class teacher herself was relatively inexperienced in drama, and diffident over working in role. However, with a clear brief she rose to the challenge of signalling her character's intentions clearly and unambiguously.

What happened	Rationale
* I introduced 'Ted' to the pupils (a real teddy), and told them that he belonged to someone called Ursula. We would let their teacher be Ursula, and the children helped her on with her hairband. Our drama would happen at Ursula's house.	Preparation for roles Establishing clear make-believe context
* We spent quite a time actually creating the 'set' for the make-believe, adapting the available space, moving furniture, etc.	Time for everyone to 'catch up'
* We 'drew' the façade of Ursula's house using masking tape on a portable screen (room divider), and at the very top put in a small window – the 'attic'. Still out of role, I explained that Ted was kept in a box up in the attic – I put the teddy in a cardboard box and placed him up high on a shelf.	Making it 'concrete'

* I then explained that in a moment the drama would begin: they would know because a pretend telephone would ring.

Talking them into the drama

* Teacher in role (teaching assistant as Ursula's mother) made the call and invited the pupils to come over because Ursula was in one of her moods again, and she desperately wanted some nice sensible children for her to play with.

Introducing a focus

Elevating their status as 'experts' at playing with toys, and immediately drawing them into the drama through the role

* The children each chose a toy to take to Ursula's, by selecting from pictures on a feltboard and then matching to the real toy from a small pile, remaining faithful to their choice.

Cross-curricular task, contextualised in the drama

* We quickly improvised a short bus ride, arriving before there were any mishaps on the way (no burst tyre!).

As teacher I had a clear agenda for this lesson, and on this occasion did not want the drama to go off at that point!

* On arriving, Ursula's mother ushered them into the lounge, whereupon Ursula burst in. (Supporting staff had been briefed beforehand.)

Teacher in role, clearly indicated by headscarf tied in a big bow on top of her head

* Ursula was stroppy, stamping and slamming about, shouting 'I want my teddy, where is he?' Some of the children pointed 'up there', but Ursula ignored them, picked up some of the toys they'd brought and started chucking them around before storming out.

Focusing attention
Negative role to illustrate what *not* to do

* The children were amazed and shocked!

If they'd made a more concerted effort to stop Ursula, I'd have gone with their responses and slowed the drama down to give them a chance to demonstrate and teach her more appropriate behaviour. As it was, it was better to go along with their response, and

	lead them to a second opportunity to instruct Ursula
* I reminded them that we knew the 'secret' of where 'Ted' really was, and if they were very quiet and sensible, I was sure Ursula's mum would let us go up to the attic: she consented, Ursula having gone off to sulk in her 'room'.	Tension of secrecy
* We pretended to climb up lots of stairs (in a line – follow-my-leader).	Physical task to involve everyone Making the shift in 'scene' very clear, moving to a different part of the 'set'
* They crawled through a small opening (human arch) and huddled up close.	Contextualised movement
* They very softly called 'Ted' all together, and he appeared	Ritual to give focus
* I talked to them through 'Ted', giving the teddy a voice, which they accepted entirely. I told them how lonely I was: could they teach Ursula how to play gently with her toys, so that I could come down from the attic?	Introducing a challenge
* They 'bought' it (appealing teddy!): Ursula was summoned, and the children told her what she should do, and demonstrated the correct way to play with the toys they had brought.	Mantle of the expert – pupils empowered through reversal of the usual relationship: an adult in need of *their* help and knowledge
* Tension was high as Ursula was handed the teddy; in slow motion, she began to stroke him and cuddle him lovingly.	Tension
* Ursula's mum thanked the children, who each in turn gently stroked Ted goodbye in a fond farewell, which brought the drama to a close.	Reflection
* I stopped the drama, and involved the pupils in putting the room straight and in helping the staff off with their props.	Making clear the make-believe had finished

. . . . DRAMA EDUCATION AND SPECIAL NEEDS

* We discussed briefly how Ursula had changed, and how they play with *their* toys. The children then followed up the drama by painting a picture of Ted in the attic and then Ted reunited with Ursula (sad/smiley mouth), reminding them that it was thanks to them that Ted had cheered up and Ursula had become kind and sensible.	Consolidating learning area

This lesson illustrates how a drama may end up diverging from the original narrative, never in fact to return to that particular storyline. To remain faithful to Jane Hissey's 'Old Bear' our drama would have had to finish at a point where the teddy necessarily would have remained in the attic. By implication, the children would have been unsuccessful in teaching Ursula appropriate behaviour. It was more constructive therefore to go for the positive ending, and for the children to see good implications resulting from appropriate behaviour. After the drama, I then read to them Jane Hissey's 'Old Bear'. I introduced it as a story about a different bear who didn't belong to Ursula: he belonged to some other children, who weren't lucky enough to have sensible friends like Ursula did …

CONCLUSION

In the examples in this chapter I have deliberately not indicated the ages of the pupils with whom these lessons were carried out. This is for two reasons:

1 Age and ability may well not correlate with pupils with severe learning difficulties, although one may expect some greater worldliness and social awareness from older pupils.

2 In drama, it is possible to achieve *differentiation by outcome*: in other words, the teacher may carry out virtually the same lesson (albeit modified according to the perceived needs of the participants), but with very different responses in terms of their sophistication according to their age and ability.

• I have used most of the lessons described in this chapter in other educational contexts (mainstream as well as special education), so I have not made them age-specific; very many of the stories contain universal issues and themes that are relevant for people of all ages and abilities. The point I wish to make is that this same approach to developing drama from story is applicable to pupils with severe learning difficulties.

• It is important that drama work is tackled in a way that is developmentally appropriate, and that it is dignified and relevant to the pupils. Certain lessons contained themes and issues more appropriate to older pupils with severe learning difficulties (e.g. 'The Willow Pattern Story' and 'Piggybook'), and some were more appropriate for younger pupils (e.g. 'Whatever Next!' and 'Old Bear').

- Many themes crop up time and again in different stories: a ripe opportunity for teachers needing to 'flog' a particular learning area with their pupils (e.g. 'stranger danger') to represent and repackage this in many different guises over several drama lessons.

- Material contained in this chapter will need to be adapted and accessed as appropriate to the needs of different groups. I have assumed, in all the examples, that a minimum of two adults is available (teacher and assistant), as is commonly the case in special schools for pupils with severe learning difficulties.

- Stories offer ready-made contexts for developing insight into how things could be different, through exploring alternative lines of development in drama. Many stories do not end happily, or else contain controversial moments. As David Sheppard said:

> *"If we offer children no vision of how things could be different, it is illogical to expect change."*
>
> D. Sheppard, 'Other people's stories'

I was once asked what I thought were the mistakes that people most commonly made when doing drama with pupils with severe learning difficulties. I gave a two-part answer. Firstly, underestimation of the potential of pupils with severe learning difficulties, particularly by those who are unfamiliar with working in this field; and secondly, a lack of understanding of the methodology of drama in education and how to apply principles for working with pupils with severe learning difficulties (M. Peter, *Drama for All*). In many ways, my answer echoed Dorothy Heathcote's lament with which I began this chapter. I hope I have gone some way towards raising awareness of what it is possible to achieve and, in a practical way, demonstrated how to enable pupils with severe learning difficulties to learn in and through drama from the rich fund of ideas, issues and themes embedded in our literary heritage. Once you have discovered its potential, I promise you, stories will never be the same again!

REFERENCES

Davies, G. (1983) *Practical Primary Drama,* Heinemann

Heathcote, D. (1984) 'Drama and the mentally-handicapped' in Johnson, L. and O'Neill, C. (eds) *Dorothy Heathcote, Collected Writings,* Hutchinson

National Curriculum Council (1990) *English: Non-Statutory Guidance,* NCC

Peter, M. (1994) *Drama for All*, David Fulton Publishers
(1995) *Making Drama Special*, David Fulton Publishers

Sheppard, D. (1991) 'Developing drama and art in primary schools', in Sullivan, M. (ed.) *Supporting Change and Development in the Primary School*, Longman
(1994) 'Other people's stories', paper delivered at the National Drama Conference, Manchester Metropolitan University, March 1994.

Woolland, B. (1993) *The Teaching of Drama in the Primary School*, Longman

Story books
Jeannie Baker, *Window*, Red Fox
Quentin Blake, *Angelo*, Jonathan Cape
    Patrick, HarperCollins
Raymond Briggs, *The Snowman*, Hamish Hamilton
Anthony Browne, *Piggybook*, Methuen
Allan Drummond, *The Willow Pattern Story*, North–South Books
Jane Hissey, *Old Bear and Other Stories*, Hutchinson
Pat Hutchins, *Rosie's Walk*, Puffin
Jill Murphy, *Whatever Next!* Macmillan

CHAPTER FIVE

FIRING THE IMAGINATION: LANGUAGE DEVELOPMENT THROUGH DRAMA

Gill Brigg

As an advisory teacher for drama I have often asked myself the question: Do there need to be any specific guidelines for teachers working with students who have moderate learning difficulties? Many such teachers come along to mainstream INSET courses eager to develop ideas specific to the needs of their students only to find that confidence dwindles once the immediate stimulus of the course has worn off. I feel that much of this is to do with the range of individual needs within teaching groups and a possible insecurity with how drama can serve that range. I hope that by trying out the sessions outlined in this chapter and by becoming familiar with the structures underpinning them, teachers will feel confident enough to devise their own material to the formats I have suggested.

All of the sessions have been tried and tested with groups with moderate learning difficulties and they were devised specifically to stimulate spoken language.

Because of the very individual needs of students, it might help if teachers see these needs as more important than the drama. That is, the stimulation of a student into spontaneous speech is actually the aim – not the creation of a perfect drama (if such a thing exists). If a teacher wants a student to achieve a specific aim, then whatever helps the student achieve it must be right!

What kinds of students might this work be suitable for? Students who:

- can concentrate on a task for at least 10 minutes
- can understand simple rules
- can work in groups
- are able to enter into an imaginary situation with their teacher.

The first three of these need to be present in order for the particular drama sessions outlined here to take place. However, if a teacher is beginning drama with a new group of students, he may not know whether the last prerequisite on this list applies to them – but it is possible to work towards it.

All of these practical ideas have been carried out in three contrasting settings where there were students labelled as having moderate learning difficulties.

What follows is a general outline of the sort of groups of students with whom these sessions have been successful – that is, the language challenges offered by the drama were appropriate for the types of learning difficulty outlined below. I shall describe the groups as a series of first impressions – the general characteristics as I encountered them at a first meeting, as a visiting advisory teacher.

SCHOOL A

A group of ten students in a school for children with moderate learning difficulties, ages 7–8

There was a high level of noise in the classroom as the students eagerly carried out their learning tasks. There was evidence of a great deal of enthusiasm and a general willingness for the students to please their teacher. Some members of the group were showing signs of hyperactivity and it was sometimes a battle to encourage them to focus during a whole group activity. Some members of the group were very withdrawn. All of the students had a degree of language impairment. The teacher was eager for them to develop listening skills through the drama as she felt this was central to their social as well as their intellectual development.

SCHOOL B

A group of ten students in an area special class attached to a mainstream school, ages 9–13

The students in this group presented a wide range of difficulties including Down's Syndrome students, dyslexia, and elective mutism. Understandably, emphasis was placed on individual programmes of learning, with some students being placed in mainstream classes for certain lessons. There was a sense of calm within the classroom as students tackled their work with care and attention. This also created a sense of isolation at times and there were few opportunities for the students to work together as a unit. The teacher was especially eager that the drama might help with this lack of unity in the group as she felt that it could offer opportunities for individual students to relate to each other for an extended period of time.

DRAMA AND LANGUAGE DEVELOPMENT – A SHORT RATIONALE

The most important reason for doing drama is that it frees the students from the present time and the present location and places them within a fiction. This fiction provides opportunities for the trying-out of language appropriate to new situations within the protected world of a drama that can be stopped at any time should the need arise. If students show signs of confusion, lack of confidence or belief, the drama can be stopped and re-started. This cannot happen in the real world.

Drama also allows the participants to bring the real world into the comfortable, familiar surroundings of the school. The teacher can encourage the group to develop life skills within a safe context.

It is important that students are given the opportunity to experience the art form of drama at first hand. It is a central way in which people make sense of the world and it is therefore important that drama operates as a learning medium within schools.

USING APPROPRIATE SPACES

In this chapter, the concern is not with physical development. The room which the students are accustomed to using for concentrated learning tasks is likely to be the most conducive space for drama. When students are taken into a large space they can either be overwhelmed with its size or tempted to test out their physical relationship with it. That is, 'Can I make myself invisible, or how fast can I run? How much noise do my feet make when I bang them on the floor? What is the maximum amount of the space that I can occupy at any one time?' All of these problems have to be overcome before the drama begins. If the group works in the classroom, the problems do not arise. In many special schools the groups are small enough to be accommodated for drama in their regular room.

A further advantage of working in the classroom is that the students are near to resources that may be useful during the drama. The computer and drawing paper may play a part.

PLACING TALKING TASKS AT THE CORE OF THE DRAMA

If language development is the most important objective to be fulfilled through the drama, the following rule of thumb can be applied to planning. If language is your priority, it is more important for your students to pretend to be 'people who live at the foot of a volcano' rather than pretending to be the volcano itself. To adopt the 'people who' approach guarantees that the language to emerge from the drama will be based in social reality and thus have some transferability to the outside world. For example, to find drama ideas from a topic such as 'The Weather', the following ideas can be generated very quickly.

THE WEATHER

- People who forecast the weather.
- People who get caught in bad weather and need help.
- People who lose their umbrella and have to borrow another one.
- People who lose their homes in a flood.
- People who have to survive in drought.

And so on.

The 'people who' model immediately suggests roles for either the teacher or the class to adopt. It provides a human framework from which to approach the drama.

KEY STRATEGIES

In all of the practical examples given in this chapter, there are three fundamental practical strategies which inform the work:

- *Contract.*
- *Structure.*
- *Circles.*

These three strategies, when applied to teaching drama, can offer security both to the teacher and to the participants, especially with groups who may have problems distinguishing between fantasy and reality, or who have problems with concentration.

CONTRACT

Making a contract with a class gives the teacher the opportunity to outline the expectations which she has for the drama time ahead. It is a chance to outline the rules and regulations by which the drama will operate. It is a way of winning agreement with the students that drama is a two-way process and that without their participation, it will not succeed. It is also a time to waylay fears and suggest that if the drama comes up against a problem then it is possible to stop and sort it out by talking it through. It may be an opportunity to state that there are often no 'right or wrong' responses and that all ideas will be accepted. Some teachers will need to use this as a way of distinguishing between fantasy and reality. It is possible to stop the drama to make this distinction as often as necessary. It is not desirable to have a student ask, 'Is this real?'

A contract at the outset of the drama time might be stated as follows:

> *"We're going to be starting work on some drama ideas now. That means that everyone must listen to what is being said at all times. We might all be working in the same play at the same time and I might be in it as well. We can always stop the drama if we need to. It isn't a competition. Remember, we'll be imagining things that aren't real for some of the time, so be brave with your ideas. Let's have everyone looking at my eyes and I'll know we're ready to talk about the first idea."*

STRUCTURE

To have a structured approach to drama means that the students perceive it as being more educationally valid than the play which happens in the playground or commonroom. This has implications for improved behaviour. Certainly the building-blocks are the same. That is, they are protected from the real world within their games, they can replay their games with different outcomes, and they are not confined to the 'here and now' of the real world within their games. The difference is that in the drama, the teacher is able to enter the play-world of the student and thus manipulate the learning as the teacher feels appropriate. It is also possible to slow down the speed at which games unfold in order to maximise the learning potential. Students feel confident in the drama if their teacher is providing them with structures which help to build belief in the fiction and make the meanings contained in the drama clear to them as they go along.

CIRCLES

Circles are useful for drama because:

- they are democratic and everyone can be valued
- the participants can see everyone in the group
- they focus attention inwards and shut out what is outside the circle
- they are a natural space in which to share ideas without having to create a 'stage' area and thus create anxiety
- if they are used at the start of all drama work, they become part of regular classroom routine offering an element of structure (see above).

For some groups, it is a challenge to make a circle efficiently and without undue fuss. The following game might help with younger students.

THE STORY OF A CIRCLE

Once upon a time there was a circle.
(Group joins hands in a circle)

Sometimes it was very small.
(Circle squashes up in the middle)

Sometimes it was very big.
(Circle stretches out)

Sometimes it moves this way.
(Group turns to the right and walks around)

Sometimes it moves this way.
(Group walks in the other direction).

Sometimes the circle breaks up into lots of little bits and moves around.
(Circle breaks up with individual students walking round the space)

And then joins up again to make one circle.
(Circle is re-formed with students being encouraged to stand in a different place in the circle)

The story is repeated faster each time it is talked through. The aim is for the group to make a perfect, still circle before the story starts again.

In the following examples of drama work, I have placed major emphasis on the structures and strategies that are most likely to make the drama succeed. This means that the teacher remains in control of both the content and form of the drama – that is, the teacher decides what the drama is about and also how the group will explore that idea.

Six drama sessions are outlined here. They are written in such a way that they can be lifted directly from the page. I have also extracted the structures underpinning each session (see 'Structure boxes') in order that they can be 'recycled' with new content.

Not all of the ideas will be appropriate for all students. Be selective, especially in terms of age appropriateness.

OBJECTS IN A ROOM

The group begins in a circle and the contract is made. A grid is marked out on the floor using adhesive tape. Each sector is labelled with the name of a room in a house: bedroom, bathroom, kitchen and lounge. The teacher has a large cardboard box full of objects which need to be placed in the appropriate room.

The teacher takes on the role of a parent who has just moved house and needs the help of the students to get everything put away in the right places. The teacher can choose the attitude of role that will best stimulate enthusiastic spoken responses from the students, e.g. forgetful, aggressive, exhausted. The teacher attempts to use questions throughout as a means of giving the students choices. The questioning sequence might sound as follows – students are encouraged to use full sentences in their responses.

The 'forgetful parent' role might say:

> *"Danny has chosen a spoon. What is it made of? I can't remember the word. I wonder which room it might need to go in? Are you going to put it in a drawer or on a shelf? Are you going to put it in the top, middle or bottom drawer? Where do you think it should go? I can't remember."*

'Objects in a Room'

These questions are assuming that the student needs a step-by-step guide through the activity. More sophisticated questions might be posed by the 'aggressive parent' role.

> *"I'm fed up with sorting these things out. You'll have to help me. What else might you put in this drawer as well as the spoon? Sometimes I get so bad-tempered I can't see straight. What things might I knock over in the kitchen if I swing my spoon around in a bad temper? What do I need a spoon for, anyway?"*

When the student has decided on a home for the object, he is invited to show us how it is used before it is put away.

This simple structure is repeated until all of the objects have been 'put away' in the appropriate room.

Variations on this activity could include objects from different buildings or rooms depending on the age and needs of the students.

This session can last between 30 and 50 minutes depending on the concentration span of the students.

THE STRUCTURE

- Circle and contract
- Choosing objects as a stimulus
- Questioning to extend vocabulary
- Mimed activity
- Close*

---

*The close

This is a statement to the group that the drama is ending and that they will be re-entering the real world. It could include some quiet introspective tasks such as looking at specific objects in the room, or listening to real sounds.

WHY ARE WE WAITING?

The group begins in a circle when the contract is made. Chairs are then moved away and the group is asked to stand in a line. A piece of rope is passed along the line and then laid on the ground.

The teacher begins by suggesting that this line could be a line that people queue along. The teacher asks the students to face her at the front of the queue. The questioning then begins: 'What might we be queueing for?' One

'Why Are We Waiting?'

of the responses is chosen by the teacher for further exploration. (For the purposes of this chapter, I will further develop the response 'We're waiting for a bus'.)

"How long have you been in this queue?"
(Responses from each group member along the line)

"Why might the bus be late?"
(Volunteer responses)

"Where is the bus going?"

(An idea from a volunteer is chosen by the teacher for further development. Let us assume it is 'The bus is going into town.')

"What jobs do you have to do when you get into town?"

The line is broken and a circle is formed. Ideas are gathered. Ideas may include shopping for clothes, going swimming, eating in a café. In pairs, students choose (or are allocated) ideas to work on. They are then asked to improvise with their partner the activity they have chosen. Pairs move away from the circle and improvise in small spaces in the room. During the improvising, emphasis is taken off physical activity and placed on spoken language by the teacher stopping the action and intervening: 'What might you be talking about if you were in that place in real life?' The improvising can then continue. After a few minutes, the teacher invites the group back to the circle and asks each pair to make a frozen picture of their activity for the others to watch. The aim is not for the observers to guess the activity but to get them to ask the 'performers' detailed questions about what is happening in the picture.

The teacher then asks the group to re-form their bus queue and to think what new character might come into this story to give them news about the late bus.

The teacher chooses a role suggested by the group and tells the students that she will be working alongside them in the drama. She needs to choose a role that will stimulate the majority of the students into spontaneous talking. The ideas from the students will be very simple but once elaborated on by the teacher may resemble one of the following:

- The exhausted bus driver who has walked a mile to break the news that the bus has broken down and needs some help.
- A frantic passenger who has heard that all the buses for the day have been cancelled, and needs to make alternative arrangements with the other passengers in the queue.

The group then improvise their ideas, with the teacher working alongside in role.

At the end of the session the group returns to the circle and the teacher might choose to ask them which bits of the drama they enjoyed the best. This helps with creating structures which she feels will increase the confidence of the group as time goes on. It is possible to build-in popular activities.

This very simple structure can be repeated as often as the teacher feels is appropriate.

THE STRUCTURE

- Circle and contract
- Create the line
- Gather ideas and work on one
- Pair or small-group improvisation
- Freeze-frame to share
- Group chooses a role for the teacher
- Improvise ideas
- Close

THE STREET

The group sits in a circle and the contract is made. The chairs are put to one side and a large roll of paper (newspaper offcut) is laid out along the floor.

Each member of the group is asked to collect a few pens and to sit themselves somewhere around the edge of the paper.

The teacher draws two lines to represent a road down the length of the paper.

The students are asked to draw every type of building they might find on a High Street in a town. (At least 10 minutes is allowed for this activity.)

'The Street'

A box of objects is provided. The objects might include:

- library book
- tins of food
- apple
- small plastic bottle of fizzy drink
- shoe
- box of plasters
- hamburger box
- newspaper.

Students choose an object out of the box and put it on the place where they would buy it in the street. Some objects can be found in more than one place. A choice can be made.

The teacher then asks the students to choose which place they could set the drama in.

> "I wonder which place we could choose from our street where we could all be at the same time? It needs to be the sort of place where there would be lots of people talking to each other. Any ideas?"

An idea is chosen and the roll of paper is moved out of the way. Students are asked to imagine that they are in the chosen location. Let us assume it is a hamburger restaurant.

"What sorts of things would be around us? We could use some of the furniture in this room to help us imagine that we are there."

Chairs and tables can be moved at this point to help create the location.

Students are settled in groups of their choice and the teacher circulates to ask each student why they are having a hamburger. Is it a special occasion? Lunchbreak from work? Students work at recreating the scene as accurately as possible. Some students and the teacher could work in role as food preparers and servers.

After a little while, the teacher suggests that to make the drama more interesting, perhaps something might happen or go wrong in the restaurant. The question is asked, 'What sort of things might go wrong in a place like this'?

An idea is chosen. Students may come up with some ideas which would be difficult to manage within the classroom, such as a riot or an explosion. The teacher needs to choose carefully an idea that has the maximum talking potential and the minimum potential for physical disruption. A workable idea would be that everyone is given the wrong food order by mistake and the problem has to be sorted out.

The mishap is dramatised, with the teacher intervening frequently to slow down the action. The following strategies will help to slow down the drama process.

- Freezing the action at an important moment in order to gently question someone within the drama. We are aiming to find out thoughts and feelings; it is a form of hot-seating. (The term 'warm-seating' is a more accurate one here as the aim is not to make the student feel threatened in any way.) Questions might be:
  'What is happening to you at this moment in the drama?'
  'How might that make you feel?'
  'What might you be thinking about at this time?'
- Freezing the action at an important moment and asking small groups to show you two freeze-frames of what might happen in the five minutes following the incident.
- Freezing the action and asking a volunteer student to phone for help on an imaginary telephone while the others listen and give advice if necessary.
- Freezing the action and the teacher asking who might come along to help sort the problem out. Teacher works in role as this character.

When the teacher senses that an appropriate amount of time has been spent on the drama, narration could be used as a device to round off the session. For example:

"After a great deal of co-operation, the people in the hamburger restaurant finally got the problem sorted out. They sat down again and were treated to a free milk shake by the management."

Rounding off the session in this way takes the pressure off the students to find a resolution to the story, and allows the teacher to sort the story out in a non-violent, conciliatory way.

The group returns to the circle where experiences can be reflected upon, praise given and the drama session rounded off.

THE STRUCTURE

- Circle and contract
- Drawn stimulus
- Placing objects in locations
- Students choose one location
- Create location
- Incident
- Resolving a problem
- Close

ACTS OF COURAGE

This session was carried out with the School C group after I had paid several visits. These drama techniques are sophisticated and may not work too well if the class is asked to try them out during their first drama session.

Part One

Group sits in a circle and the contract is made. The teacher holds up a card saying 'I feel shy when …'. Students are asked to respond verbally to this situation.

The teacher reads out a letter and suggests to the group that this might form the basis for some drama work. The letter appeared in a teenage magazine.

> *Dear Jane*
> *I hope you can help me with this problem. I really fancy this boy at school but I am very shy. I think he fancies me but he is shy, too. What can I do? Please help.*

The group has a short discussion about what general advice might be given to this person.

The circle opens out to make a horseshoe, and two chairs are placed in the gap at the end. The aim is for students to practise making conversation as if they were the advice-seeker sitting next to the person they like.

Volunteers take it in turns to sit in one of the chairs and offer a first line of conversation to the empty chair. The previous discussion will have provided plenty of ideas.

The exercise moves on to consider the responses to the first part of the conversation. Both chairs are occupied this time. Person A opens the conversation. The task is for person B to respond in two ways. Firstly they should reply with a negative or 'blocking' response, and secondly with a positive, encouraging response. For example:

Person A
'Isn't the weather lovely today?'

Person B
'I hate the sun!' (negative response)
'Yes. This bench always gets the sun.' (positive response)

'Acts of Courage'

After each of the responses, person A is asked to make an exaggerated 'statue' of how the response has made them feel. The group thinks of words to describe what the statue looks like.

Many different opening lines and responses are tried out. It is important to talk about the different effect that the positive and negative responses have on person A. Much attention is paid to the description of feelings.

It should never be necessary for person A and person B to be stuck for ideas. The teacher needs to try to place the responsibility for ideas onto the whole group.

In this exercise, the short snippets of very 'safe' drama serve as triggers for discussion. The A and B responses should never be allowed to continue into improvisation unless the teacher is confident that the students are able to deal with such a sensitive, potentially embarrassing situation.

Part Two

The teacher reads out another letter from a magazine.

> *Dear Jane*
> *Please, please help me. My son is 16 years old and he has fallen in love with a girl who goes to his school. He can't eat. He mopes about all the time. I'm worried sick.*

The teacher takes on the role of the boy in the fiction in order that the students don't feel any pressure to put themselves forward into what could be perceived as an isolated situation. The group is encouraged to ask questions about the scenario and give any advice that might be appropriate.

Again, two empty chairs are set up. A confident volunteer who will be taking on the role of the lovelorn boy is asked to leave the room while the teacher gives the rest of the group some secret information. They are all friends of the boy and they need to break the news to him that the girl doesn't like him enough to go out with him. She wishes to remain friends with him. They are asked to find various ways of breaking the news to him, hurting him as little as possible.

The volunteer comes back in and sits in one of the empty chairs. Volunteers in turn sit on the other chair and try out various ways of breaking the news. The action is stopped frequently in order that feelings and emotions can be discussed.

The session needs to end with the group making a positive plan of action for the boy.

Return to the circle and the drama closes.

THE STRUCTURE

- Circle and contract
- Stimulus
- Discussion
- Opening lines and responses
- Discussion
- Stimulus
- Teacher in role
- Secret information
- Trying out ideas
- Discussion
- Close

This structure can be used for any dilemma which the teacher wishes to explore with the group.

CONTEXT CORNERS

In this practical example, a corner of a classroom is used with the group sitting in a semicircle facing the corner. The aim is to create a corner 'set' which provides a context for language. For the purposes of this chapter, I shall use the example of a context corner created on the theme of the sea (Figure 12). The structure can be applied to any set of stimuli based on any theme. Other ideas might be the seasons, our town, farming, hospitals or shops.

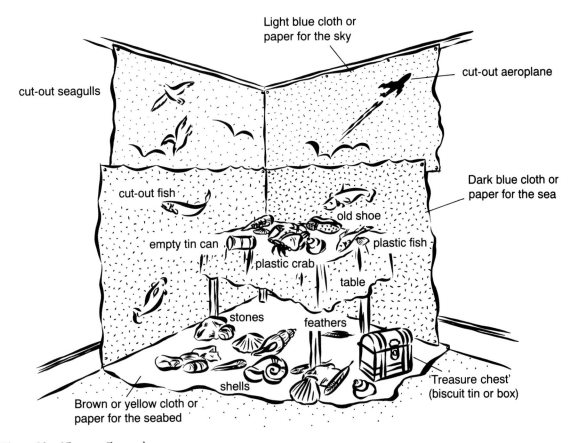

Figure 12   'Context Corners'

The teacher begins by making the contract with the group. The next step is to ask three main questions:

> *"If this was a real place, what might you be able to see – in the air, at sea level, and beneath the sea?"*

Plenty of time is given for responses.

Attention is then paid to objects on the 'set'. An object is chosen and it is passed from student to student. Volunteers are asked to contribute words that describe the object, with emphasis being given to putting the adjective in a complete sentence. For example, 'It is a *rough* shell' or 'It is a *soft* feather'.

This task is carried out with three or four objects.

The teacher then works as a narrator to move the students into drama.

> *"One day when some people were digging on the beach, something rather important was found. What might it have been?"*

The teacher chooses an idea at random from a student and the *imaginary* object is passed around the group and adjectives collected. It is important that the students feel that their idea might be chosen for the story. Criteria of 'best' ideas do not apply here. It is the responsibility of the teacher to work the object into an interesting narrative. Almost any idea is a valid one providing it is within the realms of possibility.

A decision has to be made about what to do with the object. The teacher may need to use the narrative to steer the students away from the context corner in order for the story to unfold. If the narrative becomes too convoluted or unfocused, the teacher is always able to move the action back to the beach.

An unfocused narrative might sound like this: '… and then the man got in his car and drove away … and a dog ran down the street … he got lost … the girl got some sweets from the shop.'

The teacher needs to re-direct the talking so that the students apply themselves to creating a narrative appropriate to the object and the place. Perhaps 'Let's think back a little bit to the moment when the [object] was dug up on the beach. What happened to it next?'

The aim of this session is to encourage the students to feel that there really is no 'right' or 'wrong' to a story that the group is making up as it goes along and that, in drama, it is always possible to try something else!

Throughout parts of the story, volunteer students can be encouraged to improvise moments with the others watching. This device is helpful as it focuses thinking and encourages predictive talking – that is, 'What might happen next?'

At an appropriate time, the teacher draws the group into a circle and closes.

The 'Context Corner' is a resource in the classroom for longer than just the drama session. Students can be encouraged to 'playmake' independently of the teacher.

LOST SUITCASE

Group sits in a circle and the contract is made.

The students take on the role as people who work in a lost property office at British Rail. On this particular morning the lost property manager has decided to investigate a particular item which has been in the office for a long time – all efforts are made to return the items to their owners.

A suitcase is placed in the middle of the circle and volunteers are asked to open it and have a look inside. The contents are as follows:

- gents suit
- pyjamas
- business papers
- map of a city
- family photo in a frame
- diary with a telephone number in the inside cover.

The teacher asks questions about the objects, for example: What materials are they made of? What colour are they?

Questions are then asked about who they might belong to and where was the person when the suitcase got left behind. The teacher asks for suggestions as to how they might find the owner.

It is likely that the students will suggest trying out the telephone number in the front of the diary (teacher prompting can help here).

An imaginary telephone is used. A volunteer dials the number and the teacher is the voice at the other end. The teacher is in role now as the owner of the suitcase. The aim of this exercise is for the teacher to extract detailed descriptions of the case contents from the student. The questioning might sound like this:

'Lost Suitcase'

"Can you tell me what is in the case?"

"I have so many pairs of pyjamas. Tell me as much as you can about them to jog my memory."

"Who do you think the people in the photograph are?"

"Yes. I remember now. Something really terrible happened to me the day I lost my suitcase."

(The word 'terrible' could be substituted with 'exciting', 'life-changing', 'frightening' or 'funny'.)

The drama is stopped and the students are asked to predict what happened to that person on that day. Students work in pairs or small groups to prepare and present their ideas in the middle of the circle.

The teacher needs to encourage the students to consider incidents which are likely to have happened to that sort of person in that sort of job – that is, lives which are different from their own experience. This is likely to result in the students being brave with vocabulary as they move from the familiar into the unfamiliar.

The session ends with the teacher in role as the owner arriving at the lost property office and reclaiming the case.

This structure can be applied to a variety of suitcase contents which suggest different characters to the children. Some examples:

Wedding dress
Confetti
Rail tickets
Holiday brochure

Jumper
Skirt
Slippers
Knitting
Teddy bear in a paper bag

Swimming trunks
Suntan oil
Sunhat
Novel
Address book

Students can be encouraged to invent their own sets of objects for the suitcase. Once they become familiar with the structure, they will be able to think of objects which might make the drama more exciting to explore.

THE STRUCTURE

- Circle and contract
- Putting the group in role
- Exploring the case
- Questions to extract language
- Making a telephone call and describing
- Improvising and sharing an incident
- Giving back the case
- Close

A FINAL CHECKLIST: KEEPING STUDENTS CONFIDENT

The creation of a comfortable, open-minded learning environment is central to the confidence of students in their use of language. They should not be afraid to put ideas forward within the drama. As they develop in confidence, so they will be able to engage in talk which is appropriate to the world beyond their immediate experience.

This checklist aims to help students remain confident.

- Announce to the group when you are going into, or coming out of, role.
- Develop a clear control signal. Your students need to know when it is time to stop.
- Allow periods of contemplation to follow periods of action. This gives the students time to change focus.
- Develop phrases for accepting all ideas, which will encourage the weakest students to participate.
- Real objects are useful starting points for the imagination. Try to include some in most of the drama sessions.
- Make the group feel as if they are succeeding at all stages of the drama.

CHAPTER SIX

DRAMA AND THE PHYSICALLY DISABLED

Bernard Hodgkin

'LIVES WORTH LIVING'

In 1982 The Belgrade Theatre in Education team in Coventry produced a show entitled 'Lives Worth Living'. The play centres around Mark, a young man with severe learning difficulties who is loved, respected and needed by his sister. Mark is facing up to the life he will lead in an institution. The driving tension of the play is the inner conflict suffered by his sister, Julie, who would like to look after Mark, but feels this would leave her with no life of her own. Her guilt because of this, and the fact that she is 'normal', gave the show a strong message, and challenged many of my own attitudes, both to the subject of disability and the relevance of drama to people with learning difficulties.

At the time I saw the play I was head of a big drama department at a large comprehensive school in Gloucestershire, and had been a drama teacher in comprehensive schools for thirteen years.

The show formed part of a project initiated by a local theatre-in-education company, which involved about a dozen mainstream schools. The teachers from the mainstream schools were invited to watch the show, discuss it, and prepare for a visiting performance of the show in their own schools. Having seen the show (which shocked many of my Year 10 students), each mainstream school was matched with a special school or college and they embarked on joint drama workshops. We worked together over a period of three months on a weekly basis along with a disabled member of the company who provided a sound base on which to work. There were many inhibitions and prejudices on both sides and we learned early on that the word 'handicapped' is a derisory one to disabled people.

It refers to the Victorian era, when people begged on the streets 'cap in hand' (handicapped), and has associations with the seamier side of society. Other definitions may exist, but the word itself is a *label*, not a term or even a definition; it is a statement about someone, whereas the term 'disabled' refers to the fact that a person is disabled by his or her situation, as well as by society.

I was determined to make this project work, not least because the students from my school were so keen. The potential for the project was enormous.

The special school students were also very keen but the project eventually fizzled out for three main reasons:

1 We had not set ourselves a realistic aim for the end-product, or even a realistic time-scale for such a project.
2 Pressure of timetables, exams, etc. meant that some weeks contact was lost.
3 We had not involved the managers of either school – explained to them the real possibilities of such a project – and were too carried away with the explosion of creativity.

Everyone was quite pleased it had happened, but I was left feeling empty and guilty. I was empty because the students had been allowed to dip their feet, experience genuine mutual warmth and affection, but were denied real outcomes which might have remained with them and effected permanent change in their attitudes towards one another. I was guilty because I felt that my original intentions had been compromised, and I was making an enormous number of excuses to myself about the value of it – I was 'very busy', the students had other things to do, etc. It was easier to stop; I also felt guilty because people were congratulating me and the group on our work and the value of it, which I felt was superficial.

It was another twelve months, still as a head of drama in mainstream, before I actually had the opportunity to devise a project with students which would have value and would be a genuine follow-up to 'Lives Worth Living'. The school had just begun the University of London Examinations Board Community Theatre GCSE, a one-year course, which would allow students at 16+ to obtain a qualification that would be based on one project and seen through to its conclusion in one year. This examination is to be discontinued after July 1995, but the new ULEAC syllabus for Drama (1698) will offer similar opportunities.

The initial aims of the project were negotiated between staff of both schools:

• To introduce a project whereby all pupils would work together, with equal numbers from each school.
• To set definite time-scales.
• To establish trust and confidence on both sides.
• To establish continuity in relationships and encourage spin-offs to the drama work, like outings, and invitations to work in other areas of each other's schools (this developed strongly in the latter stages).
• To produce an end-product, and possibly all the students entering for the examination, or all performing together, but to allow space and freedom for pupils to achieve their own goals, at their own level.
• To set up further projects, not necessarily confined to one examination group.

The context of the work was based for the first term on finding out different ways of working, e.g. in pairs: each person had to describe his or her journey to school, from bed to the school gates. This was done non-verbally, and also with sound-collage. This was very enlightening and for some staff and students from the mainstream school was the first encounter with over-protective parents. They discovered from the pupils themselves their home routines, and the role the parents played. For example, one boy described his breakfast, which was totally determined by his need to impress his father, and to gain his approval, without being given the opportunity to choose his clothes, his food, or aspects of his school life. This was quite alarming to many of the mainstream students.

Freeze-frame work played a significant role because it was available to all students. To hold a moment in time and examine people's thoughts or feelings was difficult for some students. Quite often small groups would enact a small drama, based around the idea or moment in the freeze-frame, but found themselves unable to crystallise the moments. However, this proved not to matter, as the small piece of drama played out by the group could still be focused thus:

> *"Now pick out the best 20 seconds of the piece, or break this play down to just a particular moment. I am going to 'open the door, look in and then shut the door and leave'. In this time, what piece of the work would you want me to see or hear, in order to get some flavour of what is going on?"*

This enactment, and re-enactment, allowed the pupils to capture the essence of freeze-frame: to focus on a moment, look at what is happening, and try to understand just why it is happening and how it is affecting people in the picture.

One piece on which the group worked involved half the group as prison warders and half the group as prisoners staging a demonstration on the roof of the prison. The situation allowed pupils from both schools to face a 'real' dilemma under safe conditions, but the group reached a type of drama like that described by Gavin Bolton, in *Towards a Theory in Drama in Education*, as a 'Type D' drama – meaning that the work had gone beyond the 'play' stage and the superficial, and participants were required to make conscious decisions and solve problems in order to move the work on. A member of staff had led the work quite strongly at the beginning, setting up the prison and creating belief in the situation. See Figure 13.

This worked really well, as it put all the pupils on a 'level playing field', and allowed everyone to have the opportunity to make decisions. It was interesting that at times there were a few sixth-formers who felt that they had to behave in a certain dramatic way, but they soon realised that the teacher, who by now had taken on the role of prison governor with one group, was quite adept at developing the work as a result of what reaction he got from

DRAMA: Prisoners on the roof, Press and prison staff

TEACHER	
GROUP A half group: prisoners	**GROUP B** half group: prison staff
STILL IMAGE life as prisoners	**STILL IMAGE** life as prison staff
DEVELOPING work as prisoners	**DEVELOPING** work as prison staff
TEACHER IN ROLE as prison warder	**TEACHER IN ROLE** as prison governor

OUTCOMES

- What happens?
- What are the consequences?
- Who takes responsibility?

REFLECTION } • in role
EVALUATION } • out of role

Figure 13   'Prisoners on the Roof'

the prisoners. There was a great deal of silence and reflection throughout the work, and concern to 'solve' the situation quickly. However, the success of this work allowed pupils to be slowed down and made to deliberate on their actions; to take responsibility for their own decisions and see the consequences of their own actions. It appeared to place the students from the special school in an extraordinary position of responsibility. Some of the prison staff group took on the role of members of the press. They became mediators in the dispute, and two different endings were composed, one peaceful, and one very violent. The choreography of the violent end generated further carefully controlled work, and stimulated a group dynamic.

This section of work was probably the most successful of the whole integrated project and it was felt by all staff that this should have been examined by an outside moderator.

The project moved along at a pace. It was decided that the group would work towards a children's pantomime, to be performed for the whole special school (ages 5–17). The work was completed, and the performance was successful. However, it was decided by the whole group that the special school pupils would take a supporting, technical role in the piece and not perform. It was difficult to accept this at first, but it was the result of open negotiation, and the mainstream sixth-form group performed in front of the moderator, the special school, and interested educationalists.

The project did not, however, stop there. One of the sixth-form students left school in the next six months and returned as a volunteer. He went on to study to become a special needs teacher. Two special school pupils took up computer classes at the mainstream school, and though personnel changed, the two schools worked on similar projects over the two subsequent years. The project attracted funding, and provoked a great deal of interest from the Special Needs Inspector in the county.

The original six aims had all been fulfilled to a certain degree. Spin-offs had included joint holidays during a week in summer involving students from both groups, leisure trips to the zoo, swimming, and joint trips to the theatre. A lot had been learned about collaboration and about why such collaboration is necessary.

NATIONAL STAR CENTRE COLLEGE OF FURTHER EDUCATION

I was told in 1990 that the National Star Centre College of Further Education in Cheltenham might shortly be looking for a Performing Arts Lecturer. I fancied the idea, but that was all. A college of a hundred students from all over Britain, all with some form of physical and/or sensory disability? Yes, but I am not qualified … Nevertheless, I got the job.

The drama department I had been working in was good and getting better, but I wondered how students who had never had the chance to 'do drama' would manage to elevate their status through expressing their own feelings in the work and operating within powerful roles. The college was providing them with the vehicle to do just this. The students had not previously had the opportunity to work in an active decision-making environment, accepting responsibility and exploring the consequences of their actions. Performing Arts did not really exist there at that time but I felt that the work should be tried on a full-time, regular basis.

The National Star Centre College of Further Education was set up in 1967. From the outside the College was viewed by some people with suspicion. It was isolated, away from the town centre, and students were withdrawn from mainstream education – how could this be relevant or correct in the 1990s?

The National Star Centre is a comprehensive college; it allows students the opportunity to get a good vocational education, which may have been denied them in the past for a number of reasons. It also offers the opportunity to take examinations. 'Comprehensive' should be interpreted as inviting people with any manner of physical or sensory disability to become students for two or three years to increase confidence, self-advocacy, status and academic standing where appropriate. The College elevates people to a position where they have more choice, or more confidence to make a choice, and enables them to catch up on what really should have occurred in the previous four or five years.

This is not to say that the College is not committed to working with mainstream colleges. It has excellent contacts with the colleges of further education in the locality and is at present pursuing the possibility of students of Performing Arts joining courses at those colleges, irrespective of their abilities.

The facilities for students of Performing Arts at the National Star Centre are superb. One million pounds has been spent on a new Creative and Performing Arts block. This includes a purpose-built 172-seat theatre which is fully accessible to audiences and performers alike. The stage has three entrances, all

Facilities at the National Star Centre College of Further Education

The theatre studio

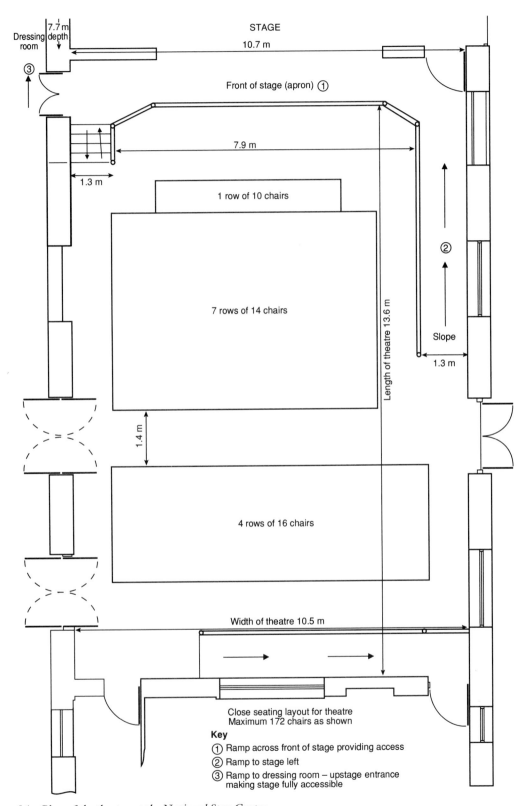

STAGE

7.7 m
depth

10.7 m

Dressing room

③

Front of stage (apron) ①

7.9 m

1.3 m

1 row of 10 chairs

7 rows of 14 chairs

②

Slope

1.3 m

Length of theatre 13.6 m

1.4 m

4 rows of 16 chairs

Width of theatre 10.5 m

Close seating layout for theatre
Maximum 172 chairs as shown

Key
① Ramp across front of stage providing access
② Ramp to stage left
③ Ramp to dressing room – upstage entrance
making stage fully accessible

Figure 14   Plan of the theatre at the National Star Centre

accessible to manual and electric wheelchairs. A lighting/sound technical studio is available to be used by all, and the dressing-room facilities are very impressive. The space is carpeted and sound-proofed. The atmosphere and ambience, and the possibilities for learning in a quiet yet stimulating environment, are inspiring. It is also a venue for small-scale touring theatre companies, Cheltenham Literature and Music Festivals, and conferences.

The National Star Centre College of Further Education is extremely fortunate in its facilities, and must be regarded as an 'ideal' to which to aspire, in terms of facilities for disabled people. Drama has a history of being taught in dining rooms, libraries, maths rooms and temporary cabins; even more commonly the space is shared with another subject area, and time is cut, in order to facilitate the next lesson, when the desks have to be replaced. *This* space, however, is accessible to everyone, and all doors, even when they are shut in blackout situations, can be pushed open with a wheelchair quite easily. The doors are designed to withstand damage, and can be pushed in or out. Once inside the theatre, there is a ramp to the stage and a ramp to the technical console. Outside the theatre a ramp gives full access to the stage, across the front and also by an entrance at the back (see Figure 14). The stage is also designed so that access can be easily negotiated behind the false back wall for the appearance of actors on both sides. The wings area is large and allows passage for one wheelchair at a time. The stage has a rubber dance floor which allows wheelchair tyres to grip, and the height of the tables in the dressing room, and lighting switches, are set at different levels to allow for adjustment to different heights for wheelchair-users and ambulant people. Four radio microphones and headset communicators allow access to language communication when there is a public performance.

When a performance is going on with an outside theatre company (these have included the Royal Shakespeare Company, Royal Court, Graeae, Theatre Centre, Royal Exchange Manchester), up to 50 per cent of the audience may be wheelchair users: effectively there are up to 60 wheelchair spaces. Theatres around the country average four wheelchairs per performance.

This description is presented here to illustrate the ideal: the facilities described allow people to be empowered and not disadvantaged as soon as they enter the space.

The space is by far the most appropriate, and stimulating, I have ever had the pleasure to use. After I got the job I was informed that, nine weeks after I started, HM the Queen would watch me teach. She was to open the new Creative Arts/Performing Arts area, so I had better sort out my lesson plans!

I have now been here four years. We teach BTEC First Diploma Performing Arts, GCSE Drama, Community Theatre, Enjoying Drama, Singing, and Dance.

Students at work in the theatre

One of the questions asked by many people (and asked by me every day in the summer of 1991 prior to taking up my post) is 'How do you teach drama for the disabled?' The only book I had ever read on such a subject was *Remedial Drama* by Sue Jennings. I read it from cover to cover, over and over, with much agonising. I really did not think I could – or indeed wanted – to teach drama for the disabled.

On that first day when I arrived here, my first question was 'Have they done any drama' – you know, the question we all ask of a new class. 'Oh yes' came the answer, 'We've done a lot of drama.' 'Dance?' I enquired. 'Oh yes, we did a lot of dance at our previous schools.' I was mortified: here I was, a teacher with 15 years of baggage, experience, enthusiasm and energy to unload on to these unsuspecting students and I was faced with a group of experienced drama types set to assess the merit of this new interloper.

DRAMA FOR THE DISABLED?

'There is no such thing as drama for the disabled.' That is true, and it is a theory and belief to which people should prescribe strongly.

If theatre companies such as Graeae subscribe to a theatre for the disabled, it is only because they believe in integration. Indeed their work now reflects integration with both actors and the production team, without necessarily highlighting people's abilities or disabilities; rather they tackle subjects for performance which may stimulate or challenge people's views. If we are to consider theatre for the disabled, do we mean the audience are disabled, or that the actors are bringing to the attention of an audience matters of disability? There is no need to label this form of theatre. To do so is isolating, and places the work on the periphery. Surely any theatre group uses the performers to communicate to another group in the most appropriate fashion? If this involves signing or using actors because they do not get a fair chance of work in the 'real world' of theatre, then this should be applauded. True integration cannot be achieved without recognising these things. In any production, the work – the 'book' – remains the constant. The interpretation is different and if a group distort the form to suit what they want to do, it really is irrelevant whether one uses a wheelchair, or sign language. The interpreted form of that particular play should be strong enough to allow the performance to have a life of its own and not rely on labelling a theatre company 'Theatre for the Disabled', or indeed 'Disabled Theatre Company'.

If one follows this route, one immediately specialises the work, which results in isolating, and marginalising; hence a return to a 'different' form of theatre. It is precisely the opposite view to the one I feel should be adopted.

There are obviously constraints when working with disabled performers which do not always apply in a mainstream situation. For example, speed or pace of work may be restricted in terms of variety, being dictated by the speed of an electric wheelchair or a person's ability to operate a manual chair. Similarly, in respect of carrying objects or working at different levels, because of physical restrictions, variety is a problem. Grouping people together for a crowd depiction or photograph is hampered by the space taken up by chairs and tends to make grouping quite formal or symmetrical, but devising ways round this is interesting.

One simple remedy is to break through the barrier and ask how many people wish to vacate their chairs if it is physically possible. It is quite amazing how many people will discard their chairs for the floor (as long as it's clean) or use another chair or cushion. In fact, in my experience, it should be positively encouraged, though for people's self-esteem it is worth getting to know a group or individual first.

For me, the key to the door as a new recruit working in special education was provided very early in my time at the National Star Centre. It was nagging away at me that I needed to understand the value of drama to my students now that I had discarded the association with the notion of 'drama for the disabled'. I had quite a shock when, in the middle of a project, I was out shopping, and I met students who the previous day had been working on a piece of drama about housing, bailiffs, social services, rights and benefits and access to work, but who were now in the middle of a shopping precinct, being treated as if they were infirm, unable to think, and 'needed help'. Two students who were organising trips, social events and improving the lifestyles of others and who, within a piece of drama, were agonising over the problem of evictions, were seemingly struggling to be identified as equals in a supposedly normal everyday environment. I could not ignore this in my work, though I did not want to do any work about disability. What I came to understand was that I did not have to, but there was no disguising the fact that approaching any piece of work, in order to make sense of it, staff, and students in particular, will approach a programme of work from the point where they are, and in effect examine attitudes and approaches without having to headline their work 'drama for the disabled'.

The point about the relationship with the disabled person and society is that in Britain those who are disadvantaged are excluded from aspects of life that we 'normal' people take for granted, although it is true to say that modern buildings, public buildings, theatres, restaurants and public places are increasingly built with the idea of accessibility in mind.

However, for all these physical constraints and freedoms, the actual debilitating factor is *attitude*. It is possible to go anywhere and do anything if the attitude and will of the host establishment, and more importantly of the people who work there, are conducive to allowing – or better, encouraging –

access to their facilities. Through regulation and explanation it can be possible to have no restrictions on access. A good example is a night club in Cheltenham. Access is poor – to get in, to get to the lavatory and to get upstairs – but students using wheelchairs are welcomed and encouraged to enjoy nights out at the club, negotiating their own arrangements for transport, access to the bar and using the facilities. They are therefore not disadvantaged, and the throng of people at the night club accept these wheelchair users as friends, peers and drinking partners.

THE WORK

EXAMPLE ONE – JO HITCHCOCK

This drama was with a group of students with a wide variety of disability, without any previous experience of drama. Everyone in the group used the spoken word. The project required a great deal of input from me. The initial objectives were:

1 To introduce the group to a new form of drama, in which a story may be created about one individual, gradually allowing the students more and more responsibility for their work, and encouraging them to find out about someone through the medium of drama.

2 To focus attention away from their own situation and towards someone else, allowing them the safety-net of make-believe to explore some of their own feelings towards other people.

3 To learn to use drama as a method of learning about themselves.

In the first instance, I introduced Jo Hitchcock by reading (singing) a poem. This work was chosen as I had used a similar project in mainstream, and this relatively new group perhaps needed to direct empathy towards others.

> *Well Jo Hitchcock, this was your life*
> *Hard-working man and a long-suffering wife*
> *Confined to barracks from an early age,*
> *Worked hard 'til then with a hidden rage.*
> *Little to show, yet the jokes you cracked*
> *Hid from us all what your life lacked.*
> *The medals you won, a testament to you.*
> *Where's it all gone? You salute the few.*
> *Well done Jo Hitchcock, you showed them how.*
> *The laughter all gone. It's all quiet now.*

A chair was placed in the middle of the space. Other props were available, and the group were invited to build a tableau of a room which included Jo's chair, surrounded by his things. If the props were unavailable, the name of the object, e.g. a scrapbook of the war, could be written on a piece of paper, and

. . . . .DRAMA EDUCATION AND SPECIAL NEEDS

the 'scrapbook' placed by the student in an appropriate place. The students defined the space, pinpointed Jo's chair on which Jo's jacket was slung, provided an ashtray full of cigarette-butts, etc. and Jo's environment was created. Once the working space was established we discussed what was known about Jo, what he was like, who else was in his life, what he had done, what he was doing now. The technique of thought-tracking, whereby a student sits in Jo's chair and the group speak out thoughts Jo may be having, elevated the discussion and brought in some interesting information.

I introduced the concept of 'teacher in role' by making the point that I was now going to be Jo by putting on his coat. The students would then question Jo, and receive only responses that Jo might give. When I took off my coat, this was a sign that I was returning to my 'normal' role.

The group then worked in pairs, picking on information derived from this work, and acted out episodes of Jo's life. When the episodes were viewed, this became part of his life history. The outline of the development of this work is set out below.

Event	Impact – Interest
1 Song	Background to Jo's life – teacher-led
2 Create living environment for Jo	Student input, develop character, investment in character
3 Teacher takes role of Jo Class respond to him/her	Students begin to take responsibility for Jo's life
4 Episodes in Jo's life – small groups	Background, all scenes are true, nothing can change
5 Frozen images Positive/negative in his life, whole group	Recognition of constraints in his life, wider view and more information
6 Focus on significant person in Jo's life – pairs	Shaping drama, choices to give Jo more depth
7 One episode: watershed in life with significant person	The story, linked in with present life of Jo
8 Developing drama to a deeper, more significant level	The fire – Jo's life now compared with previous life
9 Evaluation	• What is the drama about? • What did we learn? • What is the most poignant moment?

At point 8, when the drama deepened, the group decided that in desperation Jo and his wife had to set fire to their own house in an attempt to gain the insurance.

The ultimate scene was played with one person who, when asked whom he wanted to be at this stage, took on the role of Jo's son, and waded through the ashes of the Hitchcock home to find a photograph.

Where does the drama go from here? It could move into many areas. The group had finally taken full responsibility for the work – it was no longer necessary for me to play such a demanding role.

Learning outcomes were:

- selecting material
- focusing on one person's life
- selecting key moments from his life
- giving students responsibility for development of the work.

Evaluation, which subsequently took place, involved thoughts about old age, war, poverty, dealing with crisis, and positive thinking. At no time did the group err on the negative.

EXAMPLE TWO – THE MEMORIAL

This drama was with a group of ten students with severe learning difficulties. There were students without speech, as well as those who found it very difficult to move with any degree of freedom.

The initial objectives were:

- to construct a piece of work based out of our time
- to allow all students a role in the work, by making the stimulus a visual one
- to allow students to communicate strongly using a variety of methods
- to understand the process of change
- to introduce the concept of heritage, the environment and the understanding of local history.

In the first instance, the group discussed what they knew and understood about memorials, then split into three smaller groups. Some people used a computer communicator in discussion, one student used an alphabet board and nodded his head when the teaching assistant pointed to the correct word. This student's input was to prove crucial.

The group were asked to design a memorial which celebrated life rather than commemorated death. Using two chairs to signify gates, and a piece of string to represent a path, a special area was established in which the memorial would be found.

Where a group were unable to draw, a scribe, or artist, was brought in, but was only allowed to draw what he was told to draw. No idea was rejected; rather a consensus was reached, and the memorial completed.

We then dramatised significant events from these people's lives and pinpointed:

- the greatest moment
- the moment they remembered the most
- how they died.

Each group used a still image to start with to illustrate a character's greatest moment. Each student portrayed someone and worked out what the character might want to say or communicate. Each student (in role) was asked:

- Who are you?
- What are you doing?
- Why are you doing this?
- Where did you learn to behave like this?
- What is your deeper motivation for doing this?

These five questions were posed by freezing the action, tapping the student on the shoulder, and finding out all this information. Some groups found the concept of still image quite difficult and preferred a short piece of drama.

When the students were asked to dramatise significant moments from the life of the character depicted on the memorial, we had to discuss what we meant by 'greatest moment'. Understanding concepts is so important to this work: getting married, passing the driving test, going away to college, going home, and passing an exam, were all discussed as examples.

The group were asked to place their memorial physically. The discussions on its location were voiced so that all the group could hear. A teaching assistant became the voice of one of the students, enabling that person to take a full part. There was inevitably a ritualistic quality about the laying down of the memorial and an increased investment in the work.

The feeling of togetherness, joint decision and mutual respect was strong for these students, who had hitherto tended to operate very much on an individual basis. It was a very powerful moment.

Having established the reasons for the memorial being there, and developed the dramas surrounding it, we then brought the work into the 20th century, and asked the groups what they thought might have happened to their memorial by now.

Using whatever resources came to mind, the group had to alter the burial ground to signal the ravages of time, the neglect or care the memorial had received, and what state it was in now. One group simply cut the memorial in half and pulled the two pieces slightly apart to signal that it had been destroyed or broken into bits. Another group had it perfectly presented, and polished, with flowers constantly changed beneath it.

The whole aspect of vandalism and relevance of the past became a side issue, and one which was thoroughly discussed, though the emphasis on this work was to enable the students to feel part of an ongoing piece of work, engaging in its development at every stage. Out of role, discussion was limited.

At this point, members of each group became 'sub-committees' of people responsible for the physical upkeep of the community. They were taken around the site by individuals from the memorial groups, and each memorial and its relevance was explained to them. This extended belief and introduced an objective element to the work.

The role of the sub-committee was to decide what to do with the site. We held a meeting in which interested parties should advance to the committee what should be done about the site. In role I suggested that it was wanted by a supermarket chain, and should be demolished.

This caused uproar in some quarters, but others agreed. I then invited everyone to go back to their memorial groups, work out a response to this announcement of possible demolition, and return to a further meeting to put their case.

When this was done it was suggested that the supermarket chain might indeed triumph and move in but retain the memorials inside or outside the supermarket grounds. Alternatively the community might turn the area into an historical museum site which could serve as a tourist attraction.

We acted out both scenarios. Half the group were instructed to be the builders and surveyors and to carry out the transformation, whilst the other half formed a protest group to prevent the work physically – the protest proved unsuccessful.

The work had demanded real decisions to be made by the students, increased responsibility for people's actions within their work, and it had exposed them to a real-life dilemma.

There was a great deal of anger in the work – justified anger and controlled anger. Anger is not often encouraged from a group of young people who are at times alienated within the community. Here though the anger was tapped to promote a positive cause, to justify their arguments, to articulate their feelings, an anger felt by all disabled people, who are not always given a platform to vent anger. It was this release of anger, as opposed to constant frustration, which became important.

EXAMPLE THREE – BLOOD WEDDING

This drama formed part of the European Theatre Project in which the National Star Centre took part, along with mainstream colleges from Cheltenham, Krakow in Poland and Modena in Italy.

The production was to take place at two venues, as part of an overall celebration in which the colleges were to perform one piece of drama and work on a joint production.

It would be an enormous challenge as only six months' preparation time was available; the group were very inexperienced, and would need a great deal of confidence-building in order to perform the play.

Initial objectives were:

- building confidence to perform to a public audience
- creating self-belief
- elevating status within the group.

I began to worry. How could I produce this play, with problems of text-learning, understanding, mobility and the other potential nightmares? Some of our students have problems with short-term memory, spatial awareness and, obviously, mobility.

I decided to use a group in their first year at the Centre, brought together for drama – this was no hand-picked group of experienced thespians! I told the group we would begin in January, and finish the work in July, and perform to an audience of over 200 with full costume, lighting, and so on. They were horrified.

We did a great deal of work on love, passion, betrayal, marriage – all aspects of the play. However, I knew I was putting off the inevitable. I sat down with the group one day, and we worked out that our best way forward was to take the key scenes from the play – the moments that would hold the story together.

Our greatest strength was feeling, real feeling, and a willingness to express emotion honestly. In eighteen years of teaching I had not experienced this so poignantly as at the National Star Centre. The other thing about this play is *passion*. It is so full of passion, love, hate, war, jealousy, all strong emotions oozing from every crevice of Lorca's writing.

We worked a great deal on visual images and allowed the group to discover the play by examining its world in terms of the pace and the heat, as well as the conventions of the time: men at war, women at home tending the farms, using the children to run the home, and the women making all the big decisions.

In pairs, we improvised the rituals of giving and receiving in different situations, and reflected on the constraints there are on expressing what you really feel. We went on to use forum theatre to explore situations in which people feel embarrassed, and considered the situation of the play in which two families who have previously hated each other are thrown together in a wedding celebration. This led to working on how people greet each other in different cultures and situations.

We fixed on a framework for our performance based on four key moments:

- the first meeting
- meeting each other's parents
- the marriage
- the tragic/happy consequences.

We devised our text by basing scenes on Lorca's play and using, as far as possible, visual cues to guide us through the piece. The students soon realised they could be flexible in their use of language so long as the cues were kept in place. In the last scene, for example, where the bride finds her groom dead, the image of her leaning over the corpse became too powerful for words; the stark black-and-white costumes, the speed of the electric wheelchair on the cold and frosted stone, the cry of the jilted wife, made for effective theatre. As a link we used Dire Straits' 'Brothers in Arms'. This gave the students a security in that if the dialogue dried the music could be brought in to cover the hiatus while the cast recovered themselves.

It was a tremendously successful project in that it did not highlight physical limitations but allowed them, and the audience, to focus on theatrical strengths other than remembering lines.

'Blood Wedding'

A more recent project has brought to life Ralph Steadman's book 'I Leonardo'. This has involved working closely with Cheltenham Institute of Higher Education on a multi-media approach; a wall of video screens, pre-recorded and live music, a choir, and some marvellous gadgetry on the set along with twenty disabled actors made for an extraordinary event.

GCSE DRAMA

Having scanned the various syllabuses for GCSE Drama, it was decided to link up with the University of London Examinations and Assessment Council. The present syllabuses covered by the National Star Centre are:

- ULEAC GCSE Drama 1698 (introduced in 1994)
- ULEAC Mature GCSE Community Theatre for 17 years or over: 5580/81/82.

GCSE DRAMA 1698

When students first arrived at the College, all post-16, it was quickly established that few had had opportunities to do any formal examinations. Indeed, there is quite a major change of emphasis here, giving students the opportunity to do GCSE subjects at the College before embarking on full-time vocational courses.

At the National Star Centre the Drama course 1698 is specifically intended for first-year students. (In fact it is a two-year course, which the students cover in one year.) The syllabus for students at the National Star Centre is appealing for many reasons. Firstly, according to the rationale of syllabus, it:

> *"... allows for different approaches to teaching drama whilst highlighting a common core. It views drama as a practical, artistic subject which has its roots in exploration through improvisation. The intellectual strand is the way students use drama to explore issues, to think about their work and thus evaluate and develop it."*

The drama experience is essentially practical, concerned with imagination and communication.

One of the strengths which was observed early on when working with students at the National Star Centre was their ability to create and work in a mature fashion. Whether this is because of the small groups, or the ages, or indeed because the individual desire to succeed is stronger here than in the larger classes of the local comprehensives, it is difficult to say.

The examination is split into four papers:

1 *Improvisation,* which is externally moderated in the autumn term
2 *Evaluative Commentary,* which is course work, based on the practical work undertaken over the year

3 *Preparation for Performance,* and

4 *Performance in Acting* or *Design and Technical Skills.*

The attractive part of this syllabus is that it is continually assessed. The first term's work is actually put on video and sent to the Board, and is externally moderated, the students being assessed on the ability to:

(a) contribute to ideas within the group

(b) adopt and sustain appropriate roles

(c) communicate through language of space, movement and words.

Item (c) has proved the most attractive element. It allows people to communicate in different ways, and thereby does not disadvantage students without good speech, or students who are restricted in movement. This Board also positively encourages people with special needs to take the examination.

Non-verbal drama, puppetry and documentary drama have all been used in addition to communicating through language, and it has been a mutually satisfying educational process with administrators and assessors from the Board.

No dispensation has ever been formally requested, as it was felt that it could again isolate students from the mainstream.

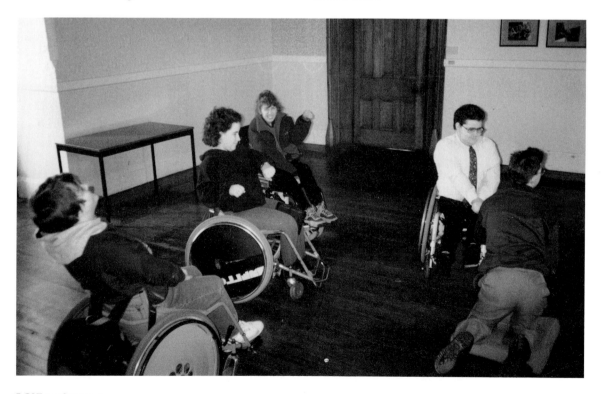

GCSE performance

Constraints

Constraints which have been evident, and which have been dealt with, have included the physical challenge of taking students to the theatre in numbers. Negotiations with theatres such as the Everyman Theatre, Guildhall Arts Centre, Gloucester and the particularly impressive New Theatre, Cardiff, have allowed lecturers and students the opportunity to discuss access and Health & Safety Regulations, and how theatre space can be adapted to suit the needs of our students.

In the New Theatre at Cardiff, instead of removing seats for wheelchairs, the whole back row of the stalls was set aside for students; while going to dress rehearsals at the Everyman allowed the students and the theatre complete freedom. The following points are offered for others in this situation:

1 Ring the theatre administration and discuss needs.
2 Make a pre-performance visit to discuss needs with administration staff.
3 Check parking/setting-down facilities, as this can take a long time.
4 Leave plenty of time before the performance to arrive and settle students into seats.
5 Double-check arrangements with the theatre the day before the event.

Other constraints have been adapting work to suit short-term memory, finding and using the strengths of students in final performance, requiring a bigger space to accommodate large electric wheelchairs, and needing a lot more time to clear work away.

COMMUNITY THEATRE GCSE 5580

The Community Theatre GCSE has really been the 'flagship' for the College since 1991. The syllabus is quite simply what it says, and because of the importance placed by the College on working out in the community, it coincides with the College's own mission statement.

The syllabus requires the following of the College:

1 In the first term, assess all theatre provision in the local area, including visiting these theatres.
2 Introduce students to work which allows them the opportunity to devise and create unprocessed work, based on issues, and curriculum themes, as well as matters relating to their own lives.
3 Target an audience to whom the work will be directed, e.g. children, employers, senior citizens, 14 to 16-year-old teenagers, etc.
4 Devise and create theatre appropriate to the audience.
5 Perform to an audience in an appropriate space.
6 The folio consists of a diary based on a practical project and is submitted by 1 June of the examination year. In a folio, evaluate the performance.

The syllabus allows students up to six months to create, devise and perform a piece of work. Some students develop technical skills such as in lighting and sound, and are examined on these skills. Administrative skills can also be assessed for non-actors.

There are constraints on where students can perform, and they must have the confidence to perform in a variety of spaces. Checking venues at short notice can also be difficult because of transport, and students' ability to initiate such visits. The College has performed in youth clubs and schools as well as in the college theatre.

Audiences have included youth clubs, work placement employers and 14 to 16-year-old students from mainstream schools.

The most recent project was on Bosnia, and was played 'in the round', with a completely white set allowing video, slide projector and colour to paint the world of refugees and hardship, a project which really fired the imagination of the students.

The syllabus gives students the opportunity to show the 'outside world' their talents, their views and, more important, their freedom of movement, expression and evaluation. Indeed the most recent group included a seminar on life in Bosnia as a talk-back at the end of their piece.

Community Theatre GCSE is to end in 1995 but should be continued as an NVQ.

BTEC PERFORMING ARTS

The staff felt that the College needed to offer the BTEC First Diploma in Performing Arts, or the GNVQ Intermediate Equivalent as it is now called. In school terms it is the 4–5 GCSE equivalent which leads on to a BTEC National Diploma, which in further education terms is the equivalent of 2–3 A Levels. It became a recognised course at the College in September 1993. It was very difficult to judge at first whether or not it was an appropriate course, whether students would cope, or whether BTEC would accept the submission.

The submission is sent as a comprehensive document, outlining facilities, staffing, teaching methods, methods of assessment, and examples of work. Having the submission accepted, and knowing that BTEC were keen for this College, as the first of its type in the country, to offer such a course, created its own pressures. Students embarking on the course were taken on interview; some had not followed the required academic route.

The course consists of units which have to be completed in one year, with a final performance project at the end of the course. There are mandatory units such as 'Performance Processes', 'Common Skills', 'Performance Project', and option units such as 'Drama Performance', 'Dance Performance',

'Understanding Music', 'Performance Technology' (students must choose three of these). In each area students have to complete three assignments, and all assignments are practically based.

Teething troubles were huge, as one would expect. Some of the students at the Star Centre found it difficult to cope with the amount of work, the deadlines, and the amount of concentrated time devoted to the units.

It was an educational process for everyone involved. In terms of dance, the course team were determined that students would do devised work, develop contemporary dance using chairs as props, and devise a means of varying speed of work. Encouragement to get out of chairs where possible was very strong.

Strong links were established with the local FE college, and a member of their staff was brought onto the course team to teach circus skills as part of Performance Processes. A performance of Shelagh Delaney's 'A Taste of Honey' as part of the Drama Performance was also a watershed. It was the first time the students had actually performed a scripted play – that is, not devised from a text, as 'Blood Wedding' was. There was much agonising over some students who had great difficulty in memorising words. The course team negotiated an agreement with the students that if words were too difficult to learn over the four-week Easter break, then the group would devise work based on the play. As it turned out, the group performed Act I using the scripted text, and Act II was devised around the play's text. This took away unnecessary pressure, and allowed the director to concentrate on characterisation and developing role.

Joint assignments such as Theatre Administration allowed the local FE students and Star Centre students to work the Box Office together for the visit of the Graeae Theatre Company to the National Star Centre.

Progression in terms of BTEC courses is very important; the link with the local FE college resulted in one student going on to the BTEC National Diploma in mainstream education, and two others did the same course in their local FE college at home.

New and innovative methods of assessment were agreed with the moderator for the second year. There was to be more learning support within lectures, and video assessment, use of dictaphone and other communications aids were to be used to complement the written assignments.

The course is essential to the College curriculum, as it gives students a real programme throughout the College:

- Lifestyles Pre-Vocational Drama
- GCSE Drama
- GCSE Community Theatre
- BTEC First Diploma in Performing Arts.

The College is now attracting students from all over Britain to come as direct-entry students to the BTEC First Diploma in Performing Arts. It is also hoped to introduce the BTEC National Diploma in the near future.

SUMMARY

- It is important when working with young people who have physical disabilities to recognise limitations, understand the nature of their disabilities, and to adapt work accordingly.
- It is important to elevate self-esteem, and to encourage freedom of expression and provoke discussion.
- It is important to combat a sometimes predominant passive nature.
- It is important to ignore the wheelchair and the sticks and concentrate on the person.
- Trust people themselves to be the (only) experts on their disability.
- Work in a constructive yet non-patronising way.
- Encourage people to make decisions, and to plan their work, and integrate people in appropriate situations – integration for its own sake can be damaging.
- Allow students to be the judge of their own limitations.
- Beware of the lazy students.
- Give students the respect they deserve by setting high standards.
- Plan learning support, class support, care provision if necessary, and contingency plans if there is a problem.
- Break down barriers of such things as roles of men and women.
- Enjoy your work!

REFERENCES

Belgrade TIE (1987) 'Lives worth living', in Redington, C. *Six TIE Programmes,* Methuen

Bolton, G. (1986) *Drama as Education,* Longman
(1979) *Towards a Theory in Drama in Education,* Longman

Jennings, S. (1973) *Remedial Drama,* Pitman

Marston, P. *et al* (1990) *Drama 14–16 – A Resource Book,* Stanley Thornes

Neelands, J. (1984) *Making Sense of Drama,* Heinemann

Further details of the ULEAC GCSE, BTEC AND NVQ courses can be obtained from:

ULEAC, Stewart House, 32 Russell Square, London WC1B 5DN
BTEC, Central House, Upper Woburn Place, London WC1H 0HH.

Useful music resources

Dire Straits	'Brothers in Arms'
Bonnie Tyler	'Total Eclipse of the Heart'
Queen	'Greatest Hits 2'
Rocky	'Eye of the Tiger'
R.E.M.	'Greatest Hits'

CHAPTER SEVEN

WORKING IN PARTNERSHIP

Jan Beats and Penny Barrett

INTRODUCTION

We are a teacher and teacher-assistant working at Addington School in Berkshire. Addington is a special school catering for the needs of 212 young people with learning difficulties ranging from moderate to severe. Within the school, the pupils are grouped according to age, and teachers and assistants work together in teams to meet their needs. The staff work together to plan, deliver, evaluate and develop the school curriculum. We have worked in the same team for a number of years, in the further education section of the school, with students aged between 16 and 19 years. Staff partnerships within the team vary throughout the week, so we do not always work together. Whilst the staff (both 'teaching' and 'non-teaching') may have specific roles within the school, essentially it is our aim to work together to support each other within the teaching and learning environment. The idea of calling our teacher-assistants 'NTAs' (non-teaching assistants) seems ludicrous, as in fact assistants in special schools spend most of their day teaching! Responsibility for the planning, organisation, delivery, evaluation and recording of the curriculum should and does lie with the teacher. However, everyone who works within the special needs classroom, which includes the assistant, has a very important role to play in all of these areas.

We are certainly *not* drama specialists. We wear numerous 'hats', and are responsible for delivering a wide and balanced curriculum. Initially we both had an interest in drama and could see its potential within other areas of the curriculum such as PSE, English, History, and Technology. Students at Addington are developmentally, cognitively and socially at a level much younger than their chronological age. Many are functioning at concrete levels of understanding, and find the use of more abstract language bewildering. Through drama we found we were able to move the students on from their concrete world and bring about an understanding of more abstract ideas and concepts. For example, enacting a scene from a part of history may bring it to life, relating it to the students' own experience. Exploring a theme such as theft within PSE may lead to a greater understanding of different viewpoints.

STARTING OUT: EARLY DAYS

When we first began working together in drama we had no real structure to our work, and often grappled around in the dark, taking ideas from books and trying to piece together useful strategies. Neither of us had any training in drama – we simply had a 'feel' for it. We began by playing lots of short drama games taken from books, then we played some more games ... and a few more ... until we finally realised that whilst 'drama games' were useful in developing simple communication skills, like following rules and working in groups, something more needed developing – but what we were not yet sure!

Students using Makaton sign language to communicate during a drama game

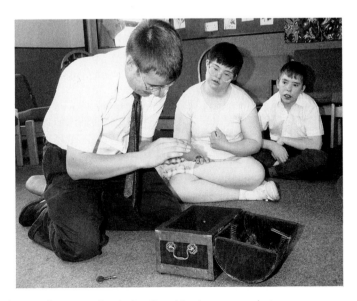

A student mimes to the group what he has found in the treasure chest

As we now had drama on our timetable, we felt under pressure to put on a performance. It seemed to us at the time that drama was about *performing*. The students were very much into the TV soaps, so we decided to work on the theme of 'a street'. The street was eventually named 'Maple Street', and students volunteered to play various parts with great enthusiasm. In our minds the students' disabilities were not a barrier in our drama work. However, we soon learned that they felt differently about this. For example, Nick, a young man with no speech, felt that he didn't want to do anything because 'you can't act without a voice'. We looked together at some video material of a theatre group who used signing in their work. This encouraged Nick to 'have a go' and he chose the role of the local policeman. Our school's liaison officer loaned Nick a uniform. This whole experience was a great boost to his self-confidence.

We used questioning techniques to set each scene. A session would go something like this:

> *"Who wants to be mum? … dad? … the shopkeeper?"*
> (Volunteers)
>
> *"OK, Stephanie wants to be mum. What are you doing, where are you?"*
>
> *"In the house."*
>
> *"Are you alone?"*
>
> *"No, my daughter's here."*
>
> *"What is she doing?"*
>
> *"She won't get out of bed! She's really getting on my nerves."*
>
> *"Who would like to play the daughter?"*
>
> *"Me – I'm tired because I was out late with my boyfriend."*

We developed a number of characters this way. One of us took a leading role as one of the residents in the street, whilst the other directed the scenes. We felt at the time that this was necessary because the students needed a great deal of 'prompting and prodding' to help them to remember what to say and where to be on stage (an area of carpet bordered by chairs). On reflection we wondered if our roles overpowered the roles of the students. We seemed to have too much control over the development of ideas within the drama. We wanted to hand this control over to the students. This was when we began to look at ways of developing our methods. One of the main things we learned from this project was that we, as adults, often view a situation differently from the students and therefore always need to be sensitive to their needs and perceptions.

In these early days we fell into the trap of believing that unless we finished each project with a 'grand performance' then we hadn't really succeeded with our drama. We needed to be looking at the evidence of learning which could clearly be seen within the process that the students were working (these are outlined below, in the section 'Identifying skills'). In our eagerness to perform our work for others, we missed many opportunities to enable the students to lead/take control of the drama. This can be a very dangerous path to work along with students with learning difficulties. Because of their eagerness to succeed they can be very easily manipulated, ending up like puppets with no real say in the drama. In spite of this, our early performances were great fun and boosted the students' confidence.

RESOURCES

In our school, space is limited and working areas have to be shared. We are not fortunate enough to have space allocated specifically for drama. We often have to negotiate space and frequently find ourselves improvising. Like most teachers we have collected an ever growing set of resources. Because of the lack of space this has had to be limited. We began by collecting hats and other pieces of costume which we used to create, confirm or clarify a role. We also have access to the Berkshire Drama Centre where we can hire more specialised costumes and props. Items that can be used flexibly are most useful, e.g. fabric and drapes, interesting artefacts, shells, boxes (like a treasure chest), pictures and photographs. It is also good to make use of items within the teaching area where you are working.

USING THE TEACHER IN ROLE

Use of costume and props has worked well for our more able students and enhanced their ability to 'get in to' and sustain a role. However, we found that some of our students with more severe learning difficulties were not able to take on a dramatic role, although they responded to their peers who were taking a more active part, so we tried out 'teacher in role'. This worked well, with the teacher in role being able to respond to and target specific students, leading to more of the group being actively involved throughout the drama.

> ### EXAMPLE
>
> *Penny (assistant) – teacher in role, dressed in a clown-type costume*
> *Jan (teacher) – session leader*
>
> The session leader worked with the group, playing some warm-up games. About ten minutes into the session, the teacher in role entered the room. The students' initial reaction was one of amazement. The session leader

began by prompting the group, encouraging them to communicate with the character. The leader was soon able to take a back seat in the main communications, only needing to give gentle prompts in the style of questions (e.g. 'Who do you think this is?', 'How are we going to find out?', 'Is there anything we could ask our character?') and ensuring that all of the students had an opportunity to participate ('Perhaps Paul could find out'). The group were asked by the character for help and advice in order to overcome a problem. The range of possibilities for suitable problems is vast, and can be tailormade to respond to the needs, experience and interests of the group. For example: the character has just had an argument with a friend, boy/girlfriend, parent; the character has lost/broken something; the character has taken something not belonging to him/her; the character has to make an important decision.

At the end of the session we were pleased with the responses and achievements of the group. However, we felt that bringing in a teacher in role with no introduction was both confusing and unfair to the group. We should have warned them that what was about to happen was in fact a drama. Most of the students quickly picked up the pretence of the situation, but some may have been a little lost at this new way of working. Throughout this session the group took more control of the drama. However, we (the session leaders) needed to improve our own planning, and perhaps include the students in this stage; for example, building a character together using 'role on the floor' (this is described in more detail later, in the project 'The Street').

IDENTIFYING SKILLS

As our learning in drama progressed, the 'production' gave way to the 'process' that we were working through with the students to develop specific individually targeted skills. These skills can be put in two main groups:

Dramatic skills

- Getting into and sustaining a dramatic role
- Relating and responding to someone else in role
- Using dramatic conventions to convey meaning to an audience
- Evaluating a piece of drama
- Improving a piece of drama.

All of these might be covered by the terms suggested in the Arts Council's booklet *Drama in Schools:* 'making', 'performing' and 'responding'.

Personal and social skills

- Working as a member of a group
- Co-operation

- Leadership
- Evaluation of own learning
- Giving and valuing opinions
- Negotiation
- Self-advocacy
- Enquiry/questioning techniques
- Empathy with others
- Flexibility
- Creativity
- Self-confidence

Because of the wide range of ability within teaching groups, students are often working on very different levels within these skill areas.

For example, evaluation of one's own and others' performance/work can be as simple as 'showing appreciation' and 'saying which part of the drama you liked best', or as complex as saying 'why you considered a piece of drama good' or 'how you could improve it'. Different students within a session could be working at all of these levels. Sustaining a role may be inappropriate for a student with very delayed development and severe learning difficulties. Instead it may be a valuable learning experience to give that student opportunities to respond to a teacher in role.

EXAMPLES OF PROJECTS

The following are examples of drama projects which we hope will reveal aspects of our own development as drama practitioners:

MILO AND THE PHANTOM TOLLBOOTH

We used the book *The Phantom Tollbooth* by Norton Juster as a structure for this drama. We began session one by reading from the first chapter. We established the main character – Milo, a boy of similar age to the students. The group identified well with the character and had great fun re-creating Milo's flat. The group also enjoyed assembling the 'Tollbooth' which would become the vehicle that would transport us each week to 'the drama setting'. We found that it was useful to link each session with common objects, signifiers or repeated routines. For example, each week we took a map and money with us on our journey. We followed a routine, created through improvisation, to work the Tollbooth, and this was repeated each week. After each session we finished with a problem to solve, or a plan, agreed by the whole group, for the following week. The character of Milo wore a simple costume – members of the group took it in turn to play the part during each session.

This all helped the students to remember the story and pick up from where we left off each week. It motivated the students well, enabling them to stay with the story throughout the session – staying in role themselves, or continuing to respond to someone else in role.

Using Milo and the Tollbooth as a means of journeying to different drama settings was a structure that enabled us to go anywhere we wanted. It could be used to explore what life was like in another time (the Second World War, the Sixties, another century, etc.), or what it might be like to live in another country or culture – the possibilities are endless. Some of our destinations were pre-planned and others were decided upon by the students.

EXAMPLE

We visited:

- The land of the unexpected, where the students worked in groups to explore a cave, overcome a storm and help someone who had fallen into a deep hole.
- The land of paradise, where the students visited a cocktail bar, worked in a market, explored the beach and visited a disco.

Whilst we wanted the drama to be fun, it was our aim to raise more serious issues in a way that the group would understand, giving them opportunities to question and make decisions about the issues raised (Figure 15).

AIMS OF THE DRAMA

☆ To encourage group/team work within the drama group

☆ To encourage the group to support and motivate each other

☆ To encourage 'non-friends' to work together

☆ Language development – give directions within the drama
 – give explanations about what has happened/might happen

☆ To recall information about characters/events/general storyline from previous drama sessions

☆ To give opportunities for individual and group decision-making – encourage the idea of compromise

☆ To encourage students to argue, discuss, defend and justify a point of view

☆ To encourage students to see situations from more than one point of view

☆ To develop assertiveness and to identify with characters in the drama and build relationships with them

☆ For the group to build and develop a character (name, age, personality including use of costume), and eventually working towards some students getting 'into role'

☆ For students to respond to and express their feelings about a character 'in role'

Figure 15   Aims of the drama

We decided that one of our visits in the Tollbooth would be to 'Cardboard City'. We hoped to explore the notion that not everyone lives in a comfortable house with mod cons, etc. and also that it is easy to have preconceptions about people who seem to be different from you. For this session we set up a classroom as 'Cardboard City' using drapes and cardboard boxes to darken the room. We used candles to give the room an eerie light and hung a makeshift washing line. In Cardboard City the students were introduced to a character called Belinda (a teacher in role). In our planning meeting, before our session with the students, we decided on certain facts about her life and aspects of her character (see Figure 16a). Later in the project we built up a character description of Belinda with the students (see Figure 16b) and compared it with our own. We felt that we had laid down the skeleton of the character, and the students had put a lot more 'meat' on the bones. This had only been possible as a result of the students gaining a real insight into the feelings and responses of the character.

This part of the project lasted for about four weeks ($1 \times 1\frac{1}{4}$-hour session each week). Throughout the project the students were highly motivated. There were opportunities for the group to develop their communication skills and experience group decision-making. Individuals were able to shape, develop and respond to the drama from within a role. The students reacted spontaneously, showing a range of emotions such as compassion, empathy, anger, fear, happiness, curiosity and sadness. Using the teacher in role was a powerful tool. It was successful in that there were two of us acting together as drama facilitators – one responding to the students from within a role, and one to guide the session and observe individuals' contributions and reactions. This enabled us to respond immediately and appropriately to the suggestions, wishes and needs of the group. This way of working, using the teacher in role, enabled us to develop students' ideas and at the same time give the drama a useful focus and a clear structure – a far more flexible and responsive approach to drama than the 'prompt and prod' method.

THE ISLAND

In this project we decided to create an island which would become the setting for the drama. The students were presented with a large outline of the island. Most of the group knew immediately what it was, and were keen to make suggestions as to what features the island possessed. They drew their suggestions on the map or indicated where they wanted to place a particular feature. This was a useful exercise involving a great deal of discussion, negotiation, co-operation and compromise. Next we decided to explore the inhabitants of the island. We did this by looking at the 'jobs' of the people who lived there. The students came up with the following ideas: medical people, fishermen, builders, cooks, church people, bosses/rule-makers, cave people. We then split into smaller groups, each choosing to look at one of the

One of the group finds Belinda

The group have many questions for Belinda

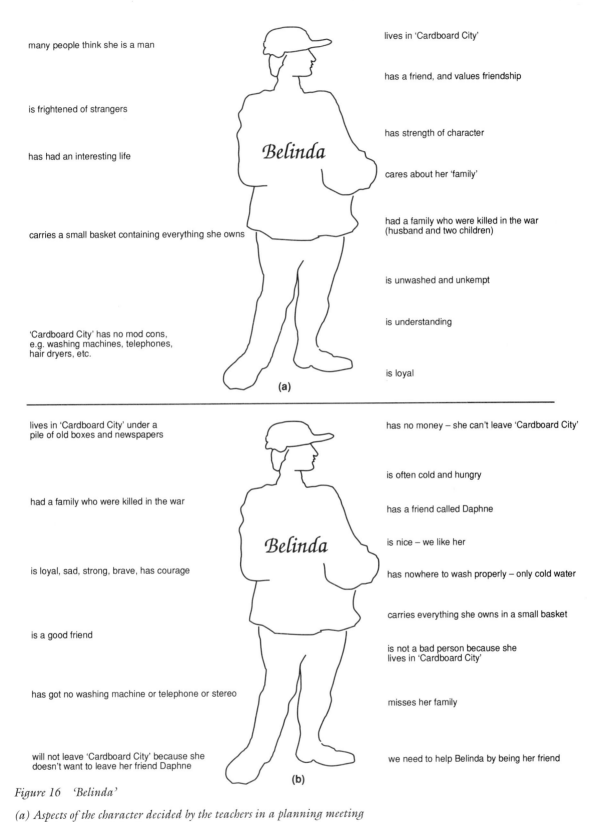

many people think she is a man

is frightened of strangers

has had an interesting life

carries a small basket containing everything she owns

'Cardboard City' has no mod cons,
e.g. washing machines, telephones,
hair dryers, etc.

lives in 'Cardboard City'

has a friend, and values friendship

has strength of character

cares about her 'family'

had a family who were killed in the war
(husband and two children)

is unwashed and unkempt

is understanding

is loyal

Belinda

(a)

lives in 'Cardboard City' under a
pile of old boxes and newspapers

had a family who were killed in the war

is loyal, sad, strong, brave, has courage

is a good friend

has got no washing machine or telephone or stereo

will not leave 'Cardboard City' because she
doesn't want to leave her friend Daphne

has no money – she can't leave 'Cardboard City'

is often cold and hungry

has a friend called Daphne

is nice – we like her

has nowhere to wash properly – only cold water

carries everything she owns in a small basket

is not a bad person because she
lives in 'Cardboard City'

misses her family

we need to help Belinda by being her friend

Belinda

(b)

Figure 16   'Belinda'

(a) Aspects of the character decided by the teachers in a planning meeting
(b) Students' view of the character

ideas. The groups mimed activities relating to their particular role. We put this to music and the students rehearsed their piece to perform to the others. This resulted in an excellent piece of movement/dance-drama.

Making tools on the island

To create tension we brought in some 'outsiders' who landed on the island in their boats. A teacher and two students in role formed the outsider group whose aim was to take up residence on the island. In this project we covered topics such as:

- cultural differences – the outsider group wore special hats which they weren't allowed to remove in public
- unemployment – were there enough jobs for everyone to do?
- fair distribution of food and resources
- rule-making and democracy – we voted on whether the outsiders could stay and under what conditions
- disability – one of the group wasn't able to work and needed special facilities.

The students in role coped well in standing up to the main group of islanders. They gained in confidence as a result of working alongside the teacher in role and with the other teacher working with the main islanders; there was a good balance to the viewpoints of each group. Finally, though this particular project was drama-based, we were able to cover many other aspects of the curriculum. In Art and Design we made the island into a three-dimensional model. Within the students' personal and social development, they learned how to co-operate with each other, negotiate, share, discuss and resolve problems; for example, one of the islanders was found to be stealing fish and the group had to decide what to do about it.

One of our biggest successes in this particular project was with Julie, who has Down's Syndrome. She was extremely introverted, especially in group sessions of any kind when she would sit with her head in her hands refusing to look up. As this project progressed and she felt comfortable and unthreatened by the methods we used, she gradually took a more active part in the drama, offering suggestions and solutions to the problems encountered by the group. Her self-confidence grew and these drama sessions became a turning point in her personal and social development.

THE STREET

The idea of using a street as a stimulus for drama came from a course we attended at the University of Reading led by Gill Brigg. We began our session at school by drawing a street on a long sheet of paper. We asked the students about the kind of buildings they might find on a street. They suggested shops, houses, a pub, a swimming pool, a fire station, a police station, etc. The students drew their suggestions on the street.

Drawing the street

One of the features chosen by the students was a bus station and several bus stops. We suggested that the students could wait for a bus to arrive. We all formed an orderly queue and chatted to each other about where we were going. One of the students volunteered to be the bus driver. We all boarded the bus stating our destinations. The passengers struck up conversations with each other. During this improvisation one of the group stated that he was the Mayor of the town. We froze the drama at this point, giving us time to review the responses and interactions within the group. When we resumed the following week, the session leader put a question to the Mayor (student in role): 'What's happened to our new swimming pool – remember, the one you promised us?' The Mayor replied, 'As it happens I'm just off to the town hall, so I'll make some enquiries when I arrive.' We asked the students to use props from around the room to create the scene at the Mayor's office in the town hall. We had plenty of suggestions and volunteers to take on roles within the Mayor's office: the manager, the clerk, and the secretary. We needed some more information about these characters so we used 'role on the floor' to build up their identities (Figure 17). We split the group into two and worked separately at this point. Each group looked at a different character. They decided, for example, how the Mayor might look and behave, where he might live and with whom, what sort of person he was, and what his interests were. Soon the students had a full description of each character, which they shared with each other.

A role on the floor!

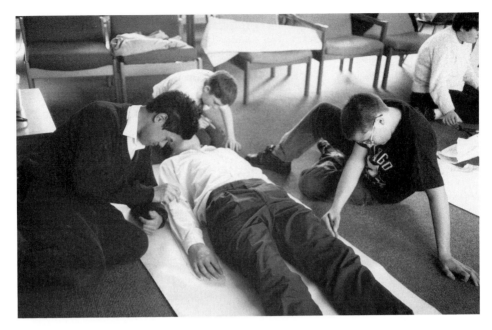

Building the character

USING THE DRAMA STRATEGY: ROLE-ON-THE-FLOOR/WALL

1 Draw around one of the students to create an outline. The outline signifies the character.

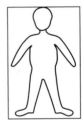

2 Inside the outline write information about the character, e.g. age, name, where he/she lives, occupation, likes/dislikes, etc.

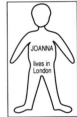

3 Outside the outline write information about other people who are involved in the character's life, e.g. family, parents, friends, workmates, how other people view the character, things that have happened to the character.

NB Decisions about the character are made and agreed by the group. This strategy gives the students opportunities to practise a wide variety of communication skills: speaking or signing, listening, agreeing, disagreeing, compromising, etc.

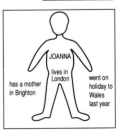

Figure 17   Using the drama strategy of 'role on the floor (or wall)'

The following session, we returned to the scene using signifiers to identify each character. For example, chain for the Mayor, tie for the manager, portable telephone for the secretary, hard hat for the builder. The students worked in role within the scene they had created, using these signifiers. After a long debate in the Mayor's office about the unfinished pool, the clerk decided to get in touch with the builder for an explanation as to why the work on the pool had been stopped. The builder (a student in role) was called to the town hall for an official meeting to sort out the problem. On arrival, he was met by a very angry crowd of people demanding to know about their pool. At this stage the whole group was working in role. We decided to use 'forum theatre' to involve everybody in the debate. This worked well with our students and led to a satisfactory solution to the dilemma (see Figure 18).

The town hall: students use simple costume to signify characters

At this point the students were highly motivated and wanted to continue working on 'The Street'. We were able to move on to create new dramas using this structure. Most of the ideas in this project came from the students, with our input initially being to provide a structure and then to keep things moving and developing, enabling the students' suggestions throughout the drama to be put into practice. In this particular project the students were introduced to and and practised a number of different drama structures and strategies, for example role on the floor, forum theatre, use of a signifier, thought tracking. They also practised their skills in negotiation, decision-making, dealing with conflict, and leadership. We felt this had been of our best work so far.

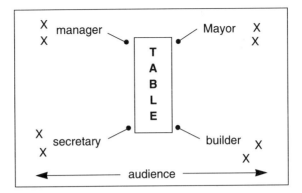
- One student in role as each character at the meeting.

- Two or three students sit behind each character (marked X).

- Meeting begins – improvised by students in role.

- Students sitting behind each character can support the character by calling 'time out' (raise hand) and advising them of what to say.

- Each character can call time out if they need help to argue their case.

- Session leader responds to time out signals. Time out lasts for approximately 30 seconds, during which time each character-group can discuss the progress of the meeting.

NB Using forum theatre is useful because:

 – it can involve more students in the scene

 – it reduces the pressure on the student who is working in role

 – it can extend discussion, giving a fuller and more balanced view to a dilemma.

Figure 18   Using forum theatre

THE ANTIQUE SHOP

We began this project by looking at the word 'old'. The group gave some wonderful descriptions of what the word meant to them. In small groups the students made up short sequences using movement to describe the word/phrase chosen. Their examples included *an old creaky house, old bones, an old attic* and *an old shop.* We decided to create an antique shop and discussed how we might do that. The students brought lots of old objects in from home, and we put together a display which later became part of the shop. Together we imagined the front of the shop, and tried different ways of making the door open. We chose our favourite – a revolving door – and used this to start the drama each week.

The antique shop

The group decided that the shop was owned by an elderly couple called Tom and Alice. The students themselves suggested that they use 'role on the floor' to build a description of these two characters. We decided that it was best to use teacher in role for the character of Tom. For the first few sessions one of us got ready before the drama began and went straight into role. Later in the project we asked the group to describe Tom. As they did so, our actor, a teacher in role, put on each item of costume until Tom looked as he had in previous sessions. The students had remembered well and they had observed our character in much greater detail than we had expected. It was clear that they were beginning to appraise performances with a more critical eye, and in this case knew just how they wanted Tom to be. In some of the sessions we used a second teacher in role for the character of Alice.

An underlying theme for this particular project was sibling rivalry. In the shop the students came across a mysterious parcel. Tom told them quite clearly 'not to touch it'. Each session the students became more curious about this package. Eventually Tom let out his long-kept secret. The parcel contained an old music book written by his talented brother many years ago. Tom had stolen the book, which had taken his brother years of work. Tom was sorry for his actions. However, his brother had died before he had had a chance to apologise. The students wanted to go back and put the story right for Tom. They acted out a number of alternative scenarios. Throughout the drama we gave opportunities for discussion. The students talked a great deal about jealousy and feelings of inadequacy, especially with reference to their own brothers and sisters. The students related to Tom's feelings of anger towards his talented brother, although they were very definite about what was right and what was wrong. In our evaluation with the students we explored Tom's feelings of regret, and what was really interesting was the group's realisation that mistakes cannot always be put right.

A student in role as Tom from the antique shop, gives a soliloquy demonstrating his regret

TRAINING

Training for us has involved attending courses, seeking help from advisory drama teachers and support groups, reading books and on-the-job practice. We have short regular planning meetings (fifteen minutes at the end of a session/day over a cup of tea), and longer meetings at the beginning and end of a project. We have built evaluation sessions into these meetings to discuss how the group is progressing within the drama structure, and individual reactions to what is happening. In this way we can make the work as relevant and appropriate as possible, and in some cases change our direction in order to meet individual needs. We have sometimes asked a third person (college student helper, volunteer, Addington student or another member of staff) to video part of the session. We have watched this together and then been able to discuss individuals' reactions and monitor their understanding of the drama. Later we have been able to use the video with the group to help with student evaluation. This ongoing assessment and evaluation (see Figure 19) has proved invaluable in our planning. It has helped us to clarify what has actually been learned by the students and given us a structure and direction for our work.

DRAMA EVALUATION
PROJECT: PROBLEM-SOLVING FOR FRANCESCA

What was good?

We worked with another school called the Avenue on this project. I enjoyed working with another school and meeting new people. We also did some warm-up games.

What was difficult?

1. Trying to get myself organised.
2. Trying to understand if people were talking as the character or as themselves.

What did I do?

We got into different groups and planned out some scenes as well. Plus I did some talking in role. I was hot-seated.

What did I learn?

1. I learned about doing drama with new people from a different school.
2. I learned some brand-new drama words - questions, character, and costume.

(a)

Figure 19   Three examples of evaluation forms completed by students at the end of drama projects

DRAMA EVALUATION
PROJECT:THE ISLAND

What was good?

I liked acting and being in role.

What was difficult?

Talking in role is hard because I keep forgetting which character I am.
Communicating with other people can be hard.

What did I do?

We drew the Island. We put lots of places on it where people live, and work. We had lots of people doing different jobs like church people, cooks, teachers, builders, firemen.
I was a teacher.

What did I learn?

I learned some new words like 'communicating' and 'in role'.
I have got better at acting.

(b)

GROUP DRAMA EVALUATION

NAME: **PROJECT:** Simon & Donna

What did I do?

I played Simon.
I helped to build the character of Donna.
I wore a hat - a signifier
Somebody drew around me to make the outline of Donna - Role on floor.
I played Simon, I had an argument with Donna.
I volunteered to be hot-seated.
I was Simon and Mark was Donna.
We worked in groups.
We took turns to show our acting.
We wrote to an agony aunt 'in role'.

What was good?

The acting was good.
I really enjoyed working with Katie.
I liked wearing the costume.
I liked being hot-seated.
The best thing is getting dressed up.
I liked the arguing.

What was difficult?

Working with other people.
Some people don't match.
It was difficult not to laugh.
To think and remember what to say.
It was hard to act.
It was difficult to look at people and make eye-contact.

What did I learn?

How to act.
How to act with each other.
What these Drama words mean - costume, role, hot-seat, signifier,
*   character.*
How to communicate better.

(c)

Another medium through which we have learned a great deal is 'The Ark', which is based at South Hill Park Arts Centre in Bracknell. The Ark is a project that provides opportunities for people with learning difficulties, artists and members of the public to be creative together and work towards a performance based on sharing. The Ark works with drama at its centre and brings together artists from every field – the visual arts, music, dance and drama. Each year a different theme is fixed upon, with the work culminating in a festival during which groups share their performances. The experience is tremendously empowering, and gives all those who take part opportunities to achieve, belong, appreciate and be appreciated. We had the privilege of taking our drama group to join the sessions which are run by professional artists. The people involved in the project are dedicated to giving equal opportunities to children and adults with learning difficulties, who otherwise might never get the chance to feel a sense of personal achievement through working in the field of the arts. The atmosphere and environment were very different from anything we had ever experienced before. We had the opportunity of working in a real theatre with professional artists, and seeing the value of a truly collaborative arts project. The Ark was a wonderful learning experience for us *all*, and one we will always remember.

A common feature of county training in education is that it is generally open only to 'teachers' and not to 'assistants'. We feel strongly that schools should extend these opportunities for training to include assistants. Within our school the idea of teamwork is strongly promoted. Therefore we, as teacher and assistant, have had opportunities to attend courses as individuals and as colleagues. We have also worked together to lead in-service training at our school in the area of 'Drama and the Arts'.

PERSONAL REFLECTIONS

At this point we feel that we need to write a little of our personal feelings about working in partnership.

PENNY'S VIEW: THE ASSISTANT

Soon after Jan and I began working together as teacher and assistant, I discovered we had a mutual liking for drama. We made a point of discussing how we could perhaps use drama to help our students. One way was to help them to express their opinions and not be afraid to speak up for themselves – this is often difficult for people with learning difficulties. Sometimes teacher-assistants find it difficult to speak up and express opinions too.

Being quite a chatty person, I began to express my ideas and opinions regarding drama (I couldn't help my enthusiasm). The good thing about this was that Jan took all my ideas on board and allowed me to use them. This teacher was accepting me as her equal. It gave me great confidence and I believe helped me to put much more into our working day. Jan gave me the chance to show what I was made of by asking me to play teacher in role. I remember thinking, 'Oh no, I'm going to blow it and will have to go back to paint-mixing again'. When I first walked into a drama session in role I was shaking inside, but by the end of the session I felt very pleased. Jan had steered the students in the right direction and they had asked all the appropriate questions. This was to be the structure for most of our sessions – with Jan leading and me working in role. By the end of the year I was able to work in role with confidence, and enjoyed the drama sessions tremendously.

Our school has a policy of equal opportunities, which enables assistants to further their career by taking part in outreach training courses. Thus I went where no NTA had been before – that is, on a drama course. The session started with a circle of course members telling each other who they were and where they came from. All of the people on the course were teachers. When it came to my turn I introduced myself as 'Penny – just an assistant'. I discovered that 'just an assistant' meant quite a lot to the people there and they treated me as their equal. I soon felt comfortable with the situation and happy that my ideas were considered of value by the group. That was the beginning of several drama courses I attended, and each one was a great learning opportunity. I was subsequently able to pass on my experience to other staff when Jan and I ran a staff training day.

Today I feel confident enough to run drama sessions by myself, and am pleased with the opportunities I have been given by my school and colleagues alike. So to all you teachers: go on, give your assistants a chance – who knows, they may have talents you didn't know existed. And to all you NTAs, take heart, perhaps one day your title too may be 'teacher-assistant', as mine is at Addington.

JAN'S VIEW: THE TEACHER

Teachers in special schools and special needs departments are accustomed to working with or alongside colleagues in the classroom. Sometimes this can be with another teacher, but often it is with an assistant. As a teacher who has worked in a number of special schools, I feel there are two very distinct ways of working:

A

With you, the teacher, taking the lead in all matters, making all the decisions, taking full responsibility for every aspect of the teaching and learning environment, asking your assistant to fit in with your way of working.

or

I have often heard assistants saying, 'I can't do that any more, my new teacher likes it done this way.' Some assistants feel subordinate to their teacher colleagues. Some teachers can feel threatened by their assistant, as if they are waiting for them to make a mistake.

As a teacher I feel that the way of working described in **A** is a rather lonely existence for the teacher. It can lead to misunderstandings between teacher and assistant, and an almost competitive relationship between two people who are there primarily to provide a rich and motivating environment for the pupils and students they teach. Surely this can be achieved more easily if the teacher and assistant have a mutual respect, and work together using each other's strengths to improve the quality of what is offered to children?

Working *in partnership* in the field of drama is essential within a special needs environment. If you have a teacher and an assistant working together in a drama session, then that session must be planned and each of you must have a clear role to play – otherwise your assistant will become little more than an observer – and what a waste that would be!

In this chapter we have discussed the use of the teacher in role within various projects. This is a useful strategy for all students, whatever their age or ability. However, we have found it to be particularly successful when working with young people with severe learning difficulties who may find it hard to understand some of the more abstract drama techniques such as hot-seating, thought tracking, and tableaux. Penny is extremely talented at working as teacher in role. She is able to respond to the students from within her role as a character in the drama. This frees me to concentrate on the responses and language used by the students. This can also be done from within role, but it is more successful if there are two session leaders – one working in role and one working the group. These roles can be interchanged, as Penny and I often choose to do. This helps you to understand better your working relationship. In our case it has given Penny a chance to feel what it is like to lead the session, and me an opportunity to gain experience working as teacher in role. Having two or more staff also means that students can receive more help and support when they are working in groups. An average size for a drama group would be 10–15 students with two staff. The staff can then move around within the smaller groups, or attach themselves to one group who may be experiencing difficulties in working together. Having a team-teaching situation in drama gives greater flexibility in using a variety of drama strategies and structures.

SUMMARY

To summarise, here are some of the main points we feel are important when working in partnership in the field of drama education and special needs

- Make planning a shared process. Teachers and assistants need to plan together.
- Consider yourselves as having joint responsibility within the teaching and learning environment.
- Let your roles become more flexible. Move away from the traditional teacher/assistant relationship. Swap roles. Share the lead.
- Recognise each other's strengths and weaknesses, and respect each other's roles within the school.
- Involve your students in evaluating each drama project. Evaluation of one project often leads to an idea or direction for another.
- Give students opportunities to direct and make choices within the drama.
- Don't be afraid to let go and give control of the drama to the students.
- Use the same techniques as any drama teacher. You may need to adapt their use, but do *not* look for a separate set of strategies. Drama is drama whatever the age or ability of the student group.
- Most important of all – enjoy your sessions.

REFERENCES

Arts Council of Great Britain (1992) *Drama in Schools*, ACGB

Juster, N. (1962) *The Phantom Tollbooth*, Collins

CHAPTER EIGHT

INTEGRATING SPECIAL AND MAINSTREAM EDUCATION

Andy Kempe

INTRODUCTION

In their research into attitudes towards integrating children with special educational needs, Paul Croll and Diana Moses discovered that while many teachers applauded the idea in principle, they were less enthusiastic about integration in their own classrooms. Lack of appropriate training and expertise were stated as the major reasons for this. Teachers in mainstream schools were, however, more prepared to accept children with a physical or sensory impairment than children with a moderate learning difficulty, despite having far more personal experience of children in this latter category. One wonders if it was because teachers had experience of the problems of integrating children with moderate learning difficulties into an already pressurised classroom situation that made them recoil from the possibility of more integration without some relief in staffing or extra training.

This chapter considers the opportunities and constraints of integrating young people from a special school with those in mainstream education through a specially designed drama project. In addition to guidance for initiating similar links, I believe the project has considerable implications for teachers working with classes of widely mixed ability pupils in comprehensive schools.

'IT'S GOOD FOR THEM!'

My first contact with young people in a special school was when I took over the drama department of a large comprehensive school. As part of the sixth-form general studies course, students could opt to join a drama project which involved working with young people with a range of physical and learning disabilities. The school was proud of the link and wanted me to keep it going.

The school had its own learning support unit which withdrew from a number of lessons pupils who were identified as having special needs in basic numeracy and literacy. That drama was particularly appropriate for these pupils was never questioned, so children were never withdrawn from drama lessons. Despite the tremendous growth of GCSE and A Level Drama and Theatre Studies courses in recent years, it is still frequently stated that drama is especially suited to children who are 'less academic'. The assumption seems to be that because drama is practical, pupils at the lower end of the academic scale may benefit from it more than their more academically able peers. This view of drama has been around for some time. Indeed, the 1963 Newsom Report into the education of pupils of average or less than average ability put considerable emphasis on the importance of all practical subjects for such children. But this assumption seems to beg a number of questions, namely:

- Is drama good for children with low academic ability because they can succeed in it and therefore their self-esteem may be enhanced?
- Is it good for them because it offers an alternative means of interpreting and commenting upon the world?
- Is it good because it promotes a number of skills such as initiative, imagination, and the ability to work as a team, and these skills are less apparent in other 'desk-and-book' type subjects?
- Or is it good because the conventional classroom set-up and traditional teacher-based approaches to the imparting of knowledge all too frequently lead to a confrontation between the agenda of the pupils and that of the teacher? In short, is it that some teachers simply cannot or do not want to contain these children in their classrooms?

The first three questions suggest another – why aren't all of these things considered good for all pupils? The concept of an 'entitlement curriculum' is important here. The 1978 Warnock Report suggested that the objectives of education should be the same for all children, though the means of achieving those objectives may be different. All children may benefit from working through drama, but some *individuals* may benefit in particular. This does not correlate with their academic ability but is dependent upon other factors in their individuality. My own belief is that drama is not necessarily any more efficacious for one *group* of children than another. On the contrary, in drama it can be very productive to accommodate a diverse range of children within one group. Drama feeds off the negotiation which occurs when different individual perspectives and ideas are released in a common framework.

The last question posed above seems cynical but I have no doubt that it reflects attitudes that many drama teachers have encountered. It is ironical therefore that the sixth-form project in which my students worked on a weekly basis with pupils from a local special school was warmly applauded by the staff as a whole. An activity that had been seen by some colleagues as a bit of a waste of time for 'bright' pupils lower down the school suddenly became a valid exercise in community relations and the development of social responsibility. Here though it wasn't drama itself that was deemed 'good for them', but the chance of mixing with people who weren't quite like them. As it turned out, in this project the amount of drama undertaken (as opposed to other purely social activities) was minimal.

What is also thrown into relief by this brief anecdote is that there is a palpable difference in the attitudes of some teachers in mainstream education to those children in special schools who, it is assumed, have clearly recognisable special needs, as opposed to those children with learning difficulties in their own schools. Put bluntly, children in special schools are afforded some sympathy (notwithstanding considerable ignorance about the diversity of reasons for which children might be there), while those remaining in mainstream education, though loosely referred to as 'having special needs', are all too often regarded as 'hard work' (to put it euphemistically).

Some years after my brief though thought-provoking introduction into the complexities of integration, I had the opportunity to join a similar project involving the same special school but a different secondary school. The project again involved sixth-formers. This time I considered carefully what exactly it was that was 'good for them' – that is, *all* the young people involved. For if the education of children with learning difficulties, be they in special or mainstream schools, is to progress, the attitudes need challenging; where better to start than with those children who are not categorised in such a way?

PERSONAL AND GROUP AGENDAS

Any project seeking to integrate young people from mainstream education with those for whom some special provision is made, must take into consideration the different agendas that participants have. Both the personal wishes and needs of each participant and the institutions to which they belong are valid factors. Geoff Gillham has usefully pointed out that, in drama, it's as if there are two plays happening simultaneously: the play for the child and the play for the teacher. In a drama about space explorers, the play for the child might be chiefly concerned with communicating with an alien that has appeared in the story. The play for the teacher might be chiefly concerned with getting the children to communicate with each other. In this example it may be seen that the activity appears to have a different purpose for the teacher and for the children but these objectives are not in contradiction with each other. In a project that may throw together young people with very different real-life experiences in the same fiction, consideration must be given to what's in it for whom, so that unproductive tensions can be avoided.

Personal needs and wishes may, of course, be enormously varied and may not always obtain the wholehearted approval of others. Many young people in mainstream education might state that they hope involvement in such a drama project will help them:

- increase their self-confidence
- bring them into contact with a wider range of people
- give them the fun and enjoyment of making and acting a story
- improve their understanding of a different social group.

These are all laudable, and the kind of personal objectives which most people would be willing to state openly. On the other hand, would-be participants may have a hidden agenda. They may, for example, wish to join the project because:

- it will salve their social conscience
- as a community project, drama is likely to be an easier option than cleaning out the local canal
- they are actually frightened of people with disabilities and feel the only way to overcome their fear is to confront it head-on
- they love showing off, and drama offers lots of opportunities for that
- people will think that they are brave, kind and generous for working with children who are not as fortunate as themselves.

And what of the agendas of the young people with special educational needs? It would be good to think that they also had a say in whether or not they actually wanted to do some drama rather than have it done to them in order to suit somebody else's needs!

Schools wanting to initiate an integrated project must take a realistic view of these personal objectives when setting objectives for the project. Offering young people the chance to become involved may have great therapeutic value for them as individuals simply as a by-product of the drama activity itself. To insist that all participants state completely honestly what their personal objectives are, will change the nature of the exercise dramatically. Some young people in mainstream education could well benefit from facing up honestly to themselves. On the other hand, asking young people who are very likely still to be feeling unsure about themselves to make such a declaration, might damage their self-esteem and effectively debar them from joining the project with a positive and open frame of mind. To respect the notion that any drama activity may have a therapeutic value is not to say that the purpose of drama is to provide therapy (as was discussed in Chapter One).

People's expectations of what they might get from drama are altered by experience. Sometimes their wishes and needs are fulfilled, while at other times what they set out to find pales into significance in the face of what they do find; they will take their own luggage with them into a drama no matter what is said or done beforehand. What the organisers of group drama projects must ensure is that solely personal objectives do not obstruct those objectives that are shared by the whole group. This can only be achieved by negotiating and explicitly stating what those whole-group objectives are. In this, the teachers and carers involved in the project must play a crucial part.

The personal, social and intellectual development that may take place through drama has been discussed in many books for drama specialists. A potential pitfall for any integrated project is to place too great an emphasis on these educational aims at the expense of considering what the drama itself, the 'play for the children', will involve. While the participants in the project will inevitably come from different educational backgrounds and may, as discussed above, have different personal needs, a key question must be, 'What will be common to all participants in the nature of the work?'

Regardless of who the participants are, a drama session will have two related elements:

> *A content:* the story told as the drama unfolds
> *A form:* the way in which the story is told

For a drama project to meet its full potential, both the form and the content must be appropriate to all the participants. This implies that all of the participants must be both excited by the content and stretched by the form.

A danger in this kind of project is that those children with special educational needs will be patronised. This may happen in a number of ways:

- *An assumption is made that because the group have learning difficulties they are immature and therefore most likely to benefit from some sort of children's story.*
  It is difficult to assess the exact relationship between physical and emotional maturity and intellectual ability. It may be safer to assume that all people need social relationships just as much as they need intellectual stimulation. Dealing with teenage relationships or plunging into a murder mystery drama is therefore much more likely to engage young people with learning difficulties than simply re-enacting familiar stories or everyday situations.
- *Seeing the physical or learning disability of their counterparts, participants from the mainstream endeavour to perform tasks for them.*
  Effectively, this is to handicap them more. The aim of the drama should be to empower all the participants by allowing them to contribute themselves.
- *Working on the notion that people with learning disabilities need plenty of stimulation, they are given too much.*
  For people who may already have a problem with focusing their attention, swamping them with visual, aural and social stimuli will handicap them by reducing their ability to understand the situation and take a part in it.

Another danger in integrated project work is that the participants from the mainstream become so engrossed with the drama themselves that they ignore the presence of their counterparts with special needs, take over the whole activity and so widen the gap between the parties rather than build on the common ground.

All of these points indicate the need to prepare the participants for the joint project in advance of the groups meeting, and to establish a number of ground rules. Ways in which groups might best be prepared are discussed below but let us first consider the implications of these hazards to the drama itself.

CONTENT

Choosing the content of the drama carefully can help safeguard against participants being patronised. If the drama is interesting and relevant to all the participants, there will be an equality to the partnership.

In answer to the question 'What shall we make the drama about?', students in both special and mainstream situations often tend to select such themes and issues as:

- teenage relationships
- isolation
- bullying
- prejudice
- finding a job.

Such a list reflects the genuine concerns of all young people. Exciting opportunities arise because children with special educational needs may well have very different personal experiences of these issues from those of their mainstream counterparts. The problem is, while a good drama explores issues, it does so through the lens created by a particular story. The task for the teacher must be to find an appropriate narrative which offers scope for dealing with these issues. Some young people, when asked what the drama should be about, will respond by suggesting a story. Here the problem is that the story is often already complete and leaves little room for creative development or exploration. For example, young people will recount the narrative of a favourite or recent television programme or film. Their expectation might be that they will be able to act this out in the drama session. This might be fun and might satisfy a number of physical and social objectives, but simply re-enacting a story is to undervalue the potential that drama has to help develop new insights by making new stories. What the teacher may do is take an element from a story and use that as a starting point in the same way that he may take any literary or pictorial stimulus to start the drama. For example, the drama may:

- focus on a particular character and investigate that person's life beyond the confines of the story
- choose a particular scene and consider what happens next to those characters who are shown in the scene but not featured in the rest of the story – for example, what happens to a particular group of passengers in a lifeboat after the sinking of the *Titanic*

- develop new scenes along the lines of those included in the story – for example, adopting the roles of King Arthur and the knights, the group set off on another, as yet untold, quest.

A strong narrative works as a motor. It isn't necessary to have all of the details of the story worked out in advance. In fact, overpreparing the narrative will present the group from exploring the things that are important to them. What is crucial is ensuring that the story is introduced in a clear and stimulating way so that all the participants know what is going on and are sufficiently engaged to want to continue with it. Chapter Four gives more detailed guidance on this aspect of drama work in the special classroom.

FORM

There is a plethora of drama strategies from which teachers may draw to help plan the work. A number of these are outlined in Chapter Three. These strategies may be seen as stepping-stones through the narrative: points at which the developing characters and storyline can be checked and refined to ensure that there is a coherence in the drama and that the underlying issues are exposed. In an integrated project, a careful structure helps the teachers involved to monitor the learning that is taking place. It also allows them to manipulate the roles taken by the students in a productive way, stopping mainstream partners from dominating the action and reinforcing the notion that all of the participants are in the same boat as far as the fiction is concerned. One particularly useful strategy to employ here is to usher mainstream students into roles where they are subservient to other characters. This allows them, when it's appropriate, to be an adviser, messenger or assistant to their counterparts from the special class without actually taking full responsibility for any decisions. At one point in 'The Party' drama described below, the group were paired off, each student with special needs being given an assistant and asked to help prepare for the party. The 'assistants' used their questioning skills to engage their partners in the work: 'Have you got the bread? Shall I butter or do you want to? What do you want me to do with these sandwiches anyway?'

In the 'Space' drama, the group were split into small groups and given the task of designing a particular piece of equipment on board the starship. It was the job of the special needs students, as 'officers', to operate the equipment but one of the sixth-formers, as an 'official guide', was delegated to explain to the rest of the class what the equipment actually did.

PRE-PLANNING BY STAFF

The amount of expertise and experience of drama which staff might bring to an integrated project is, obviously, indeterminate. What they will be able to offer, though, is a knowledge of the individual students involved, and it is from this starting point that the joint planning should begin.

Ideally, all the staff – that is, teachers, assistants and carers – should meet together before the project starts. If this really is impossible then the key initiators should ensure that there is a means of reporting back to the others involved. It cannot be stressed enough that for the integrated project to reach its full potential all the adults must be clear about the aims of the work and the methods to be employed.

Among the more straightforward items on the agenda should be the following:

- *When* In order both to establish productive social relationships and develop a meaningful dramatic narrative, the students will need to meet on a regular basis. A project of less than five weeks' duration is unlikely to give the young people enough of a chance to relax with each other. Equally damaging would be to try and maintain a project for more than a term and risk a steady fall-off of interest. Mainstream students especially may find conflicting demands on their time but their withdrawal from the project, albeit for good reasons, may be misconstrued. Teachers of young people with special needs might also be wary of their students becoming too dependent on the mainstream partners.

- *Length of sessions* Sessions need to last for at least one hour. Every effort should be made to start the session on time and given that at least one of the parties is likely to have to travel, time should be allowed for that. This is particularly important at the end of a session. The atmosphere and potency of a piece of drama, not to mention the personal relationships at work within it, can be shattered by half the group suddenly realising the time and disappearing! Bringing the students out of role and reflecting on the session may be crucial if all of the participants are to appreciate what has been achieved, and to ensure that confusion between reality and fiction is avoided. Teachers themselves will be the best judges of what the maximum duration of a session should be.

- *Size of group* This is a difficult one in that such a project might be useful or have an appeal to a large number of students from both sides. Organisers do need to be quite ruthless though when determining numbers. Certainly, there should not be more students from the mainstream than from the special sector. A one-to-one ratio can be very useful but the overall size of the group, including adults, needs to be considered. A group of more than twenty young people can be problematical. With a large group, it is harder to keep the drama focused, sharing ideas becomes more arduous, space becomes limited, the noise level may become distracting and the group over-excited. Any of the students may find too large a group over-stimulating or overwhelming.

- *Space* The obvious thing to say about space is that there must be enough of it. There are pros and cons to having the project housed in the familiar surroundings of the special school or in a new and different environment. Again, teachers will need to consider the logistics of the project in the light of their objectives for their students.

Less easy to deal with at the planning stage, and therefore demanding more time for discussion and thought, are:

- *What* Staff involved in the project may want to determine the content of the drama themselves or find some way of negotiating this with the students who will be involved. However, the comments on content above should be considered; ultimately, it is the staff who will be responsible for ensuring that the project is educationally valid; the 'play for the teacher' may have some aims which it would be unnecessary or unwise to state explicitly to the participants.

- *How* Under this heading, staff need to consider what strategies might best be used to introduce and develop the content. They also need to decide on who will have responsibility for what. Team teaching isn't easy. Teachers who try to rely on their ability to read each other's minds tend to end up looking like a bad juggling act with ideas flying in from different directions but none of them being caught and used. Until a close working relationship and shared understanding of methods and purpose have been achieved, it is far better to sketch out a step-by-step plan for each session. This implies that in addition to initial planning meetings, staff will need to discuss the work as it goes on.

The word 'drama' can be quite terrifying for many adults. It is often simply associated with the formal performance of plays. All of the adults involved in a project will need introducing to the notion that the process of the work *is* the product. They need to be realistic about their expectations for the students and also for themselves. Finally, staff who have no experience of drama can only be encouraged simply to try it out themselves.

PREPARING THE MAINSTREAM GROUP

Although teachers may not want to openly confront the personal agendas of the students involved in the integrated project, it is essential that honest discussion takes place about the preconceptions the group holds regarding people with learning or other disabilities. The discussion needs to be sensitively handled, for what will most likely become evident is that these students also will need careful support and attention during the work: for most, if not all of them, the project will be a new experience and likely to challenge their beliefs, skills and attitudes.

While their own teacher will most likely be the best one to explain the organisation of the project and the expectations from their school's point of view, a visit from the special school teacher can be very fruitful. It obviously isn't appropriate for teachers to talk about the difficulties or disabilities of individuals in great detail, but a general introduction about the kinds of problems and experiences they have is useful.

Consistency of attendance is tremendously important; people need to feel sure that they want and are able to undertake such a commitment before opting to join it. Any introductory talk should be encouraging but honest. It may be worth showing all the participants photographs or perhaps a video in which their counterparts in either school introduce themselves.

The degree to which these students become actively involved in the planning of the sessions is dependent on the size of the group, their experience of drama and the perceived needs of their partners in the special school. Certainly, there may be tremendous educational value in having a small group assist with the planning if that fits with the agenda of the students with special educational needs. What shouldn't be the case is that the mainstream students are allowed to feel that they are doing drama *to* their counterparts rather than working alongside them. In any case, teachers have a responsibility to ensure that the students are furnished with the appropriate skills for the drama. Questioning and reporting in ways that complement and support rather than undermine and patronise are examples of skills that can be developed in advance of the two groups meeting.

A number of 'ground rules' need to be established. The need to avoid patronising their partners in the ways outlined above should be discussed, as should the need to keep the drama focused. The students must be clear about their responsibilities to respect each other and to be reliable. They need to be encouraged to trust the drama and talk about their own feelings as the project moves on. There should be the freedom to drop out of the project, but students need to be aware of the implications of this in terms of their own self-esteem and the way that decision could be read by others; quitting mustn't be an easy decision.

PREPARATIONS IN THE SPECIAL SCHOOL

Students with special educational needs should, as far as possible, have a stake in the project from its inception. Consulting them about whether or not they wish to take part and on what terms is as much a part of the educational process as actually doing the drama. Teachers will, inevitably, judge the extent to which their students might usefully be involved in the actual planning of sessions, depending on their individual needs and abilities, and on the content of the drama itself. The teachers involved in 'The Party' project described below felt that, having gauged an enthusiasm on the part of the students to be involved, the most productive approach would simply be to launch into the practical work. Some teachers in special schools may feel that individuals will need to be reassured, given the prospect of such a new encounter. Again individual teachers will have their own way of tackling this, depending on the specific needs of the young people involved.

'THE PARTY': A CASE STUDY OF AN INTEGRATED DRAMA PROJECT

This six-week project came about as a result of a request from a group of 15 to 19-year-olds in an extended education unit attached to a special school. The group had worked on drama projects previously but not ones which gave them direct opportunities to draw on their own personal experiences and explore their current personal concerns. The group had discussed a range of possibilities for a drama and decided that looking at personal relationships would be useful and fun. All of the young people in the unit had physical disabilities and attendant learning difficulties.

Involvement in the project was offered to sixth-formers as an opportunity to undertake some community service. In introducing the project, the mainstream teachers involved had emphasised its social purpose. While the sixth-formers were academically very able, some lacked self-confidence or had a very narrow outlook on life. For these students, the teachers believed that both the social contact and the controlled pretence of the drama would be 'good for them'. These hopes were not explicitly stated. Rather, through open discussion along the lines suggested above, the sixth-formers set out their group objectives thus:

- to gain a greater insight into the needs of disabled people
- to offer support and assistance to their counterparts in the special school
- to engage actively and socially with a group whose needs were different from their own.

The teachers from the extended education unit saw the project in a different though not incompatible way. Their objectives were more sharply defined and worth stating here for their specificity:

- To increase the circle of acquaintances of the young people in the unit and so counteract the social isolation felt by them. The unit usually only consisted of between eight and ten students. Working in a larger group would constitute a new type of stimulus.
- To use the social activity as a stimulus for other learning. It was felt that the social contact would be stimulating in itself, but could also instigate discussion and other work related to the drama project.
- To offer a range of physically differentiated activities. Some of the young people were unable to take part in many sports activities; drama was seen as an opportunity to play a physical part in a group activity appropriate to ability.
- To increase the understanding of the world outside the unit both in terms of what might be explored in the dramatic fiction, and in terms of the new relationships the integrated project might offer. The teachers were particularly keen on giving the members of the unit the chance to see able-bodied boys and girls working in a controlled atmosphere. It was felt that all too often people with disabilities suffer from poor self-esteem because they perceive

able-bodied peers and siblings as being wholly successful. By actually working together, it was felt that they might see for themselves that their peers are also sometimes limited and need support.

THE PROJECT IN ACTION

As a result of this pre-planning, it was decided that five sixth-formers would be photographed wearing costumes to signify different young characters. One set of photographs showed the characters on their own, displaying a variety of facial expressions and gestures. A second set depicted them in pairs or groups. The students wore distinctive clothing for the photographs, for example a brightly coloured scarf or notable jacket. These items of clothing would later be used to signify the character.

Four of the five students in 'The Character Gallery'

Week One

The two groups of students were introduced to each other. A few 'name games' were played as ice-breakers. They were told that they would be involved in a drama about five characters (the five students depicted in the photographs were kept out of this session). Forgoing any warm-up games in favour of straightforward personal introductions, the class was split into five groups which mixed, as evenly as possible, students from the two schools.

Each group was given one of the photographs depicting a character. (They were also supplied with the character's real name in order to avoid confusion later on.) The groups discussed what sort of person he or she was by their expression, gesture and choice of clothing. An important aspect of this work was to have participants represent physically the character they were looking at. This 'total physical response' gave an insight into what the character might be feeling and the effect they might have on someone else. Participants were invited to suggest what the character was saying when the photograph was taken.

The ideas were recorded on sugar paper and, at the end of the session, each group talked about and demonstrated their character to the rest of the class.

The role of the mainstream students here was largely to guide and support their special colleagues, encouraging them to take charge of the physical demonstration if not the vocal description.

Week Two

The participants re-formed their five groups and considered the second set of photographs which depicted characters responding to each other. Again, through a combination of discussion, physically representing the visual images and then animating them with movement and words, each group generated ideas about the relationships perceived in the pictures.

Depicting relationships

One mainstream student from each group took on the role of 'target' character and was then hot-seated by the special students about what was happening in the photograph and what feelings were involved. The mainstream students were here being quite subordinate to their counterparts, acting as sounding boards to reflect on and develop the ideas coming forward. The students in the hot-seat were advised to come frequently out of role in order to ask for clarification on their own performance of the target character: 'Is that right? Do you think I would say that? Should I just be sitting or would I walk around?'

The purpose of this was not only to make the fiction of the situation clear, but to reinforce for the special students that they were the ones creating the character.

The groups were reminded, by the teachers, that all of their work on the characters so far had been speculative and that in the next session they would be able to meet the 'actual' characters and see how accurate they had been in their judgements.

The session ended with a brief discussion regarding the sort of situation which would bring these five characters together in a drama. It was at this point that the idea of 'the party' arose.

Week Three

In preparation for this session, the subjects of the photographs were briefed as to how characters had been constructed for them and what ideas there were about their relationships with each other.

The session started with one teacher re-capping on the work to date. Some 'smoothing out' took place here in order to make the drama more coherent. This was done both by the teacher using narration and, where ideas appeared contradictory, by asking the class which option was preferred. It was suggested, for example, that while the five characters were now at college or work, they had all been to school together.

Wearing the same clothes in which they had been photographed, the five characters were brought in and introduced. The teachers had debated long and hard as to whether it should be revealed immediately that they were in fact just sixth-formers playing the characters, or whether this revelation should be left until later. Some practitioners would argue strongly that allowing students with learning difficulties to believe a character or situation is real in a drama when it patently isn't, is exploitative. On the whole I would agree with this but in this situation our agreed feeling was that a key aspect of the learning would be lost if this revelation came at this point. Having been introduced, the characters sat with the groups who were asked to say what impressions they had formed from the photographs. This was a delicate task. Some of the things that had been said previously had not been entirely complementary. How would the group report to the character 'in the flesh' what they had assumed from a picture? The role of the other mainstream students here was to help the special students mediate what they said and sometimes play the devil's advocate by saying something indiscreet themselves. The point of the exercise was both to highlight the discrepancies between first and subsequent impressions, and to explore appropriate social language. For the most part, it had been agreed beforehand that the characters would admit to being very like the way the special students had constructed them. This gave the special students a feeling of success; a cheat maybe, but we felt it was a worthwhile one.

Working as a whole group, the class were invited to suggest other situations in which the characters might have been photographed, for example standing in the school dinner queue, or posing for their last official school photograph. The characters complied and made appropriate tableaux while the rest of the class commented on how the previously perceived relationships appeared to hold true in this new evidence.

The class were reminded that one of the characters, Helen, was planning to have a party in her parents' absence. Dividing into five groups again, the task was to explore attitudes towards the party. This involved some careful questioning and in-role work on the part of the mainstream students in order to help the special students utilise their own knowledge in the developing drama. For example:

MS1	*Des, have you ever been to a party?*
SS1	*Yes.*
MS1	*What did you like about it?*
SS1	*Food and drink.*
MS1	*Ah ha! So, what sort of food do you think Helen should get in for her party?*
SS1	*Apple pie.*
Helen	*But I don't know how to make apple pie!*
SS2	*You could buy one.*

Week Four

A teacher narrated how, in the run-up to Helen's party, a number of scenes had occurred because of the relationships between the characters. The class were asked to suggest scenes according to a very simple formula:

- Which characters are in the scene?
- Where does it take place?
- What will make the scene interesting?

The scenes were played out with the mainstream students playing the characters. This presented the possibility of handling sensitive issues suggested by the special students, without them feeling handicapped by their own limited communication skills. Again, they were given the sense of being authors and directors by use of forum theatre techniques which involved stopping the scene and checking with the special students that it was being played out appropriately. It quickly became possible to integrate some of the special students into the scenes as performers. For example:

Diane and Paul meet in a Chinese restaurant. They have been going out with each other for some time but now Diane doesn't want to go to the party with Paul. The scene develops into a personal argument. After stopping the scene and asking what should happen next, one of the special needs students intervenes as a waiter and demonstrates considerable strength of character as he tells Diane and Paul to take their argument elsewhere.

'Excuse me, you're disturbing the other customers!'

Jenny and David are sitting at separate tables in a college coffee bar. David would really like to go to the party with Jenny but doesn't know how to suggest it. The scene is established but apart from David smiling sweetly in Jenny's direction nothing happens. The teacher stops the scene and after discussion Jo, a special needs student, enters as David's friend. David pours his heart out and Jo sets about facilitating a meeting by going to Jenny and asking her to join them.

'Go and talk to her.'

Several of these scenes were tried out with the special students playing an increasingly important part in their resolution.

Week Five

It is the evening of the party. Working in five groups again, the participants get ready. The role of the mainstream students here was to suggest and support dramatic play by engaging in the fiction more actively themselves. For example, instead of simply asking 'What shoes should I wear?' more action was generated by saying (and miming):

"Look, I've got this red dress (actually a piece of material that was lying around) – here, hold it for me a minute will you – or what about this green one (mimed)? You try them on and see which one fits you best."

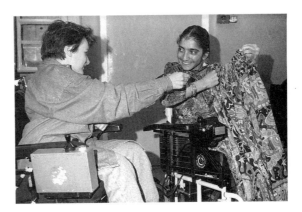

'How about this one?'

Similarly, note the difference between:
'I'll put some crisps and peanuts out' and

"Here, Desmond, could you put some bowls of crisps around for me please. Jonathan, see if you can find a big bag of peanuts in that cupboard to empty into these dishes. Thanks."

A party tape was put on and the rest of the session was spent spontaneously improvising the party, the five key characters ensuring that they talked to as many of the special needs students as possible about how their relationships appeared to be developing in the light of the action.

Week Six

This session was introduced by the teacher narrating how the party had ended and suggesting that someone had taken a number of photographs during the evening. The class were asked to suggest what was on some of these pictures. Each suggestion was then staged and at this time volunteers were asked for, to play the parts of the characters (elements of their costumes being used as signifiers). The suggestions were both mature and witty, demonstrating the appropriateness of the drama to the age-group. For example:

- two of the characters climbing the stairs together with a third glaring up after them
- David dotingly offering Jenny a cigarette with her engrossed in a football match on the TV
- two characters accidentally discovered together under a pile of coats
- one character being carried out drunk by two others.

What's he saying? What's she thinking?

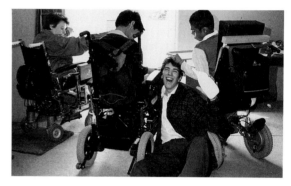

'Show me the way to go home!'

These ideas caused a good deal of hilarity but the scenes genuinely reflected personal experience and fears. Some were explored further by inviting participants to suggest thinks bubbles and speech balloons.

The session was rounded off by placing the five characters in front of the whole group and initiating a discussion with them as to how they might deal with some of the relationships that had been explored. At the very end of the session the five students dropped their characters by discarding their signifying costumes and chatting with the rest of the class naturally. It is worth noting that this attempt to distinguish between the real and the fiction was largely ignored and ineffective; the special needs students had realised our duplicity from the word 'go' and were unperturbed by it!

Evaluation

Both groups of students were helped to evaluate the drama in their own schools in the following week. For the mainstream students this took the form of a discussion around what they had learned through the integration. The teachers in the special school, however, were keener to pursue what had been learned from the content of the drama and carried on working on the theme of teenage relationships in a number of ways.

Both groups enthusiastically agreed that while being a lot of fun the drama was also, in its own way, very realistic and reflected the kind of embarrassment they had all experienced in their life outside school. Exploring it in this way had helped put it in perspective and made them realise that such feelings were common and temporary. Teachers from the extended education unit reported that the students there had 'enjoyed' seeing able-bodied characters in embarrassing situations not in any malicious sense but because, as one student said, 'it shows they are the same as us'. Conversely, the sixth-formers' teachers reported that their students had been somewhat humbled by the others. Again, this was in a positive sense in that it took the form of a realisation of the special needs students' capacity to suggest good ideas and develop them into witty and truthful dramatic images.

IN CONCLUSION

Only one example of an integrated project in action has been given here, not because it is the perfect model nor because it is the only one. Few such projects are documented and the teachers involved in 'The Party' had little to draw on, barring their own limited experience and intuition. As a result our learning curve was a very steep one and the advice given earlier regarding size of group, duration of sessions and the appropriate preparation of the groups is extrapolated from our own – and the students' – evaluation of the experience. It is hoped that by sharing the principles which we have since formulated, more students will be able to mine this rich vein of drama experience.

With regard to the teaching of children with learning difficulties in mainstream schools, I believe that the following implications need to be addressed:

- Students should be given the opportunity to appreciate and assist in the development of the creative ideas of peers who may be less able academically. Conversely, children with learning difficulties should be given the opportunity to recognise the limitations of their peers' abilities.
- This should involve facilitating discussions regarding preconceptions of what 'ability' implies and giving all students opportunities to formulate group aims for drama.
- If the content of the drama is related to age and personal experiences rather than received knowledge or perceived abilities, there will be an equality of all the participants' capacity to contribute; the teacher's job is to ensure that all the participants' contributions are, consequently, respected.
- At heart the drama should be a fiction. Through this the participants will be able to laugh at or sympathise with reflections of themselves without feeling that they are laughable or pathetic.
- Positioning children with learning difficulties in key roles in the drama while positioning others into deputy, advisory or assistant roles can develop the fiction of the drama in a productively unexpected direction while effectively teaching the participants a good deal about each other.

- Time, space and staffing, perennial problems for many drama teachers, must be given in good measure if policies of equal opportunities and support for those with learning difficulties are genuinely to mean anything.
- Encouraging pupils to evaluate openly and honestly what they have discovered about themselves and each other in the drama is a vital step towards mutual acceptance and respect.
- Finally, the drama teacher who discovers how able the 'less able' are, might usefully set about challenging the terminology used in mainstream schools pertaining to special educational needs.

REFERENCES

Croll, P. and Moses, D. (1985) *One in Five: the assessment and incidence of special educational needs,* Routledge & Kegan Paul

DES (1963) *Half Our Future* (The Newsom Report), HMSO
(1978) *Special Educational Needs: Report of the Committee of Enquiry into the Education of Handicapped Children and Young People* (The Warnock Report), HMSO

Gillham, G. (1974) *'Condercum School report'* in Bolton, G. (1984) *Drama as Education,* Longman

CHAPTER NINE

DRAMA AND DEAF CHILDREN

Daphne Payne

THE NDCS FESTIVAL OF PERFORMING ARTS

One bitterly cold morning in March 1986 I stood on the stage of a school hall in Swansea and surveyed the scene in front of me with considerable apprehension. Over one hundred children aged between 3 and 11 years were there to take part in a Festival of Performing Arts organised by the National Deaf Children's Society (NDCS). They came from a variety of schools in the South Wales area, some from special schools for deaf children, others from partially-hearing units integrated into mainstream schools. Although some of the children were hearing, a large proportion were deaf.

The Festival is an annual event, begun in 1970 by Pat Keysell with the aim of encouraging mime and drama as a means of expression for deaf children. Pat, the founder of the British Theatre of the Deaf, has many years' experience of working with deaf children. She had herself adjudicated the Festival for a number of years. She was succeeded in this capacity by a series of professional artists and workshop leaders, mostly specialists in mime. When the NDCS approached me to take over the role of national adjudicator, I had some reservations, not least among them that I am not a mime artist, and did not feel competent to judge an art form that I could not demonstrate adequately myself – much less lead a workshop in! I am, however, a qualified teacher of *drama,* with considerable experience of teaching both hearing and deaf children of all ages. There was one other factor which worked in my favour – I am myself profoundly deaf, and know from personal experience the endless creative possibilities that can ensue when an emphasis is placed on the visual and physical aspects of drama.

That year, the NDCS agreed to broaden the scope of the Festival by changing its title from the former 'Festival of Mime' to a 'Festival of Performing Arts', thus allowing a wide variety of performance forms. A hearing teacher of dance was invited to act as co-adjudicator with me. Together we spent several weeks visiting a number of venues throughout the UK, giving workshops and adjudicating the short performances prepared by the children with their teachers. At each venue, we had to select two performances (one primary and one secondary) which the children would then be invited to perform again as a culmination to the Festival.

The numbers of children taking part varied from place to place but we had not anticipated the sheer numbers that faced us that day in a school hall in South Wales. It was a daunting task, but we enlisted the help of the teachers and enjoyed an exhausting though thoroughly inspiring day.

In all the years I have been teaching drama I have never failed to be struck by the spontaneous *expressiveness* of children who suffer from the incalculable linguistic disadvantage that is the product of prelingual deafness. Children who spent much of their school day laboriously copying sentences that mean little, straining to lip-read words they cannot hear, struggling to understand a language that is, for the most part, incomprehensible to them, suddenly find a freedom of expression and communication through drama that rises above the constraints of language. Drama employs alternative means of communication – facial expression, gesture, body language, mime and movement – that are the *strengths* of deaf children and compensate for their weaknesses. For some, drama is the *only* way in which they can truly express themselves.

DEAF TEACHERS

One of the most interesting discoveries of the NDCS tour was the children's fascination with my own deafness. A surprising number had never come across a deaf adult before, let alone a teacher. A few, disturbingly, had not believed they existed. Teaching in hearing mainstream schools, my deafness had always been an 'obstacle' which had to be overcome by one means or another. It was some time before I managed to obtain the additional qualification as a teacher of deaf children. Paradoxically, it was (and still is) very difficult for a deaf person to train as a teacher, of *any* kind, in this country. I do not, of course, refer here to those teachers who become hearing-impaired *after* training, although they too face problems in the profession.

Mabel Davis, currently headteacher of Heathlands School for Deaf Children in St Albans, and herself deaf, has identified a number of problem areas which discriminate against deaf people entering the teaching profession: The following points are taken from a paper presented by Ms Davis at a combined RADAR/NUT Conference on Disabled Teachers in November 1992.

- Low expectations of deaf children, which all too often result in low educational achievements. Even where educational standards are high, few deaf pupils are encouraged to consider teaching as a career.
- The difficulty of gaining access to training, even when academic requirements for entry are fulfilled, perhaps due to a fear of the unknown on the part of the training institutions, and the lack of awareness and understanding generally that permeates so many areas of disability.

- The stumbling block of the *medical* examination to which all candidates must submit themselves and which, until a few years ago, required a candidate to 'hear' a conversation at 20 feet. (The wording of this regulation has since been changed, and any deaf person skilled in lip-reading can 'follow' a conversation at 20 feet. Much, however, still depends upon the decision of the examining doctor.)
- The practical difficulties of teacher training itself, where so much vital information is missed. It is impossible for a deaf student to watch a lecturer and take notes at the same time: one is forced to rely upon borrowed notes from other students which often make little sense. Sign language interpreters in higher education are still all too rare, and their provision (and funding) is often dependent on the charitable organisations.
- The requirement to undertake teaching practice in hearing schools is the equivalent of putting a hearing person in a class of deaf children who learn through sign language.
- For those of us who have managed to overcome these obstacles, the prejudices against deaf teachers in the more specialised field of teaching deaf children remain. For many years, the specialist training courses upheld a strict *oralist* education philosophy: that is, sign language, both as a means of communication and as an educational tool, was actively discouraged. Deaf teachers, therefore, many of whom themselves used sign language as a preferred method of communication, were perceived as a threat. This position is now slowly changing, and a more enlightened bilingual approach to the education of deaf children is becoming more acceptable.
- One of the major areas of training as a teacher of deaf children is in the assessment and teaching of *speech*. This can be a major stumbling-block for a deaf teacher, who is unable to hear mistakes being made or correct pronunciation and articulation. Indeed, some deaf teachers may themselves have problems in this area. It *is* possible to get round these problems, but the training courses need to be persuaded of this fact before they are willing to accept a deaf person for training.

Given, then, that the majority of teachers of deaf children are themselves hearing, few of these are also subject specialists; far fewer are specialists in drama. Yet the NDCS tour had shown the enthusiasm for drama, and the awareness on the part of teaching staff of its importance in the education of the children in their care. A number of teachers commented that they would like to be able to use drama more in the classroom (as opposed to the 'one-off' Festival entry), but they didn't know how to go about it.

It seemed to me to be vitally important to train deaf people to work professionally in a drama *leadership* capacity, working alongside classroom teachers, to provide the specialist tuition needed, and at the same time to provide role models for the deaf children themselves.

In 1986, a full-time training course was established within the Division of Film and Drama at Bulmershe College of Higher Education (now the University of Reading). Initially a one-year Certificate course, it aimed to train deaf, and some hearing, people with an aptitude for, or special interest in drama, and to use these skills to work with deaf children in educational and community contexts.

Few of our early candidates for this course possessed the academic qualifications that would normally be a prerequisite for entry to a college of higher education. The fact that proportionately few deaf young people are entered for formal academic qualifications, however, is no reflection of their intelligence, talent, or ability to teach. Nor did we propose to lower the academic standards of the course itself to take account of the linguistic difficulties of its students. The course was based on the philosophy that drama has its own 'language', or series of languages, which overrides the spoken and written word. If alternative means of tuition – and, more importantly, of assessment – could be found, there was no reason why the same academic concepts could not be taught as to any BA or B Ed student. In this sense, the course was, and still remains, highly experimental in its conception, with an emphasis placed upon *practical application* of academic theory.

One interesting aspect of this course has been the extent to which, almost incidentally, students' linguistic and conceptual skills improve throughout the course. Deaf people for whom reading even a newspaper had previously been considered a chore, would take the initiative to research topics of interest in the college library, and produce written documentations and analyses of their work – something they had not, hitherto, believed themselves capable of attempting. If these methods of teaching through drama worked at this level, then it can also work lower down the educational stratum, with deaf children in schools.

In 1990 the course was extended to two years, and currently leads to a Diploma in Higher Education. Since it began, a total of 45 students have successfully passed the course, 30 of them deaf. Approximately 75 per cent of the students have found work professionally since leaving college, many in children's theatre, or theatre-in-education companies, bringing drama and theatre to deaf children all over the country. When, a few years after it began, the pressures of this course regrettably forced me to give up the adjudication of the NDCS Festival of Performing Arts, the role was taken over by two ex-students who had formed their own highly successful theatre company. We had come full circle!

LINGUISTIC SKILLS VERSUS CONCEPTUAL UNDERSTANDING

Much has been made in the foregoing of the linguistic disadvantages of the prelingually deaf. Deafness is, first and foremost, a *linguistic* handicap. Yet linguistic skills must be distinguished from *conceptual* understanding. Deaf children tend to learn language 'by rote', by copying words and phrases either orally or from printed or written material. The subtleties of language, changes of meaning through inflection, intonation, or contextual use, are often beyond them. 'What does it mean?' is a constant question put to anyone who has regular contact with deaf children. This is easy enough to explain with a concrete phenomenon such as *statue* – 'I am going to ask you to make a statue …'. A picture or a quick drawing will suffice. Far more difficult to explain, however, are the conceptual ideas contained in, for example, words like 'jealous' or 'brave'.

"Superman", one 9-year-old informed me, "is brave. He fights bad men and lifts lorries and holds up a house that is falling down."

Is this really what the word means? The concept of facing fear and overcoming it is almost impossible to explain without giving lengthy (and wordy) examples, yet it is possible to set up a variety of different contexts through *drama* in which the child can experience this for herself, and thus come to a better understanding of its meaning.

Co-Sign Theatre Company's 1991 production of 'Fearless Knights', aimed at deaf and hearing primary children, was based on just this concept. The session began with a short, visually presented (and very funny!) play about three children 'sleeping over' at a friend's house, who became involved in an adventure which concerned a dragon. The dragon itself never appeared. They became more and more terrified of the dragon until, at last, one character (portrayed by a deaf actress) decided to stand up to it and battle with it – at which point it gradually shrank in size and disappeared altogether. In this case the children watching were not themselves involved in the action, but they got the point that this was not a real dragon – the 'dragon' symbolised the nameless fears of the dark, experienced by so many children. The play encouraged them to discuss the things that frightened them, and ways in which they, too, could 'stand up to them' to make them shrink away. Had time permitted, the children might have developed this theme into drama improvisations of their own. Certainly they learned that being 'brave' has nothing to do with being physically strong, and that fear itself is often the enemy.

'Emotion-words' are often among the most limited in the vocabulary of a deaf child: 'happy', 'sad', 'angry', 'frightened' are in many cases the full extent. This does not mean that they do not *experience* the full range of emotions, however. They simply do not have the language to verbalise them. This can lead to enormous frustration (another word that is difficult to explain). Drama can go a long way towards helping them, not only to extend their vocabulary in this respect, but to understand the concept behind the word. Some practical examples of this are given below.

Time

One drama exercise that I have used to help clarify the idea of *time* consists of identifying three distinct spaces in the room, labelled 'Yesterday', 'Today' and 'Tomorrow' respectively. The children go to each in turn and perform an action which took place yesterday, something that they have done today, and something that they hope to do tomorrow. This can then be changed to 'Last week', 'Next summer', and so on. For more complex historical time sequences, a 'time line' drawn on the floor of the hall can be divided up into roughly proportionate areas, each symbolising a block of time – 10 years (the year that they were born?), 100 years, 300 years, and so on. By physically walking along this time line, the children will gain some idea of the 'space' (literally) between each historical period.

Power

One of the first exercises my own students are asked to present concerns the concept of *power*. They are asked, in small groups, to present three still images. At first, these tend to be straightforward and humanised, e.g. a power relationship within a family, or within a work situation. With deeper questioning, however, some highly sophisticated and more abstract presentations have emerged – the power of alcohol, the power of the press.

As the above examples show, a deaf child who does not possess the linguistic skills to verbalise ideas or abstract thought, may still be able to receive and express those ideas through the alternative languages of drama.

It is this ability to teach *conceptual understanding* and *symbolic thought* that is one of the main justifications for teaching drama to deaf children. There are others:

- Drama encourages *self-expression* and stimulates *imagination*. Deaf children have more experience and knowledge than they can ever express in words. When a deaf child tries to explain something for which he does not have the vocabulary, it may be 'acted out'.

- Drama encourages children to *think for themselves,* to solve problems and to make decisions. Deaf children spend much of their lives 'copying' – they copy speech patterns, gestures and mannerisms, even sometimes facial expressions, without necessarily understanding them. The desire for social acceptance is so strong, and the deaf child's reliance upon observation so acute, that this habit is learned early in life. This habit may, at first, intrude into the drama session, especially in an integrated situation where the deaf child watches for, and copies, the actions of others. If the emphasis is placed upon *visual* rather than verbal clues, however, the child will gradually become more confident in the viability of her own contribution.

- A drama improvisation teaches a sense of *sequence* and *structure,* of 'cause' and 'effect': this happens, therefore it follows that … This is another aspect that many deaf children find extremely difficult. One has only to look at a story written by a deaf child. Often this will begin with the most striking *image* – usually the climax of the story. The narrative will then jump from one image to another, often with little or no coherent sequence of events. The importance of *narrative structure* in creative drama cannot, therefore, be overestimated.

- Drama encourages *empathy*. The often commented-upon 'egocentricity' of deaf children is a result of years of isolation. Someone once described deafness as like being shut permanently in a telephone box, watching the rest of the world go by. It is this sense of loneliness, of always being an observer, never a participant, that makes deafness such an overpowering disability. One cannot be an 'observer' in creative drama. Through drama one can experience an infinite range of characters, emotions and situations quite outside of oneself.

- Drama encourages *social skills, self-confidence* and *self-esteem*. Deaf children need to learn to accept and work with the ideas of others and be able to communicate their own ideas. The need for activities that will develop such skills isn't particular to deaf children, but nor should it be denied them. If drama can indeed provide such an education, then it should be a fundamental part of the curriculum.

PRACTICAL ISSUES FOR CONSIDERATION

VERTICAL GROUPING IN SPECIAL SCHOOLS

The students of the Theatre of the Deaf course work with two distinct age-groups of children while they are training:

- upper primary (8–10 years)
- middle secondary (14–15 years), in the context of a Theatre-in-Education programme.

However, where deaf children are concerned, this age-grouping must be flexible. Much depends on the schools visited. While it is possible to take a drama session with, say, a small group of three or four children, it is more likely, in a special school for deaf children with small class sizes, that two or three classes of different age-groupings will be put together to make a more feasible-sized group for drama. In this case, the age-range of the children is considerably greater than would be found in a mainstream school, and a teacher of deaf children must be prepared to work with a much wider age-range than would be usual in a normal hearing school. At Elmfield School for Deaf Children in Bristol, for example – a school enlightened enough to employ a full-time drama specialist – the entire secondary group involved in GCSE drama practical were a total of 12 children with ages ranging from 11 to 16, although of course only the most senior actually took the examination.

Chronological age in itself, however, is not necessarily an indication of linguistic or conceptual ability. Within any one age group, the *degree* and *type* of deafness of individual children may vary considerably, together with the extent to which they gain assistance from the use of hearing-aids.

A child with a moderate hearing loss (of 60–90 decibels) will experience some problems in language development, but not as much as a child with a profound loss of 90 decibels or above.

The *age of onset* of the individual child's deafness is another important variable. Children who are congenitally deaf, or become deaf before the acquisition of language comprehension (generally identified as 3–4 years) will be more linguistically disadvantaged than those children who lose their hearing *after* language has been acquired. This is true *regardless of the degree* of hearing loss. While there is, of course, a relationship between the degree of hearing loss and the severity of language deficit, even a slight or moderate decibel loss at birth or in early infancy will have a retarding effect on language development.

It is worth while, therefore, for any teacher who proposes to work with deaf children, to find out as much as possible beforehand about the audiological history of the individual children in their care. One must bear in mind, however, that this history gives only limited information: it is no indication of the child's ability to *discriminate* sound, which can vary considerably from child to child, and it is certainly no indication of the child's academic ability or intelligence. An audiogram has been described as being rather like a map: it tells you where the coastline is – it says nothing about the quality of the water!

It is possible, therefore, to have within one drama group a child of 11 years with a much greater degree of linguistic and conceptual ability than a child of, say, 14 years. While this vertical grouping of age-ranges is not necessarily a barrier in itself, it can cause problems when considering the *content* and *theme* of a drama lesson. A topic that might be of interest to, and could provide the basis for a drama session with the 11-year-old might be considered 'babyish' by the 14-year-old, even though the former child may have the greater degree of conceptual understanding.

GIVING INSTRUCTIONS AND RECEIVING RESPONSES

The practical aspects of *communication* are often the biggest hurdle for the teacher who is inexperienced in working with deaf children: 'Are they going to understand what I say, and am I going to understand them?' However carefully games, exercises and improvisations are geared towards the use of *non*-verbal methods of communication, a teacher will still have to give instructions and receive responses from the pupils.

1 *Getting attention* A teacher of drama is constantly on the move. So are the children! Calling out 'Stop' or 'Freeze' is useless: they can't hear you! Flashing the lights (the most common way to get a deaf person's attention) is not always applicable in this situation: if the lights are of the fluorescent variety, they do not switch on quickly enough, and in any case, the teacher does not necessarily want to be constrained to the location of the light switches – often in some inaccessible corner.

   If you are fortunate enough to be working in a space with a sprung wooden floor, then a sharp stamp on the floor will often suffice, as the vibration is carried through the floorboards and will be picked up by deaf children. Alternatively, a visual 'control signal' can be established between teacher and pupils at the start – an arm raised quickly in the air, a brightly coloured cloth waved.

   A word of warning needs to be stated here with reference to the use of a drum or similar instrument with hearing-aid users. A hearing-aid, however sophisticated, is merely an instrument of amplification. A sudden loud bang of this kind can cause discomfort, and, in some cases, actual pain (see 'Hearing-aids' below).

2 Once the children have stopped, and you have their attention, you need to quickly assess your own position in relation to the class as a whole. Are *all* the children within your sightline, or do you have your back to three of them? Deaf children are very quick to realise this problem, and they will move if they cannot see you, but if you do not want them to move from the space in which they have stopped, then it is up to you to position yourself in such a way that they can all see you clearly.

3 This position needs to be considered carefully beforehand. Are you standing with your back to a window, so that the light is reflected behind you and your face is in darkness? With deaf children it is best to work with overhead lights on, even on a sunny day, as this will ensure an even spread of light. Working with older children, you will need to watch that bigger members of the group are not masking you from the smaller children. You may need to raise your own position – stand on a rostrum or a chair – to ensure that they can all see you.

4 'Freeze!' – but some of the children may then be facing away from you. How do they know when to break the freeze? Similar problems occur when asking deaf children to 'lie on the floor and relax'. Both can result in some incredible contortions as they try to twist heads round to watch the teacher for the next instruction – hardly relaxing! They need to know clearly beforehand exactly what you want them to do. If, for example, it is a 'freeze/go' exercise, then it is best to say something like: 'When I raise the flag, I want you to freeze exactly where you are. Count five, then start moving again.' Relaxing will take practice, until the children have the confidence to know that they will be 'woken up', either by you or by other children whom you have roused first.

By all means ask the children to close their eyes, but they will do this immediately unless you finish your instruction first. It is better to say, 'In a minute I will ask you to close your eyes, then …'. They will also need to know when to open them again. A word of warning – never blindfold a deaf child: many experience a feeling of panic. Some forms of deafness can affect the balance mechanisms, and these children will find it very difficult to keep their balance with eyes closed. Others will experience no problems at all, but you will need to be sensitive to this.

5 *Touching* as a means of gaining attention. All deaf people rely on this to a greater or lesser extent, but it does require some sensitivity. No-one likes being poked, and it is all too easy to make someone jump when they cannot hear you approach. Again, some ground rules need to be established before you begin teaching. A *gentle* touch on the shoulder or the hand will generally be sufficient, but you will need to teach the children themselves to do this well, especially in an integrated situation where hearing children will not be used to this device.

There is one drama *trust* exercise which I find most useful here, and, in the integrated situation, serves the purpose of putting all of the children on an equal footing and increases sensory awareness. Working in pairs, **A** closes eyes, while **B** gently leads his/her partner around the room, so they are communicating with each other solely through touch. This needs to be done *very* gently, and the children being led should be encouraged to say if at any time they do not feel safe. (This exercise will give you a chance to observe if there are any children who clearly are having balance problems while moving with eyes closed. It will be quite safe because there is another child with them.) After a while, **A** and **B** switch roles. Encourage the children to discuss how they felt – what were the best methods of leading? When this exercise can be done with confidence, each pair should work out a 'touch code': e.g. tap on the head means 'stand still'; tap on the right shoulder, 'turn right'; tap on left shoulder, 'turn left'; and so on. This way the children will become used to touching and being touched, and will not feel threatened when this is used in other contexts.

6 *Giving instructions* I am assuming here that the teacher is non-signing or is relying upon total communication – that is, speech plus signs that support speech. It must be remembered that, in the English language, only 23 per cent of phonemes are visible on the lips: B, P, M look exactly the same; so do S, T, D, R, L. Some consonants – G, K – cannot be seen at all. Lip-reading is a constant guessing game, a mental crossword puzzle, while the lip-reader attempts to fill in the gaps. Often, it is only when the end of a sentence has been reached that sense can be made of it, and then time is needed to assimilate that information. Unlike the mechanisms of the ears which conduct sound, those of the eyes are made of muscle. Lip-reading can be very tiring indeed, and it is small wonder that a deaf person will quickly lose concentration if this exercise goes on for a length of time. There are a few simple guidelines which might help here:

- Always speak in short, complete sentences, and avoid going off at a tangent. Remember that a deaf person usually makes sense of what you are saying *contextually,* when you come to the end of your sentence. If it is too long-winded, they will have forgotten the first bit by the time you get to the end!

- Be prepared to *repeat* an instruction, as often as necessary. There are two possible causes of misunderstanding: (a) they did not lip-read you correctly or (b) they read what you said, but did not understand the *language* that you are using. If they do not understand the first time, therefore, then repeat more clearly. Do not over-articulate, or emphasise each syllable – this merely serves to make the work harder. Above all, do not shout. Speak normally, with normal inflection and intonation, but perhaps a little slower. If a child still does not understand, then re-phrase your wording to make it clearer.

- Give an *example* – demonstrate if necessary – but avoid a situation where they will merely copy your own demonstration.

- Do remember the importance of *facial expression* and *eye contact* when communicating with deaf people. They provide invaluable extra 'clues' in addition to the very small movements of the lips. Male teachers should take care to keep any beards and moustaches in trim: such clues can be hidden behind facial hair. Eye contact can be obscured by spectacles which tend to reflect the light (many deaf people find it impossible to lip-read someone wearing sunglasses). It is for this reason that teachers of deaf children are sometimes advised to wear contact lenses.

- Do make as much use as possible of teaching aids such as an overhead projector, flip-chart, etc. If a new word or term is introduced then *write it down*. Use diagrams or simple line drawings to explain your point. Deaf children will absorb such visual information much more readily than verbal instructions. Remember, though, that they cannot focus on two places at once, and time must be allowed for them to read what you have written/drawn before you begin to speak again.

- Try to give instructions, or to tell a story, in the *chronological order* in which events happen. One of the greatest differences between the English language and BSL (British Sign Language – the natural language of the prelingually deaf) is in its *syntax*. For example, one would say – in perfectly good English – 'I was frightened when a black cat crossed my path'. But a deaf child, thinking in visual images, would express the same sentence 'I was walking along a path, a black cat crossed in front of me, *then* I was frightened'.

This is one of the things to watch out for when choosing children's storybooks to use as a resource. So often the language is couched in a way that is very confusing for deaf children. For example: 'The Witch was furious when she arrived home and found that the children had gone. She had left them tied firmly to the chair while she went in search of the magic herb which they had told her would make her beautiful ...'. What happens *first*? Although this example has been made up, it is not uncommon. You need to take care, therefore, with instructions like:

'We are going to try to steal the Giant's treasure while he is asleep. We will have to find a way of getting into his castle, which is surrounded by a large moat ...'.

What do they have to do *first*? Set the scene carefully – in the centre of the room is a large castle; all the way around it is a moat; inside the castle the Giant is asleep; and the treasure is by his chair. We are going to try to steal it – but *first* we have to cross the moat. How are we going to do it?

The National Deaf Children's Society produces a list of children's publications suitable for or specifically written for deaf children. Not all of these, however, are useful as a resource for drama. The teacher is advised to consider well-illustrated storybooks which provide a quantity of *visual* clues.

The importance of giving clear and uncomplicated instructions to deaf children cannot be overestimated, and is one of the major areas of assessment with my own students of the Theatre of the Deaf course. Even some of the deaf students, with a greater command of the English language, find this difficult at first. They are advised to *write down* their instructions beforehand, and then to look carefully at what they have written and re-phrase where necessary; Also to identify any words or phrases used that might cause confusion or require further elucidation. For example, 'Make an *image* ...'. Will the children know what this means? The word can be introduced in the context of the session, and used thereafter, but it might be better to begin with 'Make a photograph, or a picture'.

This is not to say that everything must be 'simplified' for deaf children – that is both patronising and denies the children the opportunity to learn vocabulary as they go along – but it is a good exercise in adjusting one's own language level to that of the children. The results in practice can, at first, make for a rather stilted delivery, as inexperienced teachers tend to learn their instructions 'off by heart'. It will, however, stop you from rambling, and, with further practice, you will be able to make this adjustment with ease.

7 *Receiving responses* Communication is a two-way process. Much of the foregoing has been devoted to the children's understanding of the teacher, but one of the commonest causes of apprehension on the part of the inexperienced teacher of deaf children is the fear that she will not understand them. Newly-qualified teachers of the deaf sometimes comment on the extent to which a child's speech has improved over the space of a few months. What has actually improved is the teacher's ability to understand it. Anyone who has regular contact with deaf children (or adults) will find that, in a comparatively short time, they will 'tune in' to deaf voices.

It is very important that the teacher does not avoid this hurdle, but actively engages the deaf child in a two-way communication process as often as possible. A deaf person will be embarrassed by a breakdown in communication only if he is aware that *you* are embarrassed.

Rather more difficult is the situation where the child's first language is BSL, and the teacher/leader does not sign. One of my own colleagues once commented that she found it 'unnerving', having set a practical exercise to the Theatre of the Deaf students working in small groups, to witness the degree of discussion, argument and decision-making going on within these groups – in total silence! The clear solution to this problem is, of course, to learn to sign. This is not, however, something that can be mastered overnight; it takes a number of years and considerable practice to become fluent in sign language, but the children will appreciate the effort to learn their own language, and often make the best teachers themselves in this respect.

HEARING-AIDS

Every child who has been diagnosed as hearing-impaired is provided with a hearing-aid which is designed to make as much use as possible of this residual hearing. No hearing-aid, however, can 'restore' hearing in the same way that a pair of spectacles can restore sight. They are (as stated above) merely instruments of amplification, and they will amplify only those sound frequencies that the child may already retain. If sensitivity to sound frequency levels is lost (through damaged nerves or cochlea) then no amount of amplification will restore it. The result of such amplification is *distortion* of sound.

A hearing child will be aware of background noise – shouts from a playing field, passing traffic, etc. – but will 'rule them out' to concentrate on the teacher's voice or a discussion. A deaf child cannot do this, and the much amplified background noise can sometimes drown out what little he *is* able to hear. On the Theatre of the Deaf course at Reading University, which is situated close to Heathrow airport, everything stops at 11.00 am while Concorde passes overhead, and all hearing-aid users present (myself included) 'switch off' until it has passed. The teacher needs to be constantly aware of this problem, and avoid as far as possible any sudden loud noise which might cause such discomfort – or at least give warning to enable hearing-aids to be adjusted accordingly.

In some schools, sophisticated *radio-aids* are in use which are designed to eliminate just such background noise, and allow amplification only between the receiver and the person (generally the teacher) who is wearing the microphone. These microphones do not have wires attached, so the wearer is free to move about the room at will. The distance between wearer and receiver will make no difference to the level of amplification. These aids have proved a considerable advance in the field of education, but, personally, I find them virtually useless in the context of a drama lesson. While they do a great deal to facilitate one-to-one communication between wearer and receiver, they do not take account of the wider sphere of communication in group discussion, which is such an integral part of any drama session.

Some schools are fitted with *loop systems* in classrooms. These work in a similar way but operate in a wider area. They are generally of assistance, however, only to those children who have sufficient residual hearing to benefit from them.

At primary level, when it is considered that deaf children will gain the most benefit from the use of their residual hearing, a wide variety of aids is in use. Some of these are extremely cumbersome, involving bulky contraptions strapped to the children's bodies. These can be a hindrance to physical activity, which is frequently employed in drama. They are easily damaged and can, on occasions, be downright dangerous. It is a sensitive issue, however, to ask the children to remove them, as it is sometimes the policy of the school that they be worn at all times. The teacher will simply have to be aware of the limitations imposed by these things, and plan accordingly.

WORKING WITH AN INTERPRETER

Many of the principles stated above are true for both the integrated and the special school situations. It is perfectly possible for a non-signing teacher of drama to work in a special school for deaf children who learn through sign language, if she can be provided with a qualified sign language interpreter. The Theatre of the Deaf students frequently receive visits from professional theatre practitioners who may never have worked with deaf people before. Other course tutors, specialists in their own field, are not necessarily themselves fluent in sign language (although most have, over the years, acquired a modicum of signing skills). In both cases, a sign language interpreter is provided in order to facilitate communication. There are, however, certain ethical codes of practice which need to be observed when working alongside an interpreter in this way:

- The interpreter's role is just that – to interpret *everything* that the teacher says, for the benefit of the deaf people present, and where necessary to 'voice' in the reverse direction. The interpreter is *not* an 'assistant teacher', and should not be required to elucidate or otherwise explain the content of a lesson. If a child has a question, then the interpreter will direct that question to the class teacher.
- You should not engage an interpreter in private conversation, or discuss an individual child with the interpreter, either within or outside a session.
- Remember that the interpreter may not herself be a drama specialist. If you are using technical terminology or language which acquires a specific meaning in the context of a drama session, then it is wise to discuss this with the interpreter beforehand, so that she may consider the appropriate signs to use.
- The above guidelines on use of language and general communication still apply, but you will need to bear in mind that any interpreter, however good, will always be two or three words behind you. You do not need to stop to allow an interpreter to 'catch up' (if you are going too fast, the interpreter will stop you), but it is wise to pause occasionally to allow assimilation of information before continuing.

Working with a sign language interpreter can free you from many of the constraints imposed by communication difficulties, but it is still no substitute for direct communication with the children. Always maintain direct eye contact with the children, even when their own focus is on the interpreter (this can be unnerving at first), and encourage them to speak directly to you even if you are unsure of what they say – listen to the interpreter's voice-over, do not look in that direction yourself.

WORKING IN AN INTEGRATED SITUATION

Since the Education Act of 1981, it has become increasingly likely that teachers of drama in mainstream schools will find themselves faced with one or more deaf children integrated into an otherwise hearing class. Teachers working in mainstream schools where there is a hearing-impaired unit may find themselves in a situation where some of these children are accompanied by a support teacher from that unit, usually a qualified teacher of the deaf. The role of the support teacher is different from that of the interpreter outlined above, and this situation can present problems unless the roles of the respective teachers are clearly defined. Mainstream teachers who feel less than confident about working with deaf children may view the presence of a second teacher in their classroom as a threat, and considerable sensitivity – on both sides – is needed if good working relations are to be achieved in this situation.

Unlike an interpreter, a support teacher will clarify and elucidate instructions, and ensure that the deaf children can participate fully in the class activity. A good support teacher will encourage as much as possible direct communication between the main class teacher and the children from the unit. This can work well in classes where the teaching is 'desk-oriented', but can present difficulties in the more active and practical drama session, especially when there is more than one deaf child. There is a danger that the deaf children will stay together, under the wing of their own teacher, and this can result in their *isolation* within the class as a whole.

Other hearing children may find the presence of a second teacher in the classroom a barrier to their attempts to communicate directly with their deaf peers. An integral part of any drama session is the problem-solving, decision-making and social interaction that involves communication, in whatever form, *between the children themselves*. The educational value of an integrated group works both ways, as hearing and deaf learn from and with each other.

Such integration will not happen naturally; considerable intuition and guidance will be needed. The teacher will need to watch carefully, for example, that an improvisation or discussion does not become so verbal that the deaf child is at a disadvantage. If a drama lesson is planned in such a way that it utilises *alternative* means of communication, then many of these problems will not arise. There are many 'languages' employed in drama which utilise just those *non*-verbal communication skills that deaf children have in abundance. Indeed, it is my experience that it is the *hearing* children who are frequently at a disadvantage in this respect, with their over-reliance on oral communication, and they can learn much in this respect from their deaf peers.

THE IMPORTANCE OF DRAMA GAMES

The importance of drama games as an introduction to a session cannot be overstressed. These games are often seen merely as a 'warm-up' exercise, or a way of leading into the improvisation which will form the main purpose of the session. But where deaf children are involved they have an additional objective.

The relationship between play and child development has long been accepted in modern educational thought. Where deaf children are concerned, a fundamental factor must be borne in mind: *deaf children do not achieve the same development in spontaneous play as their hearing counterparts,* and this is not entirely accounted for by difficulties in communication skills alone. A number of independent research studies have been carried out in this field, and findings agree that hearing-impaired children:

- do not use object-substitution in their play
- are more likely to indulge in loosely structured activities such as chasing and wrestling
- play in smaller groups than hearing children
- need longer periods of habitation before using the materials that are provided in their play.

Let us consider for a moment some of the games and exercises commonly used as introductions to a drama session. There is no 'special' form for use with deaf children, but many can be adapted. The emphasis throughout should be on *non*-verbal means of communication, and should be aimed to utilise and develop the alternative 'languages' of drama.

1   There are many variations of the playground game of 'tag' which rely on ingenuity rather than speed. My own favourite I call 'Horsetail', and it has the advantage of involving every child simultaneously both as catcher and caught. Give each child a piece of material about 30 cm long, and ask them to tuck this into the back of their waistbands (squares of kitchen paper can be used instead, but these tend to tear easily). The object of the game is quite simply to gain as many 'tails' as possible, but it is wise to introduce certain rules, for example that the children may not touch each other physically except to take the tail itself. This game will involve a great deal of twisting and turning, as well as acute awareness of each other in relation to space.

2   Quieter *concentration* games can utilise and develop the deaf child's acute sense of observation. The popular 'Killer' or 'Wink Murder' can actually be problematic for some hearing children who are uncomfortable with direct eye-contact: indeed, one of the objectives of the game is to develop eye-contact. Deaf children, on the other hand, *depend* on eye-contact, and are often better at it. It is a game that they enjoy, and, when performed property, it introduces an element of suspense that can be developed into improvisation.

3   *Mirroring* is one of the best exercises that I know for developing concentration. Making human mirrors also helps to develop awareness and sensitivity to others. When it is performed properly, it promotes a heightened sense of timing, and can result in genuine harmonious contact and co-operation. It can be performed in pairs, in small groups, or with the full group. Ask the children to stand in a circle, with one volunteer as the leader. The leader moves *very slowly*, using first just hands, then other parts of the body and face. The others then move with the leader as in a mirror. It is very important to stress the *slowness* with which these movements are made: discourage any attempts to 'catch people out'.

When children are able to do this well, it is possible for the 'leader' to change from one to another *with no pre-arranged signal*, but this requires a considerable degree of awareness. It is best to try this working in pairs, with the leadership changing spontaneously back and forth.

4 *Human machines* is another exciting method for developing group communication and co-operation without the need for words. Working in small groups, one child begins a repetitive movement which constitutes a part of a machine. With *no pre-planning,* another child joins the machine to create a different component, then another, until the entire group is working. Each part of the 'machine' should be connected (though not necessarily touching) to at least one other part of the machine.

It is best to begin this in a purely abstract fashion, but once the children have got the idea they can be asked to make machines which accomplish something – a coffee-vending machine, a food mixer, a cuckoo clock.

The students of the Theatre of the Deaf course once made a machine in this way that constituted an egg-packing factory. It was an exciting ensemble, with the students at different levels, and with different rhythms of movement, yet each component connected at some point with another in such a way that it was possible to 'see' the eggs being passed along the assembly-line. Once this machine was working adequately, and the overall rhythm had been established, I introduced a box of real eggs. The result of this was to add an element of *tension* to the exercise that made for real drama – but I do not recommend it if you are working on a carpeted floor!

5 Games and exercises designed to utilise the sense of *touch* should not be neglected. The importance of touch to deaf children has already been mentioned in the context of gaining attention, but there are so many other ways in which this sense can be developed. So many of our emotions are expressed through touch: it is a powerful means of non-verbal communication, providing an almost instant awareness about another human being, and yet it is the one that we (as adults, anyway) are the most reluctant to use. I keep a 'touch box', a bag containing a variety of materials with different tactile surfaces, such as fur, sandpaper, glass, leather, something sticky like two-sided Sellotape. I pass these round the group, and ask the children to make a movement which indicates their reactions to touching this object, paying special attention to facial expression. When the children have experienced this exercise using real objects, they can be asked to pass an *imaginary* object around, and describe, through their bodies, what it feels like (another, more sophisticated, version of this exercise is described below).

6 Games designed to develop communication through gesture, facial expression and body language are, of course, ideal. My own favourite consists of a series of simple statements and questions. The children, in pairs, are asked to imagine that they are trying to communicate through a plate-glass window (sound-proofed, of course!). **A** is inside a building, **B** is outside in the street.

Communicating through a plate-glass window

They must somehow communicate the statements, given one at a time, and of gradually increasing difficulty, to each other. They must not lip-speak the words (this *would* give deaf children the advantage, and defeats the object), and they may not, of course, use sign language as such.

(Note: if working with signing children, and the teacher does not sign, you have a problem – how are you going to know if they cheat?)

Such statements could include:

- You have got my coat on.
- Your house is on fire!
- There's a lion coming down the street
- I have left my car keys on the table by the window.
- Would you like some fish and chips?
- Where do I get the Number 9 bus?

and so on.

7 Another exercise which utilises the same idea, but which can be extended into an improvisation dependent upon purely visual clues, involves a situation where two or more strangers meet who do not speak the same language, for example shopping in a foreign country. Again in pairs, **A** is the shop owner or shop assistant, **B** is the customer. *No* discussion or pre-planning is allowed. It is **B**, the customer, who decides what kind of shop it will be. He then enters the 'shop', and proceeds to try to purchase the item. **A** will have to watch carefully for clues as to the kind of shop and the merchandise being sold.

This can develop into quite lengthy, and often hilarious, improvisations. It is wise not to be too quick to 'change round', although both children should get the opportunity to lead, but to allow a promising situation to develop. If all goes well, an element of *characterisation* will begin to develop.

There are many variations around the idea of people trying to communicate when there is an inherent problem, for example:

- **A** asks **B** for directions to a place but **B** is not very sure of the way. It is amazing how difficult it is to give directions without waving one's arms about! Try getting **B** to describe *non-verbally* to **A** how to get from the classroom to some point at the other end of the school building.

- **A** is a TV reporter trying to file a report on a very exciting event taking place in the background. **B** is the studio link person. Unfortunately, the sound system has broken down. How does **A** continue to describe the event?

These types of exercise, as well as being fun to do, can go a long way towards levelling the differences between deaf and hearing children. Indeed, to begin with, deaf children will have the distinct advantage: after all, they communicate like this all the time! With practice, however, their hearing peers will develop communication skills which, hopefully, will be extended beyond the context of the drama lesson.

8 The question of 'object substitution', or lack of it in the case of deaf children, has been quoted as an indication of 'less creative' natural play. This can (and has) given rise to the belief that deaf children are in some way 'less imaginative' than hearing children. I have heard a teacher of deaf children remark that 'the problem with trying to do drama with deaf children is that they have no imagination!'. This is not true. They have just as much imagination as any other child: they need to be actively encouraged to use it. The 'copying' habit is a difficult one to break, but if one realises that it stems from a fear of failure, and creates an environment where there is no possibility of 'failure', then confidence will gradually develop – and imagination with it.

An exercise that I have frequently employed is designed specifically to encourage object substitution, and to help develop imagination. All that is required are a few props, the simpler the better – a waste-paper bin, a wire coat-hanger, a length of rope, a piece of material. Get the children into a circle, and place the props, one at a time, in the centre. The teacher should explain that she is going to use this object, not as it really is, but as something else. When the children have accurately guessed what it is, it will be replaced in the centre of the circle. Any child may then take the object and use it – but it must be as something different.

Note: Do *not* pass the object round the circle. This will create a feeling of panic. As it comes closer, the child sees her own idea used by someone else, and the mind goes blank. This *does* create a feeling of failure. Try to eliminate any element of competition – 'If you can't think of anything, it doesn't matter. Try with something else.' (I have deliberately 'gone blank' myself from time to time when participating in this game in order to emphasise this.)

Once the children have got the idea, divide them into groups, each group having *one* of the objects. The exercise is then repeated, with one child beginning to use the object, and the others joining in as they realise what it is supposed to be. As the improvisation develops, the object itself can change into something else, according to the whim of the children. I have seen entire narratives develop around a waste-paper bin, which has become, at various times, a steering-wheel of a car, a policeman's helmet, a waiting-room chair, a coffee-machine, and (sophisticated idea!) a cardiac-arrest monitor.

These are just a few of the ideas that can be developed from quite simple games and exercises. In each case, the emphasis is upon *visual* clues, and there is a deliberate elimination of a need for preliminary discussion among the children themselves. Even instructions and explanations on the part of the teacher need only be brief – much can be done by a quick demonstration.

USE OF 'PHYSICALISATION' IN DRAMA

All of the introductory games and exercises described above are essentially physical in their execution, relying as they do upon the body, rather than the voice, to express an idea. So far, however, the expressiveness of the body – movement, mime, gesture, facial expression – is seen as a *substitute for* the voice. Once the children have got used to using their bodies in this way, more abstract ideas can be introduced.

Most drama teachers will include at least some element of the use of the body to portray inanimate objects – furniture, buildings, machines, etc. This is an essential first step to the much more sophisticated notion of the physical portrayal of *concepts* and the dramatisation of *symbolic thought*.

Younger children can be introduced to this idea through a series of drawings on a flip-chart. You do not need to be a skilled artist to use this method: a few lines or quick diagrams on a piece of paper will save endless lengthy explanations and give the visual cue required. Begin with concrete ideas and real objects, and ask the children, working in small groups, to construct this particular structure ('make the shape of the object') by linking themselves together physically. It is important to discourage too much discussion and argument about *how* they are going to do it. If you have previously used some of the warm-up games described above, like making machines, then the children should be able to work quickly by picking up visual cues from each other (see Figure 20).

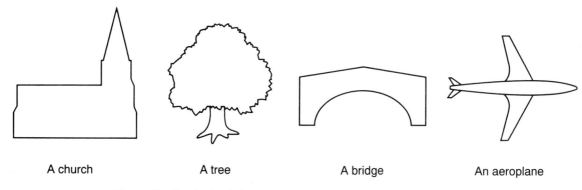

| A church | A tree | A bridge | An aeroplane |

Figure 20   Static visual clues

| A ship in a gale | A rocking-horse | A clown's face | A fairground swing-boat |

Figure 21   Moving visual clues

These depictions are essentially static: once the children have formed their structure, they do not move. The next step might be to use such drawings as a *starting point* for a wider improvised scenario involving physical movement (Figure 21). 'What does this drawing make you think of? Show me!'

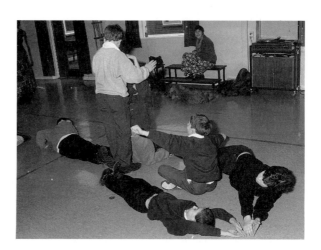

'A ship'

'A church'

Once the children have got used to working in this way, the drawings themselves can become less specific and leave more to the children's own imagination. A *window* has produced some exciting improvisations depicting what is behind it; a *circle* has been variously interpreted as a circus-ring, a spotlight, a space-ship, or a semi-religious ritual; a *locked trunk* once led to an entire improvisation involving the whole class in a search for lost treasure. In each case, the drawing itself was given with no preconceived ideas of what it might lead to: the ideas, and the drama, came entirely from the children themselves.

Physicalising emotions can be an invaluable exercise. The following was a workshop taken with the Theatre of the Deaf students, but it would work equally well with even quite young children, and can help to extend vocabulary. Deaf children who may not know the word for a particular emotion will still be able to demonstrate it, given a specified context – the word (the vocabulary) can be taught afterwards.

EXAMPLE

The scenario given in this case was that of a *fairground*. The students were asked to depict the various rides and amusements that they would encounter in a fairground, with the emphasis on as wide a *variety* of movement as possible. Roller-coasters, helter-skelters and water-chutes were interspersed with a coconut shy, a shooting gallery, a ghost train, and a 'Tunnel of Love' (watch this one!). In some cases, the students used their bodies to depict the ride itself, in others they became the consumers. Sometimes, as in the 'shooting gallery', there was a mixture of the two, with the line of student 'ducks' reacting to the inept attempts to shoot them down.

This exercise, which in itself produces some exciting work, was followed by a discussion of the various *emotions* experienced during a visit to a fairground. Fairgrounds, after all, are designed to produce a variety of sensations in their patrons: nervousness, vertigo, fright, relief, horror, pleasure, panic, astonishment, amusement, triumph, weariness, even nausea! Even though some of the students had difficulty in articulating these sensations, they were able to *show* how they would feel. The fairground was then depicted again, but this time the emphasis was placed, not on the rides and sideshows themselves, but upon the *physical depiction of the emotions* that visitors went through. They were encouraged to explore the *progression* of such emotions, for example from anticipation, through nervousness, to fear, to panic, to relief. Some of the movements employed were entirely abstract and *conceptual* in their portrayal. At a later stage, the students were asked to choose just one short sequence of movement that they had made, and to repeat this in a rhythmic way. The result approximated the rhythmic movements of the fairground attractions depicted earlier, but this time it became an 'emotion-machine' – a symbolic portrayal of the human reaction to it – rather than the machine itself.

A more complex exercise uses as a basis variations of what we call 'Abstract Landscapes'. This involves a small group of students (five or six) sitting on chairs in a straight line at the back of a performance space. The remainder observe and comment on the action. The tutor/leader calls out a word or

'Abstract Landscapes'

phrase. At *no more than ten-second intervals,* first one student then another must enter the performance space and do something that depicts this word or phrase. This can take the form of a still image, movement or gesture. While the interpretations of the word or phrase are individual, the emphasis is still placed on group composition and spatial tension, in so far as the completed depiction is very much a *group* one, not merely a collection of individuals. For example, suppose the word 'green' is called out. One person may choose to interpret this as a tree with facial expression connoting peace, while another depicts jealousy, and a third nausea. These are very individual interpretations, yet the group must still come together to form a whole. The emphasis throughout is upon *abstract* interpretations, and attempts to 'tell a story' are discouraged. Some suitable words/phrases to use include:

- spring
- death
- innocence
- loneliness
- the centre of the universe
- the state of Britain today
- the dark side of the mind.

The purpose of the exercise is to encourage *abstract* interpretations of conceptual ideas through movement and use of space. The entire exercise is 'non-verbal' – students are not allowed to discuss what they are going to do beforehand, but must work quickly and spontaneously. Often the initial spontaneous response produces more imaginative work than when students are allowed time to 'think of something'. This does introduce an element of tension, but there should be no fear of failure if a 'safe' environment has been built beforehand. Indeed, the tension itself can be productive.

This exercise is frequently used by the students themselves as a working *method,* both in creative drama and in rehearsal for a piece of theatre. If they find themselves stuck for ideas, in a situation resulting in lengthy discussion and argument, they will often stop, pick a few 'key words' or phrases, and simply 'see what happens' using this method. The visual images which result will usually go a long way towards solving their dilemma.

Perhaps the ultimate use of this kind of physical conceptualising was seen in the students' work on a recent production of Lorca's 'Blood Wedding'. Not an easy play to understand at the best of times, the poetic language in which it is written was beyond the comprehension of many of the Theatre of the Deaf students. There are numerous instances in the play of Lorca's extensive use of symbolism, but I give here just two examples of ways in which physical conceptualising helped the students to understand it. The first was a working method in rehearsal; the second was actually used in performance.

Lorca's use of colour

In 'Blood Wedding', Lorca makes a number of references to colour in relation to his various settings, in most cases with no further explanation as to why. The first scene, he insists, takes place in 'a room painted yellow' (this is the *only* description he gives of this particular setting). Act I Scene 3 puts the emphasis on pink, while Act 2 insists on 'cold blue tones', and so on. Whole chapters have been devoted to this use of colour symbolism by Lorca, and its significance is certainly open to interpretation.

The students were divided into small groups, and each group was given a piece of material of roughly the same colour but of different *textures* (thus utilising the tactile senses as described above). Using the methods of the 'Abstract Landscape' exercise, each group was asked to depict a physical interpretation of whatever this piece of material meant to them. A piece of green velvet, for example, produces a very different image from a piece of roughly-woven wool, and different again from green metallic material. The students spent some time exploring the possible symbolic ideas behind a number of different colours and textures in this way – black, red, purple, yellow, pink, blue, and white. The last four are the colours specified by Lorca in his introduction to scenes from his play. *Without having read the play,* the students came up with a number of possible ideas that would explain this specification. White, for example, was depicted variously as innocence, purity, and death – all of which relate to the final scene of 'Blood Wedding'. Having done this practical exercise, it then became very much easier to discuss this difficult concept with the students in academic terms.

EXAMPLE

The symbolism of the horse

The horse as a symbol runs throughout the play, but is perhaps most specific in the somewhat depressing lullaby that Leonardo's wife sings to her child. Lorca's lullaby tells of a weary and bleeding horse that would not drink water from a stream. Why does it refuse to drink? What is wrong with the water? The water is a *symbol* for marriage and for life; the blood a symbol for passion and for death. In many ways, therefore, his song contains within it the main themes of the play as a whole, with its emphasis on these opposing forces of water/blood, marriage/passion, life/death.

The horse's refusal to drink expresses the mutual exclusion of these two opposing principles. It is essential to understand this lullaby in order to understand the play.

Lorca's language may be difficult to understand, especially in its English translation, but he makes considerable use of essentially *visual* imagery (one of the main reasons that this play was chosen for a Theatre of the Deaf production), and nowhere is this more apparent than here. Working in small groups, the students were asked to examine this lullaby, and to draw a 'storyboard' of the main images that presented themselves. These images were then translated into a series of movements, which depicted the underlying *meaning* of the images. The groups were discouraged from too literal an interpretation – for example, the group as a whole *becoming* the horse. Instead, they were asked to think what the horse represented at any one moment.

This exercise was intended purely as a working method to get the students to explore the possible meanings underlying Lorca's lullaby, but the resulting work was so strong in its visual and physical imagery, that it was finally used in the performance itself. The horse as a sexual symbol (i.e. as a symbol for Leonardo himself) became one of the major themes of the students' interpretation of the play.

'Blood Wedding'

The students of the Theatre of the Deaf course are constantly exposed to these methods of physicalising abstract concepts and symbolic thought, and they are then able to use them when working with children in a school environment. Recently, for example, a group of students chose the theme of 'Northern Ireland' as a topic for a Theatre-in-Education programme aimed at children of mid-secondary age-range. Their own devised introductory play made extensive use of visual imagery and symbolism, especially – and interestingly – in its use of colour symbolism. The play began with an image of the Irish flag physically being torn apart. From that point on, the green was used as a symbol for Catholic Republicanism; the orange for Protestant Unionists; while the white section represented both the resultant deaths (a shroud) and the attempts at peace.

During a follow-up practical workshop with the children, the students asked them to make group statues, first of 'War', then 'Peace'. They did this one at a time, concentrating first on the theme of War. Perhaps because of their deliberate use of the word 'statue', the children inevitably reproduced likenesses of the war memorials which grace so many of our public places: soldiers, guns, flags, dead bodies, all suitably and artistically arranged. Although the student leaders rightly praised the results of this exercise, they asked the children to consider whether this was the *only* meaning of war to the people caught up in it. What other images spring to mind, for example from newsreels of wars in Africa or the former Yugoslavia? Is war only about killing and being killed? What of the victims of war? They had with them newspaper photographs which facilitated this discussion, and soon words like 'starvation', 'homelessness', 'orphans', 'disease', 'fear', and 'grief' began to emerge. A repeat of this exercise successfully depicted some of these *alternative* images of war. By sticking to the 'statue' idea, the student leaders avoided a mere reproduction of the photographs that they had used to facilitate the discussion, and came very close to a physical/visual portrayal of the *conceptual* ideas that had begun to emerge.

When it came to 'Peace', many of the children were, at first, stumped for ideas. This was perhaps inevitable, because 'peace' is purely conceptual. The student leaders began to question the groups of children closely: 'What does 'peace' mean to you?' The result was a wide variety of images and interpretations, from a straightforward depiction of a peaceful summer day, to a highly sophisticated attempt to portray the concept of the United Nations.

'War'

'Peace'

One group chose to show a game of 'Tug of War', but used the white flag as a prop to do it with. The irony of this was not lost on the children participating in the workshop, although it is doubtful that any of them could have articulated the concepts behind it. Not only did the children clearly *understand* such symbolism and abstract thought, but when presented in dramatic terms, they were able to use it to express their own ideas.

DEVELOPMENT OF NARRATIVE, SEQUENCE AND STRUCTURE

The preceding examples outline ways in which children can be taught to use visual/physical languages to express their ideas, but this in itself does not necessarily make for a drama. The development of *narrative* is of great importance in drama, and the following paragraphs outline some ways of approaching this. The *dramatic context* of a lesson presents numerous possibilities, and much will depend on the purpose behind any one session. Two examples are presented here, each with its own specific objectives.

TEACHING SEQUENCE AND STRUCTURE

As stated above, deaf children often find sequence and structure extremely difficult. The *conventions* of storytelling are, for most people, ingrained from the fairy stories of babyhood. Deaf children often lose out in this respect. They never hear bedtime stories read to them. When they eventually come to read for themselves, even the simplest books present the insurmountable problems of printed words on a page which are often meaningless.

The deaf child will think in *visual images,* not in words, and for this reason I find the 'still image' form a useful way of working in drama. It serves also to identify a *particular moment in time* – sorting out the strongest 'image' from the mass of information received. Consider what happens when we watch a play. There will be some key moments which remain firmly etched in the mind; what comes immediately before or after may have been forgotten. If it were possible to take a series of photographs of the action at these moments, then the entire narrative of the play could be shown through these photographs, *as long as* they are displayed in the correct *sequence*. The following work is based on the same principle.

EXAMPLE

Reading a visual narrative

Working in pairs, ask the children to make a shape together of given letters of the alphabet, e.g. A, W, P, O, S. As with all work of this nature, they should not be allowed to spend too much time in discussion about this, but to form the shape as quickly as possible.

When they have got the idea, ask each pair to think of a simple three-letter word – *cat, man*, etc. – and to spell out this word, letter by letter, in the same way. Allow time for them to work on this until they can move quickly and smoothly from one letter to the next. They can then show the result to the rest of the group, who should be able to 'read' it. The word 'read' here is used both literally and in its dramatic context. The children may try to guess the complete word by the time the pair have shown their second letter: sometimes they will be right, sometimes the ending will not match their expectations – *tea*, for example, may be anticipated as *ten*.

What you have taught in this very simple exercise is a fundamental principle of dramatic narrative: given a sequence of events, we are always influenced by what has gone before, and have certain *expectations* of what is to follow. The story may, or may not, fulfil those expectations, but, in order to make sense of it, the *sequence itself* must be clear.

Now, working in slightly larger groups, ask the children to 'make a photograph' (do not use the word 'image' unless you are quite sure they understand what you mean by this) which shows, for example:

- a moment from a sporting event
- a family picnic
- Christmas morning.

In each case, encourage the observing children to analyse the resulting images carefully. Who are these characters? What is the relationship, emotional as well as actual, between them? What is happening? What, or who, is the focal point? Continue this exercise until the children are able to depict situations and characters clearly in the most basic terms, through the employment of body language, use of space, facial expression, and focus.

Then ask each group to make a *sequence of three images* which together will 'tell a story'. The teacher will give the title of the story, but how they interpret this title is entirely up to them. The first 'title' that I use here is 'The Accident', but I try to discourage them from depicting road accidents, which is often the first thing that springs to mind. It is amazing what children will think of if this one can be eliminated: falling off a ladder; a child pulling a saucepan from a stove; mountaineering accidents; someone falling into a river – all of these and more have been dramatised in this way by quite young children.

The accident itself is generally shown in the *second* image, the first 'setting the scene', and the third showing the results – someone getting help, ambulances arriving, even occasionally a funeral! What the children have done, in fact, is utilised the basic components of narrative structure – *exposition*, *climax*, and *resolution*.

Visual narrative

With older children this can be repeated using more abstract ideas for titles, for example 'The Homecoming'. *Who* is coming home? To what? What is the emotional context here? The greater the scope for the children's own interpretation, the better.

SOLVING PROBLEMS IN A WHOLE GROUP DRAMA

The element of problem-solving will, of course, be a part of *any* drama session, as the children have to make decisions and come to agreement before they can produce group work of any kind. However, the following lesson was designed specifically with this objective in mind. The lesson itself is rather more loosely structured than the one described above, allowing the children greater freedom to develop the improvisation as they wished. The element of *sequence*, however – of 'cause' and 'effect' – remains integral, as the solution to one problem may lead to another.

Neither are the children restricted to a particular *dramatic form* as a method of presentation, although the emphasis on the use of visual/physical languages is contained within the main task itself. The session was designed originally for an integrated group of deaf and hearing children of upper primary age range (9–10 years), and one of its main objectives is to encourage the children to *explore* alternative methods of communication. In this case, the constraints imposed by the teacher in the above exercise are abandoned, and the children must work out for themselves the best method of communicating their ideas.

To work effectively the drama depends on the presence of a second adult 'in role', in this case as an alien who has crash-landed his spacecraft. When a second adult is available, this person can take on such a role and allow the teacher freedom to interact between the role and the children, or even to take on an additional role himself. Handled properly, the person in role has the power to focus attention and suspend disbelief, and if in some way in need of help, can elicit a genuine emotional and imaginative response, sometimes from the most unexpected children.

EXAMPLE

The session began with games and exercise, similar to those outlined above, designed to explore the possibilities of communication through facial expression, body language, and gesture. When these exercises had been completed, I produced a flat cap and explained that, when I put on the cap, I became a farmer. Donning the cap (and now therefore 'in role'), I then explained to the children that I had discovered a large hole in the middle of my potato field. It was a very deep hole, and there seemed to be someone or something at the bottom. (While I was talking to the children in one part of the room, my colleague, who had previously been watching from the sidelines, put on a *mask* and sat cross-legged on the floor at the other end of the room. *Note*: it is important that this mask is non-threatening: in this case it was a simple plain half-mask.) We did not define the area of the 'hole' itself, preferring to allow the children to do this for themselves, but it is possible to do so by drawing a chalked circle on the floor.

I then led the children to the space where my colleague sat, and the 'hole' was defined as they circled around him. He began to cower as he looked up at the children, clearly terrified. (I had not previously introduced him in role to the children, the object of the exercise being that they had to work out for themselves who he was and where he had come from.) His position on the floor put him immediately at a lower status to the children, as did his reaction of fear.

Still in role as a farmer, I pretended to be very angry about the mess that he had made of my field, and demanded that he get out of the hole immediately. I did not, however, have any ideas as to how he could do this, but asked the children what they thought we should do. (The attitude of anger on my part served its intended purpose of directing the children's sympathy to my colleague, while my deliberate unhelpfulness provoked an active response on their part.)

Two children then volunteered to 'climb down' into the hole to try to talk to him. How were they going to get down? Other children quickly organised ropes, and down they went. (Here was the first problem – how to get down into the hole. With no prompting from me this was quickly solved, and involved considerable group co-operation in the process.)

When these two children reached the 'bottom', they were faced with difficulties in communication – aliens do not speak English! Our 'alien' however, was adept at utilising gesture and managed to indicate that he wanted help to get out of the hole as quickly as possible. The ropes were employed again, but, as he was heavy, considerable teamwork and organisation went into this effort. (My colleague was able to mime these actions of climbing out of the hole without once deviating from his cross-legged position. Thus at no time was he physically higher than the children, and they never had to 'look up' to him.)

Once on 'level ground', the questioning began again. Where did he come from? What had happened to him? What did he want? It transpired that he was from outer space, had crashed his spacecraft in the field, and wanted to go home (shades of ET!). In order to do this, however, he would have to rebuild his spaceship, but he needed the help of the children in order to do this. (All these questions, and their replies, took the form of gesture and mime. Still in my role of 'unhelpful farmer' I feigned not to understand a word he was saying, thus putting the children in the position of having to 'interpret' for me – a novel situation for deaf children, and one that reverses the usual state of affairs.)

Our alien happened to have a torn section of the 'blueprint' of his vessel (a pre-arranged plan), and indicated to the children that, if they could complete the blueprint, they would be able to rebuild the ship. (Out of role at this point, I organised the children into small groups, gave each group a large sheet of paper and felt-tip pens, and suggested that they reconstruct the ship around the original blueprint. Each paper represented a section that they would then have to find somewhere in the field. Once again, group co-operation was necessary, as each section had to be 'welded' into a whole. There was, surprisingly, little argument about what this spacecraft looked like, the completed vessel bearing a remarkable resemblance to 'The Enterprise' of Star Trek!)

While the children were searching for their various sections, I resumed my role of farmer, and became angrier and angrier at the delay. (This added an element of *tension* to the improvisation, and served the purpose of confirming the empathy of the children further around the alien. Some of the children began to get genuinely angry with me.)

The spacecraft was finally put together – but it wouldn't start! (A further problem has now been introduced.) What powers a spaceship? A number of alternative ideas were tried, petrol being rejected quite early on, but none appeared to work. (It had been pre-arranged that this ship would be powered by potatoes, but if the children were unable to work this out, or if they came up with a more imaginative idea, then the 'alien' would accept one suggestion. Much depended upon the *time* available in the session: it was important to bring the improvisation to a satisfactory conclusion.)

At this point, communication was in danger of breaking down, until one child, quick off the mark, handed the alien a piece of paper and a pen. (This child has now instinctively introduced yet another means of communication – that of drawing.) A few quick scribbles and ... of course – potatoes! The ship is powered by potatoes! I objected strongly to having 'my' potatoes dug up, but the children ignored me. One child deliberately distracted my attention whilst, behind my back, the others began frantically digging. Enough potatoes were gathered, the spaceship shuddered into motion, and the alien was on his way home.

Although this session is perhaps more structured than I would normally use, it still leaves plenty of scope for the children to have a stake in the direction that the drama will take. More importantly, it serves its main purpose of presenting the children with a series of problems which they have to solve. Furthermore, there is a logical *sequence* to solving these problems – first get the alien out of the hole, then find out what he wants, find the pieces of the ship, build the ship, find out what powers it. My own role was primarily to place a series of obstacles in their way and to introduce the element of *conflict*. The children had to find their own solutions to those obstacles.

The biggest obstacle of all, however, was the communication barrier. It is amazing how quickly this barrier was broken down by the children themselves, employing every possible means of communication at their disposal. Most importantly, it placed the children in a position of *power*, equalising deaf and hearing children in this respect. Their feelings of *empathy* with the alien were genuine – only they could help him – and their antipathy to me reversed the usual teacher/pupil role, and forced them back on their own resources.

Conclusion

Deaf children are special children. They have problems which are not necessarily solved by bigger and better hearing-aids, or by more intensive schooling. Deafness is not merely an inability to hear. It impairs a child's entire perceptual experience, which, in turn, can lead to an impairment of intellectual, emotional and social development.

> *"Although the defect is limited to his ears, it is the total person who has deafness."*
>
> H.R. Myklebust, *The Psychology of Deafness*

Yet deaf children also possess inner resources which enable them to compensate, to a greater or lesser degree, for the disability that they face. In a world where the primary mode of communication between human beings is verbal language, they are forced to utilise *alternative* languages in order to make themselves understood at all. Drama can utilise these same languages in a constructive and positive way to enhance the learning experience, and to remedy some of the deficiencies that deafness entails. The very nature of educational drama, involving as it does an essentially social form of self-motivated learning, makes it eminently suitable for the deaf child.

It is hoped that the wide selection of exercises and drama lessons illustrated here gives some indication of the rich possibilities in this kind of learning experience, and will motivate teachers of drama who may have no prior experience of deaf children, to work in this field.

In conclusion, I will return once more to the Theatre of the Deaf course. Some of the more recent students first met me, so they tell me, when I visited their schools years ago as a workshop leader or in the capacity of adjudicator for the NDCS Festival of Performing Arts. In truth, I do not remember them. They were children then – just faces among many others. What I do remember is the fun, the creative talent, and the amount of genuine communication that was going on, by whatever method. Now, as adults, they have come to develop the skills that they began to acquire then to their fullest potential. Some have gone back into those same schools to become teachers of drama themselves, an achievement that once they would not have considered possible. It was *drama* that gave them the motivation to realise their potential, not just in a specialised field, but as whole people. Perhaps some of those children that they are teaching now will one day become student teachers themselves. I do hope so!

REFERENCES

Myklebust, H.R. (1964) *The Psychology of Deafness,* Grune and Stratton

FURTHER INFORMATION

The culmination of the NDCS *Festival of Performing Arts* takes place every May with a public performance of the final presentations at the Arts Theatre in Leicester Square, London. Further information about the Festival may be obtained from: The National Deaf Children's Society, 45 Hereford Road, London W2 5AH.

Further information about *hearing-aids,* their uses and limitations, may be obtained from the National Deaf Children's Society (for address see above), or from: The Royal National Institute for the Deaf (RNID), 105 Gower Street, London WC1E 6AH.

A register of qualified *sign language interpreters* can be obtained from: The Council for the Advancement of Communication with Deaf People, Pelaw House, School of Education, University of Durham, Durham DH1 1TA.

SECTION THREE

CHAPTER TEN

ORGANISING DRAMA FOR SPECIAL NEEDS

DESIGNING A POLICY

Drama is included in the brief for OFSTED inspectors to report on (OFSTED, 1994). The guidance given to the inspectors states that:

> "At all four Key Stages pupils' achievements in drama should be judged within two main categories: creating and performing drama; and appreciating and appraising it.
>
> Standards should be judged in the following aspects of pupils' achievements: using imagination, with belief and feeling; creating drama with conviction and concentration; responding sensitively to their own work and that of others in drama; using a range of dramatic skills, techniques, forms and conventions to express ideas and feelings effectively; grasping and using dramatic concepts appropriately; recalling, recording and evaluating their own work and that of others."

This may appear to be an awesome demand for many situations in special education. Teachers should draw on all the elements of drama over a Key Stage but will obviously need to consider how to focus the work and what to stress to suit the particular situation of their school. Writing a policy will give you an opportunity to reflect on and state your thinking.

The policy statement for drama, as for any other subject, does not need to be long. It certainly shouldn't be loaded with complex specialist terminology, as it must be accessible to parents or any other non-specialists who are interested in what the school is trying to achieve.

In the past there has all too often been a temptation to justify the inclusion of drama by making reference to vague, overarching aims, many of which are in fact highly questionable. For example, what does the statement that 'drama gives children the opportunity to express themselves' really mean? Is it always a good thing for people to express themselves? Teachers frequently encounter children whose 'self' appears to need controlling or modifying rather than liberally expressing. The use of these broad yet ultimately dubious aims have led to drama being mistrusted and derided as 'woolly' or 'arty-farty' by some fellow professionals and parents. A policy statement should avoid using any language with which the staff themselves are not fully confident.

One way of formulating a policy statement for drama is to ask:

- What do we want children to know?
- What do we want them to understand?
- What do we want them to be able to do?

Knowing who Shakespeare was, understanding that his plays may be interpreted in a variety of ways, and being able to demonstrate this through different methods of performance, may not be appropriate for the young people you teach. On the other hand, learning that not all drama is reliant on verbal communication, understanding that space, movement and gesture can be used to convey meanings, and being able to utilise these aspects of dramatic art to re-enact a story, may be of the utmost importance to them.

Another key question that warrants a sentence or two in a policy statement is:

- Why include drama in the whole school curriculum?

You will need to consider whether what you have identified in terms of knowledge, understanding and skills is at one with the overall policies of the school. If, for example, giving children a sense of self-worth is central to the school's general policy, the policy for drama might incorporate a statement such as this:

> *"Students will be given the opportunity to forward their own ideas and helped to develop and communicate these in their drama work."*

Other elements of the whole school policy which may be particularly well reflected in drama work might include, for example, equal opportunities:

> *"In drama, the pupils will be encouraged to work in mixed ability and mixed gender groups. Source materials will be drawn from a wide variety of cultures."*

Your policy statement should make clear the relationship between the drama undertaken in the school and the rest of the curriculum. Is drama used to support work in other subjects? Or is it perceived as having a value in its own right and therefore stands alone within the timetable? You may wish to refer back to Chapter Two to review these questions.

Finally, but very importantly, make it clear in your policy statement what the entitlement of each child will be in drama. You should mention:

- the space to be used for drama
- the equipment available to support the work
- the amount of drama time allocated for each group
- any annual drama events open to or for the students
- what opportunities are provided to take children to the theatre
- the provision made to bring theatre companies into the school (see note under Resources, pages 227–28).

The statements you make in the policy will be exemplified in your schemes of work. (See Figure 22.)

A POLICY FOR DRAMA

☆ *Intentions*

[State what you want the students to:
- know
- understand
- be able to do.
- be able to do.
in drama].

☆ *Drama and the whole school policy*

[State how you see drama reflecting the overall values and aspirations of the school.]

☆ *Drama and the curriculum*

[State how drama will relate to other subjects. Is it used as a method or presented as a subject in its own right?]

☆ *The students' entitlement*

[Give details of space and equipment available, staffing, time allocation and special events in the drama diary.]

Figure 22   A template for a policy for Drama

SCHEMES OF WORK

Schemes of work demonstrate how the school intends to put its policies into practice. The schemes are a kind of map of the students' drama career in the school. Their purpose is to ensure that students don't experience unnecessary repetition in the curriculum and that some sort of logical progression of knowledge, understanding and skills is being provided for.

In drama, the schemes of work for each teaching group should describe how the work undertaken will relate to other National Curriculum subjects in addition to stating what will be achieved in terms of knowledge, understanding and skills in drama. It may be that at a particular stage you will want to use drama to enhance the language skills of a group, in which case the work should clearly relate to the Attainment Targets for English, especially speaking and listening.

With another group you may want to utilise drama's effectiveness as a vehicle for the teaching of history or science, in which case close reference would be made to the Attainment Targets and/or the Programmes of Study set out in those documents.

In both of the above cases, however, it would be necessary to make clear what it is that the students in each group are being expected to *make, perform* and *respond to* in terms of drama in that particular scheme (note how the OFSTED guidelines refer to 'creating and performing; appreciating and appraising').

In essence, a scheme of work is

> *"a summary of how the school intends to deliver its planned curriculum within specific groups and subjects: what is identified by each school as a proper area for a scheme of work will be determined by their own curriculum organisation."*
>
> NAHT, *Guidance Note 7: Schemes of Work,* 1993

In order to plan a scheme of work in drama you might devise a matrix such as the one shown in Figure 23. For each unit of work in the scheme you should state:

- key elements of drama to be tackled
- which NC Attainment Targets and/or Programmes of Study are being addressed
- when and how the work will be assessed.

Year	Term Autumn	Spring	Summer
7	Persephone	The Family	Festival
8	–	–	–
9	–	–	–

Figure 23   Scheme of work for Key Stage 3

UNITS OF WORK

Having established a coherent scheme, the work is broken down into smaller units. A unit therefore may consist of a few drama sessions within a larger class project on a particular theme (for example, 'The Persephone Myth', outlined below), or it may be a series of lessons leading toward a predetermined dramatic outcome (for example, working towards a short presentation as part of an arts festival). Again, in either case, the practical work in those sessions will be greatly aided if the teacher has carefully considered why she is doing this in terms of knowledge, understanding and skills. Figure 24 is an outline for a unit of work, designed by Marigold Ashwell.

AIMS

Each unit should have clearly stated aims. In essence, the aim is a description of what is being focused on in the course of the sessions.

The purpose of drama is often seen primarily as one of social education. Co-operation and working as a group are often forwarded as the aims of the work. But one might justifiably claim that these social aims should be present

UNIT PLANNING SHEET FOR DRAMA

UNIT TITLE   PERSEPHONE AND THE SEASONS

APPROXIMATE TIME   6 weeks   YEAR/KEY STAGE Year 7 KS 2/3

TEACHING OBJECTIVES
What do I want pupils to:

Understand

- How masks and movement can convey character traits.
- How stories can be re-told through drama.

Be able to do

- Make a simple mask appropriate to the story.
- Use movement and sound to suggest character.
- Re-tell the story in their own way.
- Re-enact some scenes using elements of drama.

SUGGESTED TASKS/ACTIVITIES

- Tell the story. Re-tell it around the circle, inviting each pupil to contribute a part.
- Pupils write/record their own re-telling.
- Make and decorate a simple card mask for different characters.
- Experiment with ways of moving with masks and adding appropriate sounds.
- Make still images and soundscapes of the seasons.
- Experiment with ways of showing light/dark, cold/warmth through movement.
- Work in role as Zeus: pupils to plead for the release of Persephone.

ASSESSMENT OPPORTUNITIES

Making

- Did they find a way of re-telling the story themselves?
- Were they able to make a simple mask representing a character from the story?
- Did they, with assistance, manage to structure and engage in a dramatic scene from the story?

Performing

- Could they use the mask to create a sense of drama?
- Did they employ movement and sound to reflect character and atmosphere?

Responding

- Were they able to comment on the difference between telling the story in drama and in other ways?
- Did they see a connection between the myth and aspects of their own lines?
- Comment on the differences in their own/each other's work.

RESOURCES

- Edited text of the Persephone myth from <u>The God Beneath the Sea</u> by Leon Garfield and Edward Blunden.
- Recorded extracts from Vivaldi's <u>The Four Seasons</u> and Offenbach's <u>Orpheus in the Underworld</u>.
- Card, scissors, poster paint, felt pens.
- Cassette recorder, tapes.
- Rostra to suggest different locations.

COMMENTS

Figure 24   Unit planning sheet for drama   *Source:* Marigold Ashwell, Inspector for Drama, Berkshire

regardless of the subject being taught. In planning for drama it might be more productive to think in terms of what's being explored in the drama (the content) and how the drama is actually working (the form). The content may well have an explicit social element to it; the drama might be about a person who is being bullied, for example. The social learning might, on the other hand, be implicit in the way the children are being asked to work; advising each other through forum theatre on how to develop a scene is an example.

In the unit outlined in Figure 24, the *content* is indicated in the title. The drama work focuses on the myth of Persephone. Through this unit, the pupils will come to know the story of how Hades kidnapped the beautiful daughter of Demeter, the goddess of the harvest, and took her to be his queen in the Underworld. Demeter grieved so much that all the fruits withered and the plants died until her daughter was restored to the surface of the Earth – but only on condition that she spent half of each year in the Underworld.

Such a story offers opportunities to help pupils investigate, for example, concepts such as light and dark, the seasons and perhaps even life and death. Teachers might want to tie in all sorts of elements of the curriculum with the project but they shouldn't lose sight of the fact that, beyond being a vehicle for the National Curriculum, it is a jolly good story and worth knowing for its own sake!

What the pupils will come to know, understand and be able to do in terms of the *form* of drama can be stated as specific teaching objectives.

OBJECTIVES

Some *objectives* can be described as being 'instructional' – that is, they involve teaching the pupils a particular skill or imparting a specific piece of knowledge. So, for example, an instructional objective for the Persephone unit might be to teach the pupils how to make a simple mask out of card. Eliot Eisner (1969) has described other objectives as 'expressive', suggesting a more circumspect and reflective approach which will lead the pupils beyond doing and towards understanding. In the unit outlined here, the objectives focus on what elements of the drama form are being addressed. There is no limit to the number of objectives you may wish to identify when planning units of work. Remember though that they are tools to help you assess the progress of each child in the group. If long lists of objectives are stated it may be impossible to assess the progress made by individuals with any accuracy (a fatal flaw of the early orders of the National Curriculum).

LESSON PLANS

A number of activities are outlined for the 'Persephone' unit in Figure 24. Some of them are already very specific and could be used immediately as the basis for a lesson or a part of a lesson. Other ideas would need to be structured more carefully in order to make it clear to the pupils what, exactly, they are to do.

There is no right or wrong way of making a lesson plan. Indeed, several lessons are described in this book, representing a range of ways of planning. Some teachers, having once started on a drama, will carry on the narrative for a number of sessions in the same way that a serial on television does. As the narrative unfolds they incorporate an ever widening range of strategies and information as opportunities present themselves. At other times it is more appropriate to set a more rigid structure to ensure that certain bits of knowledge or particular skills are introduced, reinforced and utilised.

A NOTE ON PROGRESS AND PROGRESSION

Progress and progression are two separate but related aspects of the acquisition of knowledge, understanding and skills.

Progress concerns the development made by each individual child. Teachers have been made increasingly aware of the need to monitor, record and report on each child's progress but there is no consensus on how this is best done. What is clear, though, is that the more carefully delineated and appropriate to the group the objectives are for any unit of work, the easier it is to assess the extent to which each child in the group has attained them. Reference to the Programmes of Study and end of Key Stage statements in the Arts Council's *Drama in Schools* booklet will give you an idea of the kind of benchmarks that could be used to plot how any individual child is making progress.

The term *progression* is applied not to the child but to the activities undertaken. The different units of work making up the scheme should have some logical sequence to them which will offer the children the opportunity to engage with an increasingly sophisticated and ever widening repertoire of drama work. Teachers may sequence units in order to develop specific skills such as language or social skills; or they may wish to offer groups a range of ostensibly unrelated units in order to give the children a broad range of drama experiences, for example puppetry, dance/drama, mask work, storytelling. In either case, it is up to the teacher to ensure that the scheme of work does offer a progression towards what is stated in the school's drama policy.

ASSESSMENT

As you will see in the unit outlined in Figure 24, the headings of 'Making', 'Performing' and 'Responding' have been used in order to help the teacher identify the differences in the nature of the pupils' achievement in drama. The questions posed in this section should relate to the objectives and help the teacher identify what each pupil has actually achieved. Like the current national driving test, this sort of assessment is largely, but not entirely, criterion-referenced in that it registers the pupils' ability to do something rather than qualifying how well they have done it. In the driving test, for example, the candidate is required to reverse around a corner; the speed and panache with which this is performed is irrelevant against the importance of being able to do it at all!

At the end of each unit, the teacher may want to write a brief comment on each pupil's progress and development. Every school will have its own system for assessing children and reporting on their progress. Some systems incorporate elaborate tick charts and graphs to replace the now thankfully outdated practice of giving one letter-grade for Attainment, another for Effort, and a general comment, often to the effect that

'Jenny has worked well this year and can express herself quite effectively'.

Neither of these approaches helps parents, or the children themselves, understand what the unit was about and what was learned through it. Many schools are now realising that providing a printed description and rationale of the work undertaken gives more sense to the individualised comment that follows it. Figure 25 is an example of one such assessment slip.

PROGRESS REPORT FOR DRAMA

Child's name: ⎯⎯⎯⎯⎯⎯⎯⎯⎯⎯⎯⎯⎯⎯⎯⎯⎯⎯⎯

Year/Group: ⎯⎯⎯⎯⎯⎯⎯⎯⎯⎯⎯⎯⎯⎯⎯⎯⎯⎯

Work undertaken this term:

    The group has been working on the myth of Persephone to support their topic work on 'The Seasons'. The drama project has involved storytelling, making masks and using them with movement to show different characters.

Teacher's comment:

Pupil's comment on the work:

Figure 25   Assessment slip for drama

EVALUATION

In addition to assessing the pupils, the teacher will want to evaluate the effectiveness of the activities and the purpose of the unit itself.

It is probably true that all teachers evaluate every session they teach, one way or another. But in a good deal of drama work an informal, wholly mental evaluation of the session simply isn't enough. In an ongoing drama, for example, the teacher needs to make a note to remind himself of where the narrative got to at the end of the lesson in order to be able to start from that point in the next session. (One answer to this problem is to ask the class what happened in the previous lesson but, if the teacher doesn't know himself, he is missing an opportunity to assess just what the children have assimilated.) I would argue that in the special needs situation, where progress is often slow and difficult to recognise, the need for conscientious – albeit brief – evaluation of each session is imperative in order for the teacher to be able to reinforce learning without simply repeating the activity.

Evaluating whole units of work can certainly help teachers in their future planning by recording those elements of the work that were successful and therefore worth trying with other groups, and those that weren't. The proforma in Figure 26 would be one way of keeping such a record. You will note that a four-point scale is used: no sitting on the fence here – be definite in your judgements!

UNIT EVALUATION

Group: _____ Term: _____ Year(s): _____

Unit title:
Description of work undertaken:

Cross-curricular links:

Personal reaction to the success of the project:
Very successful   Unsuccessful
   1   2   3   4

Perception of group's reception of the unit:
Very positive   Hostile
   1   2   3   4

Extent to which pupils were able to:
  Make drama   1   2   3   4
  Perform drama   1   2   3   4
  Respond to drama   1   2   3   4

Extent to which pupils learned about the content of the drama:
A great deal   Very little
   1   2   3   4

Extent to which the social health of the group developed:
A great deal   Very little
   1   2   3   4

Which particular drama activity worked best?

What problems were there with organisation and management?

What resources/strategies need rethinking?

What are the main points arising for consideration in the planning of future units?

Figure 26   A unit evaluation proforma

REFERENCES

Arts Council of Great Britain (1992) *Drama in Schools*, ACGB

Eisner, E.W. (1969) *Instructional and Expressive Objectives: Their Formulation and Use in Curriculum*, AERA Monograph Series on Curriculum Evaluation, Rand McNally & Co.

Kempe, A. and Holroyd, R. (1994) *Imaging: A Teacher's Guide*, Hodder & Stoughton

National Association of Head Teachers (1993) *Guidance Note 7: Schemes of Work*, NAHT

OFSTED (1993/94) *The Framework for the Inspection of Schools*, HMSO

Woolland, B. (1993) *The Teaching of Drama in the Primary School*, Longman

RESOURCES

The contributors to this book were asked to note down what particular resources they have found useful to instigate and support their practical classroom drama work. The choices are therefore obviously personal but we hope they will spark off ideas of your own.

MUSIC

Lilting instrumentals such as music by Enya or Kenny Gee.

Old favourites like 'Stranger on the Shore' by Acker Bilk might seem clichéd to teachers but may be new to young people.

Classical music is obviously full of riches. Pieces used for adverts work well perhaps because of their familiarity.

More 'experimental' music can be exciting and offer strong rhythms and atmospheres. Try:

'Revolution'	Jean Michel Jarre
'Volume One'	Soul II Soul
'Below the Waste'	Art of Noise
'In No Sense Nonsense'	Art of Noise

Some work by Philip Glass such as 'Powaqqatsi' and 'Mishima' is suitable, as is music from other cultures such as the South American pan pipes (try the soundtrack for the BBC series 'Flight of the Condor'), African drumming and the Aboriginal didgeridoo.

Film sound-tracks: some instantly recognisable ones such as James Bond themes or themes for westerns can be used to establish characters or settings. Others are very suggestive of atmosphere; try, for example:

'The Killing Fields'	Mike Oldfield
'The Mission'	Ernio Morricone
'The Piano'	Michael Nyman
'Chariots of Fire'	Vangelis
'Inspector Morse'	Barrington Phelong

VISUAL AIDS

- Old sepia photographs of families or street scenes.
- Old postcards – these often have intriguing messages on the back.
- Pages torn from a diary or filofax.
- A photograph of a person torn to suggest that the missing half also showed a person.

- Maps: replicas of county maps printed on parchment have a pleasing look and feel about them. Simply adding a few mysterious signs or arrows can lead to interesting dramas.

PROPS

Watch out for things that denote character, for example:
- a 'lost' wallet or handbag filled with some expected and one or two intriguing things
- a suitcase packed with clothes that clearly belong to a certain kind of character
- a walking stick – the more unusual the better

or places, for example:
- telephones
- an airline ticket
- seashells
- keys (the bigger the better)

or some sort mystery, for example:
- an old soft toy with some sort of note attached
- a bottle with a message in it
- decorated and unusual boxes
- a magic wand.

COSTUME

All manner of hats but of particular use:
- a peaked cap (denoting authority)
- a very obvious woman's hat
- a very obvious man's hat
- a unisex straw hat
- a flat cap.

Scarves, shawls and ponchos of different colours and materials (these can often be used as things other than what they are).

Particularly useful single items:
- waistcoats
- a tweed jacket
- a striped suit jacket
- a monocle
- a pair of mirrored sunglasses
- an absurdly large pair of shoes.

STORYBOOKS

A number of storybooks have been referred to in individual chapters (see especially Chapter Four). In many respects the possibilities are endless given that the success of drama is likely to depend on what angle you've taken on a story, rather than the story itself.

Stories such as folk and fairy tales are useful because the characters and key actions are usually very clear.

Stories such as quests offer the possibility of adding new episodes. Myths and legends can fall into this category but so too will books like *The Phantom Tollbooth* (see Chapter Seven).

Other stories to watch out for are those where there seems to be some significant jump in the attitude of the characters or a sudden change in the situation. *I'll Take You to Mrs Cole* by Nigel Gray is a very good example of a story in which something must have happened to a character but the reader is not told exactly what; the drama can explore this gap.

DRAMA BOOKS

There are a great many useful and interesting books on drama in education generally but very few which relate directly to drama and special education. However, given that all the authors of this book agree that there is no 'special' sort of drama for children with special needs, practical books produced for use in mainstream education can justifiably be plundered for ideas. Those marked with an asterisk* below offer practical suggestions, while the others serve as a broader grounding.

Arts Council of Great Britain (1992) *Drama in Schools,* ACGB

*Bird, G. and Norris, J. (1983) *Worlds of English and Drama,* Oxford University Press

*Boal, A. (1992) *Games for Actors and Non-Actors,* Routledge

Bolton, G. (1992) *New Perspectives on Classroom Drama,* Simon & Schuster

*Brandes, D. and Phillips, H. (1977) *The Gamesters' Handbook,* Stanley Thornes

*Burgess, R. and Gaudry, P. (1985) *Time for Drama,* Open University Press

Cattanach, A. (1992) *Drama for People with Special Needs,* A & C Black

*Davies, G. (1983) *Practical Primary Drama,* Heinemann

DES (1989) *Drama from 5 to 16,* HMSO

Jennings, S. (1973) *Remedial Drama,* Pitman

(1987) *Dramatherapy: Theory and Practice for Teachers and Clinicians,* Routledge

Johnstone, K. (1981) *Impro,* Methuen

*Kempe, A. and Holroyd, R. (1994) *Imaging – A series of resource books: Evacuees, The Great Bath Road, A South African Scrapbook, Teacher's Book,* Hodder & Stoughton

McClintock, A. (1984) *Drama for Mentally Handicapped Children,* Souvenir Press

Morgan, N. and Saxton, J. (1987) *Teaching Drama,* Hutchinson

*Neelands, J. (1990) *Structuring Drama Work,* Cambridge University Press
  (1992) *Learning Through Imagined Experience,* Hodder & Stoughton

*Peter, M. (1994) *Drama for All,* David Fulton
  (1995) *Making Drama Special,* David Fulton

Sherborne, V. (1990) *Developmental Movement for Children,* Cambridge University Press

*Spolin, V. (1963) *Improvisation for the Theatre,* Northwestern University Press

Tomlinson, R. (1982) *Disability, Theatre and Education,* Souvenir Press

*Woolland, B. (1993) *The Teaching of Drama in the Primary School,* Longman

WORKING WITH THEATRE COMPANIES

A number of theatre companies and individual professional artists offer programmes that are suitable or even specially designed for special education. Unless the company, or their tour, is being subsidised, the cost of such special events may be prohibitively expensive. Companies offering their services to schools usually make it clear where any subsidy is coming from: you may have cause to be suspicious of any companies which seem remarkably cheap yet are not subsidised!

In our experience you can't be too careful when booking companies. You might usefully check with the local education authority drama adviser or inspector about their reputation. Your local arts association should also have details of their previous work and standing (addresses of the national Arts Councils are given overleaf).

Questions which can give you an insight into the professionalism and usefulness of the company to you include the following:

- Do the company offer any kind of teachers' meeting or workshop in advance of their tour to explain the aims and content of the programme?
- Alternatively, would a member of the company be prepared to make a brief visit to the school before confirming the booking?

- What sort of technical support do the company need? Are they a self-contained unit? If they have particular requirements, do they make this clear in their advance publicity?
- What expectations other than technical ones do the company appear to have of the school? Do they, for example, require you to prepare the students in any way – if so, have they made it clear what you are to do?
- Do the company offer any sort of teaching pack to use in following up the programme? Are examples of previous packs available for inspection in advance? How clear and well presented are they?

Information about local events and companies working in the area should be obtainable from the Arts Council or regional arts boards:

The Arts Council of Great Britain
14 Great Peter Street
London SW1P 3NQ
Tel. 0171-333 0100
The Arts Council of Great Britain is the national body established to foster the arts throughout Britain.

The Welsh Arts Council
Museum Place
Cardiff CF1 3NX
Tel. (01222) 394711
The Welsh Arts Council is responsible for the arts in Wales.

The Scottish Arts Council
12 Manor Place
Edinburgh EH3 7DD
Tel. 0131-226 6051
The Scottish Arts Council is responsible for the arts in Scotland.

The Regional Arts Boards
The ten Regional Arts Boards (RABs) in England have funding responsibility for most of the arts organisations in their regions and are accountable to the Arts Council.
The RABs will supply information about the professional performing arts and education in the regions.

Eastern Arts Board
Cherry Hinton Hall
Cherry Hinton Road
Cambridge CB1 4DW
Tel. (01223) 215355

East Midlands Arts Board
Mountfields House
Forest Road
Loughborough
Leicestershire LE11 3HU
Tel. (01509) 218292

London Arts Board
Coriander Building
20 Gainsford Street
Butlers Wharf
London SE1 2NE
Tel. 0171-403 9013

Northern Arts Board
9-10 Osborne Terrace
Jesmond
Newcastle-upon-Tyne NE2 1NZ
Tel. 0191- 281 6334

North West Arts Board
12 Harter Street
Manchester M1 6HY
Tel. 0161-228 3062

Southern Arts Board
13 St Clement Street
Winchester SO23 9DQ
Tel. (01962) 855099

South East Arts Board
10 Mount Ephraim
Tunbridge Wells
Kent TN4 8AS
Tel. (01892) 515210

South West Arts Board
Bradninch Place
Gandy Street
Exeter EX4 3LS
Tel. (01392) 218188

West Midlands Arts Board
82 Granville Street
Birmingham B1 2LH
Tel. 0121-631 3121

Yorkshire and Humberside Arts Board
21 Bond Street
Dewsbury WF13 1AX
Tel. (01924) 455555

INDEX